Sigmund Freud
and the
Jewish Mystical Tradition

Sigmund Freud and the Jewish Mystical Tradition

by
DAVID BAKAN

BEACON PRESS *BOSTON*

Dedicated
to the memory of
my grandfather
Yitzchak Yosef Rosenstrauch
(1859-1947)

Copyright © 1958 by David Bakan

First published as a Beacon Paperback in 1975
by arrangement with David Bakan

Beacon Press books are published under the auspices
of the Unitarian Universalist Association

Published simultaneously in Canada by Saunders of Toronto, Ltd.
All rights reserved

Printed in the United States of America

9   8   7   6   5   4   3   2   1

Library of Congress Cataloging in Publication Data

Bakan, David.
    Sigmund Freud and the Jewish mystical tradition.
    Reprint of the ed. published by Schocken Books, New
York.
    Includes bibliography.
    1. Freud, Sigmund, 1856–1939.   2. Mysticism —
Judaism.   I. Title.
BF173.F85B23   1975   150'.19'52
74–31136
ISBN 0–8070–2963–7

Table of Contents

Part III.—The Moses Theme in the Thought of Freud

Part IV.—The Devil as Suspended Superego

CONTENTS

We know that genius is incomprehensible and unaccountable and it should therefore not be called upon as an explanation until every other solution has failed.

Everything new must have its roots in what was before.

Few tasks are as appealing as inquiry into the laws that govern the psyche of exceptionally endowed individuals.

—Sigmund Freud

Preface

The purpose of this essay is to explore an hypothesis concerning the intellectual antecedents of Freudian psychoanalysis. From the point of view of the history of ideas, psychoanalysis presents a special problem. Movements of thought of the stature of psychoanalysis usually have prominent antecedents in the history of man's thought. Although there are giants in every great movement of thought, rarely do their contributions seem to arise full-blown, like psychoanalysis, as the work of a single person.

Freud is sometimes viewed as an inexplicable genius who burst upon the world, left his profound and complicated message, and departed. In seeking to understand the intellectual history of psychoanalysis one can find many features of Freud's thought in the history of ideas in the main streams of Western civilization. Yet the basic mood of psychoanalysis is so radically different from all these other modes of thought, that the question of its origins is still unsatisfactorily answered.

The hypothesis of this essay is that a full appreciation of the development of psychoanalysis is essentially incomplete unless it be viewed against the history of Judaism, and particularly against the history of Jewish mystical thought. This does not mean that we will be able to read psychoanalytic propositions directly out of Jewish mystical expressions. Our point is rather that Freud's repeated affirmation of his Jewish identity had greater significance for the development of psychoanalysis than is usually recognized. He was a participant in the struggles and the issues of Jewish mysticism; and where it was appropriate he drew from the Jewish mystical armamentarium for equipment in these struggles.

As we hope we will make clear in the course of this essay, Jewish mysticism played a special role in connection with Jewish contact with the Western world. It was a movement within Judaism which, especially after the seventeenth century, was revolutionary with respect to the classical Jewish modes of life. It served to weaken the classical patterns within Judaism and thus facilitated the entry of the Jews into the wider streams of the Western world. Thus, our presentation of Freud as a participant in the tradition of Jewish mysticism need not do any violence to our basic conception of Freud as a Western scientist and research worker.

A critical image in our analysis is that of Sabbatai Zevi, the false Messiah of the Jews of the seventeenth century. Although he has been fully repudiated in the history of the Jews—and we believe, rightly so—the social eruption which surrounded this figure was critical for the whole subsequent development of the Jews. Sabbatai Zevi and the Sabbatian movement are, in a certain sense, paradigmatic for some of the essential features of Freud's problems. What the Sabbatian movement stood for in terms of emotional and social Messianism, Freud grappled with as a scientific problem; and perhaps therein lies his genius.

Our attempt to understand Freud in terms of Jewish history should not be taken as indicating that we believe Freud to have been a secret scholar of Jewish lore. An image of him poring over Kabbalistic books in the dead of night is not supported by the facts; although to have done this would not have been inconsistent with the patterns of the Jewish mystical leaders. Nevertheless, Jewish mystical thought was in the air in those parts of Europe from which his parents and large proportions of the Jews of Vienna came. Jewish mystical thought was largely embodied in the common oral expressions of the Jews. We can suppose the kind of transmission which takes place when a parent or grandparent makes a comment on this or that problem of the day. The communication can take place by way of stories or jokes of the kind which Freud himself collected.

When the lore of Jewish mysticism is set down in books, it often comes in the form of little nuggets. For example, the *Hasidic Anthology,* edited by Rabbi Newman, is hardly an anthology of theological essays. It is rather, as described on the title page, "The parables, folk-tales, fables, aphorisms, epigrams, sayings, anecdotes, proverbs, and exegetical interpretations of the Hasidic masters and disciples; their lore and wisdom." [1] When a writer is interested in presenting us with the social and political conditions of the Chassidic Jews, he feels perfectly justified in basing such a treatment on an analysis of the legendary material rather than on other forms of historical data.[2] And the books of legends, which constituted the major printed vehicle of transmission, are innumerable.[3]

In attempting to understand the development of psychoanalysis as an expression of Jewish mysticism, it has been our endeavor to emphasize the word *mysticism* as much as the word *Jewish.* Jewish mysticism was undoubtedly the major vehicle of transmission. It operated, perhaps, by developing within Freud a certain perceptual and emotional readiness, and by defining some basic patterns of reaction in connection with the problems he encountered.

The author is aware of the fact that all forms of mysticism have features in common, and that historically there has been a considerable amount of cultural diffusion among the varieties of expression of the mystical impulse. No effort has been made to separate out the lines which have fed into or issued from Jewish mysticism. For example, Pythagoreanism undoubtedly affected Jewish mysticism; and we know that Goethe, for whom Freud had great respect, studied Kabbala. These relationships are far too complicated to be dealt with in this essay. In our treatment of Jewish mysticism we have contented ourselves with the idea that we are dealing with *characteristic* features, and that *characteristic* does not mean *unique.*

The question has repeatedly arisen, in discussions concerning this essay, as to what the author's own views concerning mysticism may be. At this stage the author does not feel that he can formulate and defend a satisfactory evaluation. Yet he cannot but feel that within mysticism there is a depth and fecundity which are often lacking in contemporary intellectual endeavors. The author is fully aware that with mysticism there are linked a number of ideas and beliefs which no modern scholar can respect. But perhaps in our rejection of mystical modes of thought, we have rejected a great deal more than superstition.

In our attempt to link Freud to the tradition of Jewish mysticism, we have sought to avoid generating the impression that psychoanalysis is reducible to the peculiarities of the mental life of its originator. The glib technique of *ad hominem* reductionism is a repudiation of the essential creativity in man. There exist in the literature several attempts to dispose of the Freudian contributions in this way. But the argument *ad hominem* is correctly counted among the logical fallacies in textbooks on logic.

We have sought to make the essay comprehensible to persons who are well versed neither in psychoanalysis nor in Jewish history. Wherever possible the references have been to sources available in English. The reader who is interested in pursuing some of the material on Jewish mysticism is directed particularly towards Gershom G. Scholem's *Major Trends in Jewish Mysticism* and the Soncino Press's edition of *The Zohar,* translated by Harry Sperling, Maurice Simon, and Paul P. Levertoff.

The present essay falls into five major parts and an epilogue. In the first part the question of the development of psychoanalysis as a problem in the history of ideas is raised, and an attempt is made to show some of the relationships between Freud and the Jewish tradition. In the second part a brief sketch of some of the features of Jewish history is provided. In the third part we deal with Freud's writings on Moses, where, we believe, Freud permitted himself to be most revelatory with respect to the role of his Jewishness in his thought. In the fourth part we deal with the image of the Devil, an image which contains, in a metaphorical sense, some of the critical features of the development of psychoanalysis. In the fifth part, we deal with some of the written works in Jewish mysticism in their relevance to psychoanalysis. In the epilogue we have tried to come to a somewhat deeper appreciation of the meaning of Freud's Jewish identification, using as a fulcrum Freud's analysis of "Heimlichkeit" —the word which he also used to characterize his Jewish feeling.

Of greatest personal importance in the writing of this essay is my grandfather, Yitzchak Yosef Rosenstrauch, to whose memory this essay is dedicated. He was a man who made the deepest impression upon me in my early life. He was, by any of the usual standards, an uneducated man. His literacy was limited, until he was about sixty-five, to the recitation of the prayers in a *Siddur* or *Machzor*. He knew the meaning of only a few Hebrew words. At the age of sixty-five he learned to read Yiddish, and gave the remaining years of his life to devotion to God and to a handful of Yiddish books that had come into his possession. He understood the meaning and signifi-cance of devotion better than any other person I have ever met.

When I was young he would spend hours reading to me the fan-tastic legends of the Chassidic leaders. Our favorite was Moishe Leib of Sassov. I still recall Moishe Leib's words that one who does not devote one hour to himself every day is not a person, and that to help someone else out of the mud one must be willing to get mud on himself.

As I grew into secular sophistication and cynicism I used to chide him unkindly, "Mr. Itsche (this was the way we used to address him), why do you *davon* (recite the prayers in the prayer books) when you don't even understand the words?" His reply was always the same, "Why do I have to understand, if the One Above under-stands?"

D. B.

Columbia, Missouri
September 1958

The three quotations facing the Preface are drawn from *Moses and Monotheism,* trans. Katherine Jones (New York: Vintage Books, 1955), p. 81; *ibid.,* p. 22; and Freud's Preface to M. Bonaparte, *The Life and Works of Edgar Allan Poe* (London: Imago Publishing Co., 1949), p. xi.

1. Louis I. Newman (ed.), *The Hasidic Anthology* (New York: Bloch Publishing Co., 1944).
2. Menashe Unger, *Chassidus un Leben* [*Chassidism and Life*] (New York, 1946).
3. Cf., e.g., the selections in Martin Buber, *Tales of the Hasidim,* trans. Olga Marx (2 vols., New York: Schocken Books, 1947-1948).

Preface to the Paperback Edition

Some have referred to this essay as a "detective story." The material which I had available at the time of writing it left one question which I had no way of resolving at the time: Was Freud *aware* of the role of the Jewish mystical tradition as a factor in the development of psychoanalysis? Some pieces of information which have come to my attention since I wrote the essay increase the likelihood that he was aware of it.

Jung's *Memories, Dreams, Reflections*[1] appeared after my book was published. In it there is an appendix containing some letters that Freud wrote to Jung. In a letter dated April 16, 1909, Freud has a numerological discussion of the number 62 similar to his discussion of it in "The Uncanny," which is discussed in this book (pp. 307 ff.). The suspicion that it was autobiographical is completely confirmed in Freud's letter. But furthermore, that such an analysis arises from the numerological penchant in the Jewish mystical tradition as relatively conscious in his thought is indicated by Freud referring to this analysis in the following manner: "Here is another instance where you will find confirmation of the specifically Jewish character of my mysticism."[2]

A meeting that I had with Chaim Bloch, the eminent student of Judaism, Kabbala and Hasidism, was particularly illuminating.[3] He wrote to me that he had seen a review of *Sigmund Freud and the Jewish Mystical Tradition*, in the *Day-Journal*, and wanted to inform me that he had been acquainted with Freud. He enclosed a clipping on himself from a biographical dictionary to let me know who he was. He asked me if he might have an opportunity to look at my book; although he could not read English, he might, with the help of his children, be able to get the meaning out of it.

I read Chaim Bloch's letter with some amount of excitement. In this book I advance the thesis that there are certain relationships between the development of psychoanalysis and the Jewish mystical tradition. But I provide little or no *direct* evidence of any such connections; indeed, I have several reservations concerning the importance of a direct connection, and especially of the importance of Freud's having had a *scholarly* interest in Jewish mysticism. Nevertheless I could not help but be very much interested—for, I also mention the fact that Freud conversed on such matters with Chaim Bloch. It had not occurred to me that I might be able to communicate with the same Chaim Bloch.

I immediately wrapped up a copy of this book and sent it to Bloch at his home address in New York. Since I was myself going to New York in several weeks, I wrote and asked if I might come and see him. He replied affirmatively, telling me that he had some information on Freud which I would find interesting.

I arrived at his home in the Bronx, carrying a tape recorder, in order to have a permanent record of the conversation. He did not let me use it, saying that his children would object because it reminds them too much of Nazis and that sort of thing. We spoke in Yiddish. He inquired about my background, especially the parts of Europe where my parents came from. Rapport was quickly established when he found out that I too was a *Galicianer*.

Then he told me his tale. He had been closely associated with Joseph Bloch, one of the leaders of the fight against anti-Semitism in Vienna. Joseph Bloch (to whom he was not related) had been a kind of mentor to him, and had urged him to do a translation of the works of Chaim Vital, the 16th–17th century Kabbalist. He began the work, but somehow found the ideas of Chaim Vital not to his taste. Still, he kept working on it as long as Joseph Bloch was alive. When Joseph Bloch died, he abandoned the work.

But once he had a dream in which Joseph Bloch appeared to him, shook his finger in his face, and asked him why he did not bring the work on Chaim Vital to a close. He arose out of the dream and energized himself sufficiently to complete the task. Yet the ideas of Vital still seemed so unsavory to him that he could not bring himself to publish the book on his own responsibility. He therefore sought someone to write a foreword to it: in effect, he wished for someone to help him bear the responsibility for its publication. He approached Sigmund Freud.

Freud, said Chaim Bloch, was beside himself with excitement on reading the manuscript. "This is gold," Freud said, and asked why Chaim Vital's work had never been brought to his attention before. He agreed to write the foreword, and even volunteered assistance in getting the book published.

Then Freud turned to Bloch and told him he too had written a book on Judaism; and took out the manuscript of the *Moses and Monotheism*. Bloch was openly aghast. "Anti-Semites," he said, "accuse us of killing the founder of Christianity. Now a Jew adds that we also killed the founder of Judaism. You are digging a trap for the Jewish people." And, "Have you examined the birth records and death records of ancient Egypt and found conclusive evidence that Moses was an Egyptian and the Jews killed him?"[4]

Freud was incensed with Bloch and told him that he would have nothing further to do with him, and nothing to do with the work on Chaim Vital. Freud left the room in anger.

Bloch did not know what to do, he said. He was loath to leave at once for fear of appearing impolite, and so he stayed in the room. On the desk were both manuscripts, his on Vital, and Freud's on Moses, both having been written on the same kind of paper.

The manuscripts were somewhat strewn. Bloch said that the *yetzer hara,* the evil impulse, spoke to him saying that it would be a completely "understandable" error if the two manuscripts became mixed up, and he took them away; and that would have been the end of *Moses and Monotheism.* But, he thought, if Freud should have a copy of the *Moses,* what would it avail?

The significant piece of information for me, however, was the following: while waiting, Bloch occupied himself by looking over Freud's books. In Freud's library was a large collection of Judaica (which is absent from the presumptive "Freud library" which is now housed in the library of the New York Psychiatric Institute). Among the books were a number of books on Kabbala in German, and, most importantly, a copy of the French translation of the *Zohar!*

In this book, I give considerable attention to the *Zohar,* since it is without question the most important work in the Jewish mystical tradition. A number of features in the *Zohar* strongly suggest relationship to the psychoanalytic movement—among them the concept of man's bisexuality, and concepts of sexuality in general. There is also in the *Zohar* the notion that man can be studied by the exegetical techniques associated with the study of Torah; and a theory of the nature of anti-Semitism almost identical with that contained in Freud's *Moses and Monotheism.* Perhaps even more important, there is an atmospheric similarity—one which cannot, indeed, be conveyed in any brief description.

Although I had felt it was very probable that Freud had had some contact with the *Zohar,* I did not wish to assert this without some actual supporting data. As a matter of fact, I even wrote in the Preface: "Our attempt to understand Freud in terms of Jewish history should not be taken as indicating that we believe Freud to have been a secret scholar of Jewish lore. An image of him poring over Kabbalistic books in the dead of night is not supported by the facts; although to have done this would not have been inconsistent with the patterns of the Jewish mystical leaders."

This new bit of information from Chaim Bloch has made me wonder. Freud did indeed know of the *Zohar,* and his connection with Jewish mysticism may thus have had a scholarly feature.

D. B.

NOTES

1. Jung, C. G., *Memories, Dreams, Reflections* (New York: Pantheon Books 1961).
2. *Ibid.,* p. 363.
3. What follows is reprinted, with slight modification, from a short article I wrote in the January 1960 issue of *Commentary,* copyright © 1960 by the American Jewish Committee; it is presented here with the kind permission of the editors.
4. Bloch has published parts of this interview: "An Encounter with Freud," in *Bitzaron,* November 1950.

Acknowledgments

In the course of the work on this essay I have received assistance from many quarters, although all responsibility for what is being said is my own.

My principal debt is to Professor David C. McClelland. Owing to his efforts I was appointed a Visiting Lecturer and Research Associate in the Department of Social Relations at Harvard University and was greatly encouraged in this enterprise. He has been a constant and continuing source of advice and encouragement and has made many suggestions which I have followed. I am certain that without his aid I could not have brought this essay to its present state of completion.

In the summer of 1955, I was awarded a research professorship by the Graduate Research Council of the University of Missouri, which was provided with the means to go to New York City so that I could use the libraries there.

I owe a special kind of debt to the B'nai B'rith. Rabbi Morris Fishman, who was Director of the B'nai B'rith Hillel Foundation at the University of Missouri, helped me to overcome the initial difficulties associated with this research. I cannot but feel a certain pleasure in the fact that I first presented some of these ideas there, just as Freud first presented his ideas on dream interpretation to the members of the B'nai B'rith in Vienna. In the same way as I was helped in Missouri, I was helped by the B'nai B'rith Hillel Foundation at Harvard. Rabbi Richard L. Rubenstein, Director of the Foundation at Harvard, gave unstintingly of his time to me and again made accessible to me the facilities of the Foundation library.

In a work of this kind, the accessibility of libraries and the cooperation of librarians are *sine qua non*. My first debt is to the library of the University of Missouri, particularly for their pains in acquiring materials by purchase and loan which were not immediately available. I am deeply indebted for an eminently high degree of cooperation and assistance to the following: Mrs. Eva J. Meyer and Mr. Robert Melton of the Abraham A. Brill Library of The New York Psychoanalytic Institute; the late Dr. Jacob Shatzky and Mr. William C. Bryant of the library of the New York Psychiatric Institute; the staff of the Judaica Collection of the New York Public Library; the staff of the library at YIVO in New York; Mrs. L. C. Mishkin of the library at the Hebrew Theological College in Chicago; Mr. Harry L. Poppers of the Leaf Library of the College of Jewish Studies in Chicago; and the staff of the Widener Library at Harvard University.

Many people have given fully to me of their time. The warmth with which some of the ideas of my book were met was a constant source of encouragement in overcoming the many difficulties I encountered on the way. My students at the University of Missouri and at Harvard University listened and commented with astuteness and interest as I was in the throes of developing point after point.

I have discussed the ideas in this essay with each of the following persons and have received inestimable assistance of a kind that cannot be repaid by mere mention of their names: Dr. Leslie Adams, Professor Gordon W. Allport, Mr. William Aron, Professor Jerome Bruner, Miss Josephine L. Burroughs, Professor Reuel Denney, Mr. Harvey Fischtrom, Professor Marvin Fox, Dr. James Frank, Mr. Nathan Glazer, Dr. H. Raphael Gold, Mr. Clement Greenberg, Professor Abraham J. Heschel, Professor Elihu Katz, Dr. Herbert Kelman, Professor Isadore Keyfitz, Mr. Irwin Kremen, Professor Abraham Maslow, Rabbi Abraham Pimontel, Professor Simon Rawidowicz, Mr. James Reiss, Rabbi Menachem Mendel Rubin,

Professor David Riesman, Dr. Theodore Reik, Dr. A. A. Roback, Professor Carl Schorske, Rabbi Joseph B. Soloveitchik, Professor Lewis Spitz, Rabbi Judah Stampfer, Mr. Menashe Unger, Professor Meyer Waxman, Professor Kurt H. Wolff, and Dr. Mark Zborowski.

I would like to acknowledge my debt to my colleagues at the University of Missouri and at Harvard University, who patiently gave me support and cooperation when these were needed.

My wife, Mildred, has given me so much in connection with this enterprise that I cannot speak of it. My children, Joseph, Deborah, and Abigail, kept bringing me back to immediate reality from the Kabbalistic and psychoanalytic reaches; and my debt to them is great for the "instinctual renunciation" with which they engaged in noble efforts—sometimes successful and sometimes unsuccessful— "not to bother Daddy while he is working."

For secretarial assistance I am indebted to the Dean's Office and the Psychology Department at the University of Missouri, where Mrs. Carol Lawson typed up some of my preliminary notes on this essay; and to the Psychological Clinic at Harvard University, where Mrs. Elizabeth Morse Atwood strove valiantly to decipher my miserably handwritten manuscript to produce a legible typescript. The final typescript was the work of Mrs. Irene Chase. The Index was prepared by Mrs. Katherine F. Bruner.

For permission to quote I would like to express my appreciation to George Allen and Unwin, Ltd., *American Imago,* Beacon Press, Inc., Basic Books, Inc., Ernest Benn, Ltd., E. P. Dutton and Co., Inc., The Free Press, Harvard University Press, The Hogarth Press, Ltd., The Jewish Publication Society of America, Alfred A. Knopf, Inc. (the quotations from *Moses and Monotheism* are from the Vintage Books edition, reprinted by permission of Alfred A. Knopf, Inc.), Liveright Publishing Corporation, Philosophical Library, *The Psychoanalytic Quarterly,* Schocken Books, and The Soncino Press, Ltd.

D. B.

Part I

The Background of Freud's Development
of Psychoanalysis

1

The Problem of the Origins
of Psychoanalysis

The year 1956 marked the hundredth anniversary of the birth of Sigmund Freud, a man whose long life spanned almost half of the nineteenth century and over a third of the twentieth. His essential modernity leads us to overlook how much of his life was spent in an age which most contemporaries cannot remember, and to ignore the historical factors that may have played a role in the development of psychoanalysis.

Freud was evidently aware of the deep moment of his contributions with respect to man's self-evaluation. He once indicated that there have been three major blows to man's narcissism. Copernicus delivered the cosmological blow; Darwin delivered the biological blow; and psychoanalysis delivered the psychological blow.[1] In addition to his profound effect upon our ideas of the treatment of mental disorder, Freud has had an overwhelming influence on psychology at large, the arts, the social sciences, social reform, child rearing, and indeed every problem involving human relationships.

3

The psychoanalytic movement seemingly originated as an effort on the part of a physician to cure certain ailments that were resistant to other forms of treatment; and it was in this guise that it first presented itself to the world. Yet, shortly after this introduction, it reached out to touch, infiltrate, and encompass practically every other form of intellectual endeavor.

The far-reaching consequences of Freud's thought are paradoxically confirmed by the degree to which his contributions are taken for granted. Freudian concepts are used freely in the contemporary intellectual world to win insight into other problems, even as this essay, which is an attempt to understand the genesis of psychoanalysis itself, will manifest. The literature of our day uses Freudian terminology without mentioning the source, as though it were gratuitous to do so. In a world in which the method of allusion has in general gone out of fashion—because writers cannot be confident that allusions will be understood—allusions to Freudian notions are made freely in full confidence that they will be appreciated by the reader.

So much for the impact of Freud on modern thought. We turn now to the major question of this essay: *Against what backdrop of the history of ideas shall we place these momentous contributions of Freud?* The tremendous impact of psychoanalysis makes the problem of its origins all the more important, especially since we have learned from Freud that only by the penetration of the mystery of origins can we come to a full understanding of either the individual or society. The editors of the letters and notes which Freud wrote to his friend Fliess gave them an appropriate title beginning with the word "origins," used in the sense that it has for our question;[2] and the atmosphere of excitement which accompanied the publication of the letters and notes confirmed their significance to the intellectual world.

In thinking through the problem of origins it is important to take note of the findings of Freud and his followers about the way in which distortion along these lines can take place. Indeed such distortions have already been set in motion. As an amusing example, when the citizens of Freiberg, Moravia, Freud's birthplace, decided to put a memorial tablet on the house where he was born, they misread the birth records and put Freud's birthday two months ahead of his actual birthday. Since Freud was born almost exactly nine months after the marriage of his parents, such an error would have thrown doubt on his *biological* legitimacy, something which would have gladdened the hearts of some of his critics. The lessons of psychoanalysis suggest that such an error may be an unconscious aspersion on the legitimacy of the origins of psychoanalysis.[3]

Just as we must guard against the processes which would undermine psychoanalysis, so must we guard against the genotypically similar processes which would lead us to overvalue and idealize Freud. In this essay we will try to steer a middle course. As pointed out by Ekstein, in the same way that the death of Freud's father brought to Freud an awareness of the ambivalent nature of his feelings towards him, so it seems "as if the death of Freud permits us now to learn more about him, his life and consequently about Psychoanalysis. . . . Our own ambivalence, another example of the Oedipal theme, is converted into scientific curiosity that aims at better insight into and integration of the work he left us." [4] A new generation may perhaps scrutinize him more objectively, in the absence of emotions stirred among those people who knew him intimately and whose thoughts about psychoanalysis were conditioned by their expectations of Freud's own reactions.

NOTES TO CHAPTER I

1. Sigmund Freud, *Collected Papers,* ed. James Strachey (5 vols., London: Hogarth Press, 1950-1952), V, p. 173.
2. S. Freud, *The Origins of Psychoanalysis: Letters to Wilhelm Fliess, Drafts and Notes: 1887-1902,* eds. M. Bonaparte, A. Freud, and E. Kris; trans. E. Mosbacher and J. Strachey; introd. E. Kris (New York: Basic Books, 1954).
3. Cf. L. Adams, "Sigmund Freud's Correct Birthday: Misunderstanding and Solution," *Psychoanal. Rev.,* 1954, 41, 359-362.
4. R. Ekstein, "A Biographical Comment on Freud's Dual Instinct Theory," *American Imago,* 1949, 6, 210-216.

2

Hypotheses Relating the Origins of Psychoanalysis to Freud's Personal Life

It is one of the major paradoxes of contemporary psychoanalytic thought that whereas it places so much of its emphasis upon the analysis of "origins," it itself seems to be without origins. Let us consider what the apparent origins of psychoanalytic thought are.

We note that Freud's intellectual life falls into two distinct periods, the one that preceded the psychoanalytic period and the psychoanalytic period itself. In the first period Freud concerned himself largely with biological problems, and there are only bare hints of an interest in psychology,[1] indeed not much more than might be expected from any typically well-educated person. His pre-psychoanalytic bibliography [2] was already such as to earn him a respectable, although perhaps not outstanding, place in science. He had made several noteworthy contributions, including his pioneering work on the properties of cocaine.[3] It was not until he was in his late thirties that he showed any indication of what was to come from him. The change which took place in him has been aptly characterized as follows:

> When Freud startled his contemporaries with his first publication on the neuroses he was in his late thirties. He had behind him years of training, research, and practice in anatomy, physiology and neurology. With every step he took in his new venture he became more of a stranger to his colleagues. They could see no link whatever between those years of solid and fruitful medical research and his new interests and methods. Later, many psychoanalysts used to take the opposite view of the first part of Freud's working life: they looked at it as a time spent in a foreign land, at best a period of preparation, at worst a waste of precious years as far as psycho-analysis was concerned.[4]

In pointing out the difference between the two periods, Jones comments on how Brücke, Freud's materialistic-minded scientific mentor, would have reacted to the shift.

> Yet Brücke would have been astonished, to put it mildly, had he known that one of his favorite pupils, one apparently a convert to the strict faith, was later, in his famous wish theory of the mind, to bring back into science the ideas of "purpose," "intention," and "aim" which had just been abolished from the universe.[5]

Freud himself, prompted by the question whether psychoanalysis might be practiced without medical training, spoke of his own medical background, which was associated in his mind with neurology, physiology, and the like, as follows:

> I have been engaged in the practice of medicine for forty-one years and my self-knowledge tells me that I have never really been a true physician. I became a physician owing to a compulsory deflection of my original purpose, and the triumph of

my life is this: that after a very long way round I have regained the path in which I began. . . .[6]

Jones writes:

To medicine itself he felt no direct attraction. He did not conceal in later years that he never felt at home in the medical profession, and that he did not seem to himself to be a regular member of it. I can recall as far back as in 1910 his expressing the wish with a sigh that he could retire from medical practice and devote himself to the unraveling of cultural and historical problems—ultimately the great problem of how man came to be what he is.[7]

If Freud had a psychoanalytic type of interest at this early period, it was certainly not being developed in any deliberate work. Jones aptly characterizes what we may call the suspension of whatever psychoanalytic interest he may have had in the pre-psychoanalytic period, and writes of a mood in which Freud

would be a laborious and painstaking student, but one not likely to excel in the "exact" sciences. Biology offered him some understanding of the evolution of life and man's relationship to nature. Later on physiology and anatomy would teach him something of man's physical constitution. But would this arid path ever bring him nearer to his ultimate goal, the secrets of man's inner nature, towards which the deepest urges impelled him? We know that the medical study of man's physical afflictions brought him no nearer, and perhaps impeded his progress. That, however, he finally attained his goal, though by an extraordinary circuitous route, he rightly came to regard as the triumph of his life.[8]

It is clear that, if we seek some explanation of Freud's psychoanalytic developments in the formal preparation and the professional work of his pre-psychoanalytic years, we find little there to give us insight. The tradition of severe materialism of Brücke, Helmholtz, and the like with which he came in contact was certainly not one which he seemed to draw upon in any essential way for psychoanalysis. It is even difficult to maintain that the tradition prepared him for his later work in the sense of providing him with issues on which he could take a contrary position. The evidence provided by Freud's psychoanalytic writings does not even begin to support the hypothesis that these writings are a reaction to the tradition with which he had been involved in his pre-psychoanalytic years. The psychoanalytic writings seem rather simply to ignore this other tradition and to strike out in completely new directions.

If the scientific background with which Freud was intimately acquainted does not provide us with any cogent clue to the question of the origins of psychoanalysis, what other hypotheses might be advanced? Five types of explanation are available, somewhat related to each other and referring primarily to the person of Freud rather than to any tradition.

The first is that *the idiosyncrasies of Freud's personal life were such that they formed him into a very special kind of being who could make the kinds of discoveries which he did.* As instances of this kind of hypothesis we may include the varieties of explicit and implicit assertions that Freud's writings are simply the work of a disordered mind and are to be discounted as one would discount the assertions of a mentally disturbed person.

Indeed, we also find this kind of hypothesis advanced in one way or another by persons who are sympathetic to Freud. Even Jones occasionally permits himself to be somewhat victimized. For example: "In tracing, as best we can, the genesis of Freud's original discoveries, we therefore legitimately consider that the greatest of them—namely, the universality of the Oedipus complex—was potently facilitated by his own unusual family constellation, the spur it gave to his curiosity, and the opportunity it afforded of a complete repression." [9] Such arguments may be appealing. However, by focusing attention on such factors as an "unusual family constellation" or an "opportunity . . . of a complete repression" they can at best provide only a partial explanation. They divert attention from the roles of history and culture on intellectual production, even though these must be channeled through an individual's life experiences.

The second of these "personal" hypotheses is what may be called the *"flash" or "revelation" hypothesis*. This hypothesis claims that the insights of psychoanalysis simply "came" to Freud. For example, Sachs puts it as follows:

> In what way his ideas germinated is anybody's guess. What was at first a small clue in psychopathology widened out by the untiring concentration of an original mind, until eventually it grew into a fundamental concept, of psychology, of human civilization, and lastly of all organic development. Some of the sudden enlightenments which marked a step in this evolution have been described by Freud, for instance how the concept of sublimation—that is, the process by which the primitive object of a drive is exchanged for a higher, socially adapted one—was revealed to him. It happened while he was looking at a cartoon. . . . [10]

Freud himself, as Sachs says, tends to lead us in the direction of the "flash" hypothesis. For example, he writes that he thinks of a marble tablet to be placed on the house where he had his critical dream of Irma's injection [11] inscribed as follows: "In this house on July 24, 1895, the Secret of Dreams was revealed to Dr. Sigmund Freud." [12] And in the preface to the third (revised) English edition of *The Interpretation of Dreams* he says of the book, "Insight such as this falls to one's lot but once in a lifetime." [13] Aside from the various considerations which remarks of this kind are subject to, such as the possibility that they are "stylistic," or that they are motivated by a kind of grandiosity, or that they are passing and idle, they succeed in generating the impression of a "flash," *de novo,* revelatory character for his discoveries.

These two hypotheses, the hypothesis of personal idiosyncracy, and the "flash" hypothesis, are not unrelated to a third, the *hypothesis of genius.* This is the hypothesis that from time to time the world is given individuals of profound and gigantic gifts and that the nature of these gifts is inscrutable. Such an hypothesis must be set aside for at least the reason that it stops investigation by substituting reverence for analysis. Freud himself cautions us against succumbing to its lulling effect. He says quite specifically: "We know that genius is incomprehensible and unaccountable and it should therefore not be called upon as an explanation until every other solution has failed." [14]

One of the important corollaries of the three hypotheses mentioned, and a fourth one in its own right, is that *Freud had unusual psychological insight into the nature of man, and* *that the psychoanalytic work simply provided him with a technical framework for its formulation.* It is undoubtedly true that he had a profound appreciation of the nature of man. However, it is a far cry from psychological insight to, for example, the method of free association, the detailed techniques of the interpretation of dreams, and the theory of bisexuality. The actual technical contributions of Freud go far beyond the kind of psychological astuteness that is manifested by such writers as Shakespeare, Proust, Dostoevsky, Ibsen, Melville, Hawthorne, and the like.*

The last of our hypotheses of a personal nature regards psychoanalysis as the result of a *germinal idea or a germinal observation dropped on the soil of an extremely rich mind.* We find this hypothesis developed in a paper by Paul Bergman.[15] It is one which Freud himself would have us accept and is advanced in his essay "On the History of the Psychoanalytic Movement." He asserts that he is "the real originator of all that is particularly characteristic" in psychoanalysis.[16] He then

* The presence of profound psychological understanding as it existed in the literature of Western civilization prior to Freud is beyond the scope of this essay. Understanding of man abounds in the literature of our culture. To illustrate this point we might cite but one example from what is seemingly so remote a source as Oliver Wendell Holmes, who wrote: "We not rarely find our personality doubled in our dreams, and do battle with ourselves, unconscious that we are our own antagonists. Dr. Johnson dreamed that he had a contest of wit with an opponent, and got the worst of it; of course, he furnished the wit for both. Tartini heard the Devil play a wonderful sonata, and set it down on awakening. Who was the Devil but Tartini himself? I remember, in my youth, reading verses in a dream, written, as I thought, by a rival fledgling of the Muse. They were so far beyond my powers, that I despaired of equalling them; yet I must have made them unconsciously as I read them." We note that Holmes had already fully understood that which we tend to regard as basic to Freud's theory of dream interpretation, the projection of ourselves into dream personages.——Oliver Wendell Holmes, *Pages from an Old Volume of Life* (Boston: Houghton Mifflin Co., 1883), pp. 282-283, essay entitled "Mechanism in Thought and Morals," delivered at Harvard University, June 29, 1870.

goes on to tell how he came upon the basic idea of the sexual etiology of the neuroses.

> There was some consolation . . . in the thought that I was taking up the fight for a new and original idea. But, one day, certain memories collected in my mind which disturbed this pleasing notion, and gave me instead a valuable insight into the processes of human activity and the nature of human knowledge. The idea for which I was being made responsible had by no means originated with me. It had been imparted to me by no less than three people whose opinion had commanded my deepest respect—by Breuer himself, by Charcot, and by the gynæcologist of Vienna University, Chrobak, perhaps the most eminent of all our Viennese physicians. These three men had all communicated to me a piece of knowledge which, strictly speaking, they themselves did not possess. Two of them later denied having done so when I reminded them of the fact; the third (Charcot) would probably have done the same if it had been granted to me to see him again. But these three identical opinions, which I had heard without understanding, had lain dormant in my mind for years until one day they awoke in the form of an apparently original idea.[17]

He then goes on to relate three incidents in which these men discussed their patients, all suggesting that the disturbed condition was due to sexual frustration. Breuer remarked, "These things are always *secrets d'alcove!*"; [18] Charcot had said, *"Mais, dans des cas pareils c'est toujours la chose génitale, toujours . . . toujours . . . toujours"*; [19] Chrobak had indicated that the prescription for the malady which the patient was suffering from, which could not be ordered, was:

R. *Penis normalis*

dosim

repetatur! [20]

There are several things in this account which would make it less significant than Freud would have us believe. Freud's complex theory of sexuality, particularly the role of infantile sexuality in the development of neurosis, is considerably beyond these communications. The "piece of knowledge" that Freud says they imparted to him is not more than the age-old awareness of the psychological consequences of frustration of sexual satisfaction. It is difficult to imagine Freud's having been so sheltered that at least this much of the world's common knowledge of the importance of sexuality in the adolescent and adult should not have reached him earlier. Freud's statement that these communications had "lain dormant," etc., can only be interpreted as the ascription to them of an importance which had been displaced from something else. An hypothesis concerning the latter is the subject of this essay.

The passage quoted has all the earmarks of what Freud calls a screen memory,[21] the retention in memory of an everyday and indifferent event which could not produce any deep effects, but which in its recollection has overgreat clarity. Its function is to cancel from consciousness some other, related, repressed material. As Freud writes about the screen memory, "There is a common saying among us about shams, that they are not made of gold themselves but have lain beside something that *is* made of gold. The same simile might well be applied to some of the experiences of childhood which have been retained in the memory." [22]

With respect to screen memories, Freud also tells us that the force of the actual repressed material is quite strong and that the screen memory is a compromise. He tells us further that the screen memory may, in spite of its evident clarity, actually be false. If we look back over the episodes recounted by Freud, we note that Breuer and Chrobak denied that they took place. Either Breuer and Chrobak were mistaken or Freud was mistaken, and we shall never be able to ascertain which. Of Charcot, Freud himself adds, without the opportunity of actually checking, that he would have denied it. A psychoanalytic interpretation, that this presumed denial is the press of the actual repressed material forcing itself to the fore, announcing, in effect, "This is a screen memory," seems to suggest itself with considerable cogency. Moreover, the fact that Freud was subject to screen memories is clearly demonstrated by Bernfeld's analysis [23] of such a screen memory in Freud.

Under any circumstances, whether or not we accept the possibility of this having been a screen memory, the objective considerations make it very dubious whether Freud received the sexual theory from Breuer, Charcot, and Chrobak in the way that he describes.

Freud's lack of clarity concerning the sources of his ideas recurs on several occasions which we shall enumerate below. This characteristic forces us to the conclusion that the origins of his psychoanalytic thought are related to repressed or at least suppressed material. To further demonstrate this characteristic in him and to demonstrate the clearly unsatisfactory nature of his explanations, we will cite three other instances from his writings.

When he addressed the group at Clark University on his trip to America in 1909, he said that it was Breuer who was chiefly responsible for psychoanalysis. As he relates it in "On the History of the Psychoanalytic Movement,"

> The occasion was a momentous one for my work, and moved by this thought I then declared that it was not I who had brought psycho-analysis into existence. The credit for this was due to another, to Josef Breuer, whose work had been done at a time when I was still a student occupied with my examinations (1880-82).

Freud goes on to say that since he, and not Breuer, has been the object of "criticism and abuse," he must conclude that he, Freud, is the originator.[24] It is remarkable that neither his reason for first ascribing it to Breuer, nor his reason for changing his mind, are particularly cogent with respect to the objective question of the real sources of his thought.

The possibility that his own utterances with respect to the origins of psychoanalysis are without reliability is clearly indicated also by the following passage about his relationship to Fliess. This concerns the idea of bisexuality, an instance in which he evidently did get an idea from someone and forgot the source:

> In the summer of 1901 [1900], I once remarked to a friend with whom I was then actively engaged in exchanging ideas on scientific questions: "These neurotic problems can be solved only if we take the position of absolutely accepting an original bisexuality in every individual." To which he replied: "I told you that two and a half years ago, while we were taking an evening walk in Br. At that time, you wouldn't listen to it."
> It is truly painful to be thus requested to renounce one's originality. I could neither recall such a conversation nor my friend's revelation. One of us must be mistaken; and according to the principle of the question *cui prodest?*, I must be the one.

Indeed, in the course of the following weeks, everything came back to me just as my friend had recalled it. I myself remembered that at that time, I gave the answer: "I have not yet got so far, and I do not care to discuss it." But since this incident, I have grown more tolerant when I miss any mention of my name in medical literature in connection with ideas for which I deserve credit.[25]

The last example in this connection has to do with the presumed source of the method of free association. Freud's paper, "A Note on the Prehistory of the Technique of Analysis," [26] deals with the source of the method of free association. Freud, in an anonymously published, third-person answer to a suggestion that he might have gotten it from J. J. Garth Wilkinson, who wrote in 1857, replies that free association was written of even earlier, by Schiller in 1788, but "it is safe to assume that neither Schiller nor Garth Wilkinson had in fact any influence on the choice of psychoanalytic technique. It is from another direction that there are indications of a personal influence at work." [27] He then goes on to tell of a writer by the name of Ludwig Börne,* who wrote an essay in 1823 which clearly anticipates the method of free association. When Freud was fourteen years old he had been given the works of Börne and was still in possession of them fifty years later. "Börne . . . had been the first author into whose writings he [Freud] had penetrated deeply." [28] "Thus it seems not impossible that this hint may have brought to light the fragment of cryptomnesia which in so many cases may be suspected to lie behind apparent originality." [29]

* Ludwig Börne (1786-1837) was a Jewish-born writer whose original name was Löb Baruch. He changed his name when he embraced Christianity in 1818.

The material of these three instances illustrates both the way in which Freud would lead us to accept the hypothesis of the "germinal" idea, as well as the unsatisfactory nature of such an hypothesis. At best, the material suggests that Freud was unconscious of his sources, and that, exerting an effort to present an honest picture (and in some sense aware of drawing on something), he points, rather inadequately, to one or another incident which does come to mind as the possible source of his ideas.

NOTES TO CHAPTER 2

1. Cf. R. Spehlmann, *Sigmund Freud's neurologische Schriften* (Berlin: Springer-Verlag, 1953).
2. H. Gray, "Bibliography of Freud's Pre analytic Period," *Psychoanal. Rev.,* 1948, 35, 403-410.
3. Ernest Jones, *The Life and Work of Sigmund Freud* (3 vols., New York: Basic Books, 1953-1957), I, pp. 78-97.
4. E. Stengel, "A Re-evaluation of Freud's Book 'On Aphasia': Its Significance for Psycho-analysis," *Int. J. Psychoanalysis,* 1954, 35, 85-89, p. 85.
5. Jones, I, p. 45.
6. S. Freud, "Concluding Remarks on the Question of Lay Analysis," *Int. J. Psychoanalysis,* 1927, 8, 392-398, p. 394.
7. Jones, I, p. 27.
8. Jones, I, p. 35.
9. Jones, I, p. 11.
10. Hanns Sachs, *Freud, Master and Friend* (Cambridge, Mass.: Harvard University Press, 1944), pp. 99-100.
11. S. Freud, *The Interpretation of Dreams,* trans. and ed. J. Strachey (New York: Basic Books, 1955). This dream is discussed on pp. 106 ff.
12. Freud, *Origins,* p. 322.

13. Freud, *The Int. of Dreams,* p. xxxii.
14. Freud, *Moses and Monotheism,* p. 81.
15. P. Bergman, "The Germinal Cell in Freud's Psychoanalytic Psychology and Therapy," *Psychiatry,* 1949, 12, 265-278.
16. Freud, *Col. Papers,* I, p. 288.
17. Freud, *Col. Papers,* I, p. 294.
18. Freud, *Col. Papers,* I, p. 295.
19. Freud, *Col. Papers,* I, p. 295.
20. Freud, *Col. Papers,* I, p. 296.
21. Freud, *Col. Papers,* V, pp. 47-69.
22. Freud, *Col. Papers,* V, p. 52.
23. S. Bernfeld, "An Unknown Biographical Fragment by Freud," *American Imago,* 1946, 4, 3-19.
24. Freud, *Col. Papers,* I, p. 288.
25. S. Freud, *Basic Writings,* trans. A. A. Brill (New York: Modern Library, 1938), p. 101.
26. Freud, *Col. Papers,* V, pp. 101-104.
27. Freud, *Col. Papers,* V, pp. 102-103.
28. Freud, *Col. Papers,* V, p. 103.
29. Freud, *Col. Papers,* V, p. 104. On the method of free association, cf. pp. 75 ff., below.

3

Psychoanalysis as a Problem in the History of Ideas

If the personal hypotheses seem to be at best fragmentary we can find only a little more satisfaction in what may be regarded as the scientific forerunners of psychoanalytic thought. It is certainly possible, after the fact, to *assign* a place to Freud in the intellectual history of our civilization. This place would be connected by lines of similarity to the tradition of Leibniz, Herbart, Schelling, Schopenhauer, Nietzsche, Brentano, Carus, von Hartmann, Du Prel, etc.[1] There is certainly evidence to indicate that Charcot played some part in "starting" Freud. We can point to direct contact between Brentano and Freud,[2] and the writings of Carus are present in the part of the personal collection of Freud which is now housed in the library of the New York Psychiatric Institute. Carus in particular may be worthy of attention. For example, in a work published in 1846 he had already written that the key to the understanding of the life of the mind is in the region of the unconscious; and that all of the difficulties and the presumptive impossibilities concerning the secrets of the mind become clarified thereby.[3] Carus also strongly suggested that some diseases are due to repression into the unconscious, and that rapid cures may be effected by bringing to memory events which have been repressed.[4]

In addition there were general forces within the culture which were moving along "Freudian" lines. A breakthrough to the scientific and realistic study of sexuality had already been made; and what we would today recognize as the unconscious was touched upon by the academic group at Würzburg under Külpe in the first decade of the twentieth century quite independently of the psychoanalytic movement.[5]

In spite of the existence of such harbingers of psychoanalysis, the movement of thought which Freud developed still stands as a mystery from the point of view of the history of ideas. Although we can retrospectively assign a place to psychoanalysis in a series of intellectual developments which articulate with it, the question of its roots is still open. We do not deny Freud's creativity; but we look for the tradition within which he was creative.

A system of thought such as was developed by Freud, made up of so many different propositions, so consistent in its mood, containing so many far-reaching implications, and with subject matter so diverse, could only be the result of a culture; and by a culture we mean the achievement of at least several generations, involving relatively large numbers of people, whose life experiences pool themselves into a characteristic entity, a socially carried and organized personality. Psychoanalysis is at least a theory of development, a theory of neurosis, a theory of healing, a theory of culture, a theory of the role of sexuality, an armamentarium of devices for interpretation of human imaginative productions, a pattern of interpersonal relationship, and a philosophy of religion. And all of this is seemingly the work of a single individual. It is difficult to maintain that the whole tapestry of psychoanalysis could have been drawn out of seeming historical nothingness. As Pumpian-Mindlin happily expresses it, "Psychoanalysis did not spring full born from the head of its Zeus, Freud. . . ." [6] No matter how high our opinion of Freud may be—and what is being said here is not to be interpreted as in any way to Freud's discredit—it would be a violation of all that we know of cultural development to characterize the work of Freud as the *de novo* work of a single individual, especially in view of the fact that the work comes late in his life and appears as a burst over a relatively short period of time, attached, as it were, to a life that had previously been busy with other things.

NOTES TO CHAPTER 3

1. For an excellent review of the material on the unconscious that existed before Freud cf. H. Ellenberger, "The Unconscious Before Freud," *Bulletin of the Menninger Clinic,* 1957, **21,** 3-15.
2. P. Merlan, "Brentano and Freud," *J. Hist. Ideas,* 1945, **6,** 375-377; and "Brentano and Freud—A Sequel," *J. Hist. Ideas,* 1949, **10,** 451.
3. Carl Gustav Carus, *Psyche* (Jena: Eugen Diedrichs, 1926; originally published in 1846), p. 1.
4. Carus, *Psyche,* p. 66. Other works of Carus of interest in this connection are *Symbolik der menschlichen Gestalt: Ein Handbuch zur Menschenkenntnis* (Leipzig: Brockhaus, 1853): *Über*

Lebensmagnetismus, und über die magischen Wirkungen über-haupt (Basel: Benno Schwabe, 1925).
5. The latter is discussed in D. Bakan, "A Reconsideration of the Problem of Introspection," *Psychological Bul.*, 1954, 51, 105-118.
6. Ernest R. Hilgard, Lawrence S. Kubie, and E. Pumpian-Mindlin, *Psychoanalysis as Science* (Stanford, California: Stanford University Press, 1952), p. 125.

4

Anti-Semitism in Vienna

The thesis of this essay is that the contributions of Freud are to be understood largely as a contemporary version of, and a contemporary contribution to, the history of Jewish mysticism. Freud, consciously or unconsciously, secularized Jewish mysticism; and psychoanalysis can intelligently be viewed as such a secularization. As we hope will become clear in the remainder of this essay, Freud was engaged in the issues set by this history. Considerable illumination of the nature of psychoanalysis may be arrived at by tying it into this context. By separating the supernatural elements in mysticism from its other content, Freud succeeded in making a major contribution to science. We believe that this pattern, from mysticism to science, is one of the more important historical characteristics in the development of general science.* We have but to think of such major scientists as Newton, Kepler, and Fechner, who, deeply immersed in theological traditions, succeeded in so rationalizing the phenomena with which they were con-

---

* Cf. Bertrand Russell, "Mysticism and Logic" in *Mysticism and Logic* (New York: Doubleday and Co., 1957).

cerned that the supernatural elements, which were an integral part of their thought, could be abandoned as gratuitous. As E. Caro, a rationalist of the nineteenth century, aptly put it, "Science has conducted God to its frontiers, thanking him for his provisional services."

Let us attempt to get some idea of the circumstances in which Freud found himself at what he called the "turning point" in his life. The burden of proof rests very heavily on our shoulders to demonstrate the importance in Freud's development of a tradition to which he makes but scant reference. In this section we will try to demonstrate that *Freud had a most excellent reason for not specifying this tradition—if, indeed, he was conscious of its role in his thought. The reason is actually an eminently simple one: anti-Semitism, in which Jewish literature was a primary object of attack, was so widespread and so intense at the time that to indicate the Jewish sources of his ideas would have dangerously exposed an intrinsically controversial theory to an unnecessary and possibly fatal opposition.*

As a reference date in Freud's life let us take June 1882, about a month after Freud's twenty-sixth birthday. He had been working in Brücke's Institute as a demonstrator and had some hopes of rising in the academic hierarchy. Freud says of this time, "The turning point came in 1882, when my teacher, for whom I had the highest possible esteem, corrected my father's generous improvidence by strongly advising me, in view of my bad financial position, to abandon my theoretical career." [1]

Jones comments on this event, wondering ". . . why that important talk took place just when it did. Nor does one see what Brücke had to contribute to what Freud must already have known." [2] We believe that we can find the answer to the problem raised by Jones by considering what was then taking place in that part of Europe.

The year 1882 was a year of tremendous anti-Semitic agitation. In the preceding year a Jew by the name of Joseph Scharf had been brought to trial in Tisza-Eszlar in Hungary for presumably having murdered a fourteen-year-old girl by the name of Esther Solymossy for ritual purposes.

> The antisemitic press of all countries discussed the case with a passion characteristic and worthy of the middle-ages. A great antisemitic congress took place in Dresden and the Hungarian agitator, member of the "Landtag" Geza von Onody appeared there, bringing an oil painting of the Jewish martyr Esther Solymossy done from memory for agitation.[3]

We know that Freud was interested in this case from the fact that he commented on the psychiatric diagnosis of the chief witness in a letter.[4]

The synagogue at Tisza-Eszlar and the house of the caretaker were destroyed. In Pressburg, close to Vienna, excesses against the Jews were taking place. Count Egbert Belcredi gave money to the agitator Ernst Schneider to turn the fury of the people against the Jews in connection with an anarchist crime against a police officer. The Archduchess Maria Theresa made funds available for the appearance of the first anti-Semitic newspaper, the *Oesterreichischer Volksfreund* [Austrian Friend of the People].

The work of August Rohling, Professor at the University of

Prague, had appeared. This was a pamphlet entitled *The Talmud Jew,* which had seventeen editions; thirty-eight thousand copies of the sixth edition alone were distributed free in Westphalia. Rohling wrote,

> The Jews are authorized *by their religion* to take advantage of all non-Jews, to ruin them physically and morally, to destroy their lives, honour and property, openly by force, as well as secretly and insidiously; all this the Jews are allowed to do, nay, they even should do it *for the sake of religion,* so as to acquire power and domination over all the world for their nation.[5]

After Rohling's appointment at the University of Prague he offered himself as an expert to courts of law with respect to the truth of accusations of ritual murder.

> Rohling's challenge of the Talmud resounded like a declaration of war against Judaism through the streets of Vienna. Immediately all the newspapers of the world heard the echo of this great event. If he should triumph then all the pyres upon which Jews had been burned, all the edicts by which the Jews had been exiled, all the persecutions which had ever claimed Jewish martyrs would now be justified.[6]

Bloch, who was a major figure in the events of the time, writes:

> The year 1882 was not yet ended when a furious agitation against the Talmud raged through the streets of the Austrian capital, and that came about in the following way.
> An antisemitic agitator, Franz Holubek . . . had on the 4th of April 1882 under the presidency of Georg Ritter von Schönerer summoned a meeting of Christian tradesmen at the "Three Angels," a large hall in Vienna, 36 Grosse Neugasse where he made the following speech:

"The Jews are no longer our fellow citizens, they have become our masters, oppressors and tormentors.

"The Christians are to be weakened, annihilated, defamed, in the metropolis of the Empire of the Habsburg. Matters have come to such a pass that we must tremble to confess ourselves Christians.

"A nation which was already signally stigmatized by Tacitus has set up as our master, and is there nothing left for us but to bear this yoke?

"Judge if such a people has any right of existence amidst civilized society. I don't intend to stir you up, but hear and judge! This book, the Talmud! Do you know what this book contains? The Truth! And do you know how you are described in this book? As a herd of pigs, dogs and asses!" [7]

Such were some of the events that provided the social and political context of the "turning point" in Freud's life. These events serve perhaps to clarify Jones's query as to "why that important talk took place when it did." We cannot tell from the available literature whether the remarks by Brücke were merely advice or constituted an interview in which it was more strongly suggested to Freud that he separate himself from the Institute. Under any circumstances, even if Freud were not dismissed, it is clear that inevitably the pressure of anti-Semitic agitation was upon him. He must have been aware that the attacks which were taking place were directed not only against the Jews as people but also against the whole Jewish tradition and culture. Among the various charges made was one to the effect that the *Zohar,* the most important document in Jewish mysticism, which we will discuss presently, taught the Jews to sacrifice Christian virgins for God's pleasure.[8]

In the last two decades of the nineteenth century the ritual murder theme arose again and again in Europe, deeply affecting the Jews of Vienna and elsewhere. On June 29, 1891, the body of a boy was found at Xanten in Rhenish Prussia, and his death was attributed to the Jewish penchant for collecting blood.[9] In 1893 a pamphlet appeared entitled *A Ritual Murder, Established as Fact by Official Documents of a Trial,* by Father Joseph Deckert. This pamphlet told of a trial in 1474 of Jews accused of ritual murder. Deckert had engaged a Jew by the name of Paulus Meyer, presumably a "Tsaddick[10] pupil," who alleged that he had been a witness to ritual murders in Russia.[11] Accusations of this kind were prevalent in Russia, especially after the ascension of Nicholas II in 1894. There were blood accusations and riots against the Jews in Irkutsk, Shpola, Kantakuzov, Vladimir, and Nikol.[12] In 1899 a Jew by the name of Hilsner was convicted of ritual murder in Bohemia.[13]

The "Jewish Question" was a frequent topic of conversation. Karl Lueger * and the anti-Semitic Christian Socialist Party which he headed were powerful and influential. That Freud

---

* It is one of the ironies of history that a person of Jewish descent (though partial) like Lueger should have played an indirect but important role in the worst massacre of the Jews in history, that which took place under Hitler. Hitler said that it was Lueger who first convinced him of the correctness of the anti-Semitic position. Lueger was Hitler's hero. Hitler read the *Volksblatt,* which Lueger controlled, with great avidity.—A. Hitler, *Mein Kampf* (New York: Reynal and Hitchcock, 1939), pp. 71 ff. Lueger himself was a descendant of a Jewess who had permitted herself to be baptized rather than be burnt in an affair in which 240 Jews were killed. "In this descendant of the Jews saved from the stake the anti-semitic faction got a highly gifted commander, who knew how to excite the masses, to concentrate and keep them together, to change the catchword according to the necessity of the moment, and to give the lead to suit the desires of the crowd."— Bloch, p. 229.

concerned himself with these affairs is indicated by remarks in his letters. For example, in a letter to Fliess in which he talks of his struggles to stop smoking he says that he "only over-indulged one day for joy at Lueger's non-confirmation in of-fice." [14] He also discusses the Dreyfus affair.[15]

It is difficult, in the perspective of modern America, where the Jews are under less oppression than ever before in their history, to fully appreciate the intensity and reality of anti-Semitism at that time. The events which were taking place in Vienna can best be understood from the fact that they led eventually to the complete annihilation of 6,000,000 Jews, whose lives were systematically extinguished in places such as Bergen-Belsen, Auschwitz, Dachau, and Buchenwald. It was this mas-sacre-in-preparation which provided the social and political background in which psychoanalysis was being developed.

NOTES FOR CHAPTER 4

1. Freud, *An Autobiographical Study,* trans. J. Strachey (London: Hogarth Press, 1935), p. 16.
2. Jones, I, p. 6.
3. Joseph S. Bloch, *My Reminiscences* (Vienna and Berlin: R. Löwit, 1923), p. 30.
4. Jones, I, p. 190.
5. Bloch, p. 29.
6. Max Grunwald, *History of the Jews in Vienna* (Philadelphia: Jewish Publication Society of America, 1936), pp. 432-433.
7. Bloch, p. 61.
8. Bloch, p. 146.
9. Joshua Trachtenberg, *The Devil and the Jews: The Medieval Conception of the Jew and Its Relation to Modern Anti-semitism* (New Haven: Yale University Press, 1943), p. 138.

10. A *Zadik* was a Chassidic leader. Cf. pp. 110 ff., below.
11. Bloch, pp. 375 ff; Grunwald, pp. 445-446.
12. Jacob S. Raisin, *The Haskalah Movement in Russia* (Philadelphia: The Jewish Publication Society of America, 1913), pp. 275 ff.
13. Grunwald, p. 429. Actually the charges of ritual murder did not quite come to an end in the nineteenth century. In 1935 in New York City, two pamphleteers, Raymond J. Healey and Ernest F. Elmhurst, reasserted the libel that the Talmud commands Jews to kill Gentiles for ritual purposes.—*The Jewish Encyclopedia,* Vol. II, p. 401.
14. Freud, *Origins,* p. 133.
15. Freud, *Origins,* p. 245.

5

The General Question of Dissimulation

In Chapter 4 we indicated that Freud would have had good reason to deliberately conceal his sources if he were conscious that psychoanalysis was a development in the tradition of Jewish mysticism. In this chapter we will offer some ideas about dissimulation in publication generally, and later we will review some of the facts of Freud's life which may have some bearing on the question.

We are fortunate in having at our disposal the excellent analysis of the problem of dissimulation-in-writing by Leo Strauss.[1] He says,

> Modern historical research, which emerged at a time when persecution was a matter of feeble recollection rather than of forceful experience, has counteracted or even destroyed an earlier tendency to read between the lines of great writers, or to attach more weight to their fundamental design than to those views they have repeated most often. Any attempt to restore the earlier approach in this age of historicism is confronted by the problem of criteria for distinguishing between legitimate and illegitimate reading between the lines. If it is true that there is a necessary correlation between persecution and writing be-

tween the lines, then there is a necessary negative criterion: that the book in question must have been composed in an era of persecution, that is, at a time when some political or other orthodoxy was enforced by law or custom.[2]

Freud was indeed writing at a time when persecution was taking place. Strauss demonstrates with great clarity that when persecution is taking place the great writer will express himself so that he will not be personally persecuted. He will write in a way to avoid censorship on political or social grounds; and in spite of such censorship he will somehow succeed in getting his ideas across to those with whom he is interested in communicating.

Strauss characterizes the opposed scholarly view, what we can consider the "face value" approach, as follows:

The only presentations of an author's views which can be accepted as true are those ultimately borne out by his own explicit statements. [This] ... principle is decisive; it seems to exclude a priori from the sphere of human knowledge such views of earlier writers as are indicated exclusively between the lines. For if an author does not tire of asserting on every page of his book that *a* is *b*, but indicates between the lines that *a* is not *b*, the modern historian will still demand explicit evidence showing that the author believed *a* not to be *b*. Such evidence cannot possibly be forthcoming, and the modern historian wins his argument: he can dismiss any reading between the lines as arbitrary guesswork, or, if he is lazy, he will accept it as intuitive knowledge.[3]

In the context of modern views about integrity in writing, the idea that we are advancing, that there may have been a concealment of his sources, even if he was aware of them, might indeed be taken as a sign of disrespect for Freud and his work. Strauss says on this point,

> Every decent modern reader is bound to be shocked by the mere suggestion that a great man might have deliberately deceived the large majority of his readers. And yet, as a liberal theologian once remarked, these imitators of the resourceful Odysseus were perhaps merely more sincere than we when they called "lying nobly" what we would call "considering one's social responsibilities." [4]

Strauss analyzes three writers in detail to make his point about dissimulation-in-writing and its relation to persecution. He chooses for his treatment three Jewish writers, Maimonides, Halevi, and Spinoza, although he does not argue that this kind of writing is unique to Jewish writers. In the history of the Jews, persecution is a commonplace, repeated century after century. Strauss's analysis of Maimonides is particularly interesting because it deals directly with the problem of presenting Kabbala, the Jewish oral mystical tradition, in a way to provide against unfortunate consequences.

We believe that Freud often wrote with obscurity, that he was motivated, consciously or unconsciously, to hide the deeper portions of his thought, and that these deeper portions were Kabbalistic in their source and content. The Kabbalistic tradition itself has secrecy as part of its nature and deals with secret matters. The Kabbalistic tradition has it that the secret teachings are to be transmitted orally to one person at a time, and even then only to selected minds and by hints. This is indeed what Freud was doing in the actual practice of psychoanalysis, and *this aspect of the Kabbalistic tradition is still maintained in the education of the modern psychoanalyst. He must receive the tradition orally (in the training analysis).* As the modern practicing psychoanalyst is quick to tell anyone, psychoanalysis is not to be learned from books!

On this point Strauss's analysis of Maimonides' *The Guide for the Perplexed*[5] is very helpful. His analysis leads him to believe that Maimonides permitted himself to violate the tradition by *writing* because the Jews seemed to be doomed to a continuing diaspora which made the matter of the dissemination by oral communication too hazardous. "Indeed," he writes, "as it seems that there existed no Kabbalah, strictly speaking, before the completion of the *Guide,* one might suggest that Maimonides was the first Kabbalist."[6] As a consequence of the double pressure to record the teachings and at the same time not to violate the tradition by recording it, Maimonides set the teachings down in such an obscure way that only a small number of people would be able to penetrate and understand them, presumably only those who *should* receive this holy secret tradition.*

If we accept Strauss's analysis of Maimonides, Halevi, and Spinoza, it would seem that there exists a tradition in Jewish thought, forged in the crucible of persecution, to write in such a way that what is being expressed is veiled. If we accept the idea that Freud is in the mystical tradition (though a scientist too) then the communication of his ideas in a veiled way is even further supported by the intrinsic nature of the tradition. A further consequence of these considerations with respect to our understanding of Freud is that we cannot hope to obtain

---

* Even the Talmud was not set down until persecution threatened its loss, and when it was set down, there arose a protest that its living quality was thus destroyed.

any convincing evidence of the effect of Jewish mysticism on Freud by pursuing the question of what Freud read. As we will see later on, the Jewish mystical tradition translated itself from esoteric doctrine to large-scale social movements in the culture of Eastern European Jewry. With these developments the number of Jews who were personal bearers and transmitters of the tradition becomes quite large. In our analysis of the effect of Jewish mysticism on Freud we will resort to citations from the mystical literature, since these are what are directly at hand. However, this does not mean that Freud had necessarily read in this literature. Rather, the argument must rest on the historical continuity of the Jewish mystical tradition as it was embodied in the culture out of which Freud arises. As we shall see, when we analyze the features of Freud's self-identification as a Jew, it is this essential identification which emerges as critical.

NOTES TO CHAPTER 5

1. Leo Strauss, *Persecution and the Art of Writing* (Glencoe, Ill.: Free Press, 1952).
2. Strauss, pp. 31-32.
3. Strauss, p. 27.
4. Strauss, pp. 35-36.
5. Strauss, Chap. 3, pp. 38-94. "The Literary Character of *The Guide for the Perplexed*"; Moses Maimonides, *The Guide for the Perplexed,* trans. M. Friedlaender (2d ed., New York: E. P. Dutton, 1936). Maimonides was born in 1135 and died in 1204.
6. Strauss, p. 51. Although Strauss is *essentially* correct, the existence, for example, of the *Sefer Yetzirah* (cf. pp. 69-70, below) prior to Maimonides might lead one to qualify this assertion.

6

Did Freud Ever Dissemble?

Our hypothesis pertains to the Jewish mystical tradition, and not to whether Freud's participation in it was conscious or unconscious. Although the available evidence is completely inadequate on the conscious-unconscious question, it is still interesting to see if there is any evidence to indicate that Freud ever pursued a strategy of concealment. One can, of course, readily cite the reservations which he avows in *The Interpretation of Dreams*. There he stops short of further analysis because of considerations of discretion, and he tells us that he is doing so. But here the manifest reason is that the concealed material is personal.

Beyond this avowed use of discretion, it is of note that Freud is sometimes discreet without avowing it. We have a paper by Bernfeld in which he convincingly demonstrates that a presumptive case discussed by Freud is really Freud himself. Bernfeld says, "Here Freud resorts to outright lies. He disguises his identity radically by means of contrast, assuring us that Mr. Y's * profession is far distant from psychology." [1]

---

* The choice of the letter Y is interesting. The *yod* (Y) often designates a Jew.

An instance of concealment of another kind is the manner in which he published his essay "The Moses of Michelangelo." As we shall later see,[2] this essay is of particular significance with respect to our hypothesis concerning the role of Jewish mysticism in Freud's thought. Freud published the essay anonymously in *Imago* in 1914 with the following note by the editor:

> *Although this paper does not, strictly speaking, conform to the conditions under which contributions are accepted for publication in this Journal, the editors have decided to print it, since the author, who is personally known to them, belongs to psychoanalytical circles, and since his mode of thought has in point of fact a certain resemblance to the methodology of psychoanalysis.*[3]

Besides showing that Freud would engage in concealment, this note by the editor also makes another point manifest. As will be seen, this paper can be interpreted as a contribution to the Jewish mystical tradition, and the "certain resemblance to the methodology of psychoanalysis" is accordingly worthy of note.

Significant evidence that Freud would withhold or conceal out of consideration of consequences is present in his *Moses and Monotheism*. He indicates that his original intention (before he went to England) was to withhold the last and major part from publication.

> We are living here in a Catholic country under the protection of that Church, uncertain how long the protection will last. So long as it does last I naturally hesitate to do anything that is bound to awaken the hostility of that Church. It is not cowardice, but caution; the new enemy *—and I shall guard against

* i.e., German National Socialism.—Translator.

doing anything that would serve his interests—is more dangerous than the old one, with whom we have learned to live in peace. Psychoanalytic research is in any case the subject of suspicious attention from Catholicism. I do not maintain that this suspicion is unmerited. If our research leads us to a result that reduces religion to the status of a neurosis of mankind and explains its grandiose powers in the same way as we should a neurotic obsession in our individual patients, then we may be sure we shall incur in this country the greatest resentment of the powers that be. It is not that I have anything new to say, nothing that I did not clearly express a quarter of a century ago.† All that, however, has been forgotten, and it would undoubtedly have some effect were I to repeat it now and to illustrate it by an example typical of the way in which religions are founded. It would probably lead to our being forbidden to work in psychoanalysis. Such violent methods of suppression are by no means alien to the Catholic Church; she feels it rather as an intrusion into her privileges when other people resort to the same means. Psychoanalysis, however, which has travelled everywhere during the course of my long life, has not yet found a more serviceable home than in the city where it was born and grew.

I do not only think so, I know that this external danger will deter me from publishing the last part of my treatise on Moses. I have tried to remove this obstacle by telling myself that my fear is based on an overestimation of my personal importance, and that the authorities would probably be quite indifferent to what I should have to say about Moses and the origin of monotheistic religions. Yet I do not feel sure that my judgment is correct. It seems to me more likely that malice and an appetite for sensation would make up for the importance I may lack in the eyes of the world. So I shall not publish this essay. But that need not hinder me from writing it. The more so since it was written once before, two years ago, and thus only

† Freud is evidently referring to *Totem and Taboo*.

needs rewriting and adding to the two previous essays. Thus it may lie hid until the time comes when it may safely venture into the light of day, or until someone else who reaches the same opinions and conclusions can be told: 'In darker days there lived a man who thought as you did.' [4]

This diary-like entry by Freud shows clearly that he would conceal material on the grounds of social, religious, and political considerations. It indicates that he had a conscious conception of strategy with respect to the publication of the work on Moses, and we can perhaps infer that such considerations could have been operative in connection with his other writings, with more or less deliberateness. Indeed, in *The Interpretation of Dreams,* Freud tells us that dissimulation is a frequent social event in his life and specifically refers to writing. In his discussion of distortion in dreams he writes:

I will try to seek a social parallel to this internal event in the mind. Where can we find a similar distortion of a psychical act in social life? Only where two persons are concerned, one of whom possesses a certain degree of power which the second is obliged to take into account. In such a case the second person will distort his psychical acts or, as we might put it, will dissimulate. The politeness which I practise every day is to a large extent dissimulation of this kind; and when I interpret my dreams for my readers I am obliged to adopt similar distortions. The poet complains of the need for these distortions in the words:

> Das Beste, was du wissen kannst,
> Darfst du den Buben doch nicht sagen.*

* From Goethe's *Faust,* Part I, Scene 4, spoken by Mephistopheles. "After all, the best of what you know you may not tell to boys." The editor adds that "These were favourite lines of Freud."

A similar difficulty confronts the political writer who has disagreeable truths to tell those in authority. If he presents them undisguised, the authorities will suppress his words—after they have been spoken, if his pronouncement was an oral one, but beforehand, if he had intended to make it in print. *A writer must beware of the censorship, and on its account he must soften and distort the expression of his opinion. According to the strength and sensitiveness of the censorship he finds himself compelled either merely to refrain from certain forms of attack, or to speak in allusions in place of direct references, or he must conceal his objectionable pronouncement beneath some apparently innocent disguise* [our italics]; or for instance, he may describe a dispute between two Mandarins in the Middle Kingdom, when the people he really has in mind are officials in his own country. The stricter the censorship, the more far-reaching will be the disguise and the more ingenious too may be the means employed for putting the reader on the scent of the true meaning.[5]

Freud was eminently aware that the material he was writing would arouse resistance on the basis of its content alone, as well as because he was Jewish. The resistance would probably have redoubled had he indicated the Jewish sources of his thought. He concludes his essay, "The Resistances to Psycho-analysis," which enumerates several sources of resistance, with the following:

Finally, with all reserve, the question may be raised whether the personality of the present writer as a Jew who has never sought to disguise the fact that he is a Jew may not have had a share in provoking the antipathy of his environment to psycho-analysis. An argument of this kind is not often uttered aloud. But we have unfortunately grown so suspicious that we cannot avoid thinking that this factor may not have been without its effect. *Nor is it perhaps entirely a matter of chance*

that the first advocate of psycho-analysis was a Jew [our ital-
ics]. To profess belief in this new theory called for a certain
degree of readiness to accept a position of solitary opposition—
a position with which no one is more familiar than a Jew.[6]

In this passage, in the italicized sentence, we find the clearest
indication by Freud of a linkage between his being Jewish and
his creation of psychoanalysis. Yet the qualification, or the
explanation, which he adds, is that the Jewish characteristic
to which he has reference is the ability to stand alone in the
face of opposition. We can certainly accept this explanation on
Freud's part, although one cannot but wonder about its historical adequacy. The ability of the Jew to withstand opposition has historically been based in the Jewish *community*
rather than in individual heroes. In instances in which individual Jews have stood alone in the face of opposition or in
the willingness to accept martyrdom, they have done so with
a sense that they were defending a tradition, rather than as
"solitary opposition" for the sake of a radical innovation.

If we are skeptical of his explanation as to why it was not
"entirely a matter of chance that the first advocate of psychoanalysis was a Jew," an "explanation of the explanation" readily presents itself. On the one hand, if he wanted to suggest
that psychoanalysis is related to the Jewish tradition, he here
indicated it clearly. On the other hand, for him to say it in
its bare clarity, without qualification, would invite even greater
resistance than that which is the subject of his paper.

43

NOTES TO CHAPTER 6

1. S. Bernfeld, p. 16.
2. Cf. pp. 121 ff., below.
3. Freud, *Col. Papers,* IV, p. 257.
4. Freud, *Moses and Monotheism,* pp. 67-69.
5. Freud, *The Int. of Dreams,* pp. 141-142.
6. Freud, *Col. Papers,* V, pp. 174-175.

7

Freud's Positive Identification as a Jew

Thus far we have indicated that the question of the "origins" of psychoanalysis is an open one, that the usual hypotheses for explaining its origins are unsatisfactory, that great writers engage in dissimulation-in-writing when they are under conditions of persecution, that there was persecution of Jews at the time Freud was writing, that he was capable of dissimulation, and that he specifically talked of dissimulating-in-writing. These considerations are background material for our attempt to demonstrate that psychoanalysis is to be understood as developing in the tradition of Jewish mysticism.

We turn now to a consideration of some of the information available concerning Freud's self-identification as a Jew. A deeply grounded sense of identification with a culture is not by itself evidence of the effect of that culture upon a person's intellectual productions. Owing to the great fractionation of intellectual effort, there are many instances in which there is little manifest relationship between intellectual or professional pursuits and the original culture from which the person stems. Yet there are noteworthy differences among pursuits. The ethnic background of a chemist is no doubt less significant for the appreciation of his work than is, say, that of a novelist.

In the case of psychoanalysis, its development is closely related to the ethnicity of its originator. For there has hardly been a scientific pursuit which was so spun out of the being of the investigator. The images which Freud uses to describe his work on dream interpretation are pertinent in this connection. He writes of it: "None of my works has been so completely my own as this; it is my own dung-heap, my own seedling and a *nova species mihi (sic!)*." [1] Freud's major work, *The Interpretation of Dreams,* is unique in the history of science and medicine in that it draws so heavily and directly on the most intimate features of the investigator himself.

Drawn as it is from his personal being, that being is necessarily the locus of our investigation. And for our purposes we are interested in this locus as it contained within it a culture.

We consider first the opening of Freud's autobiography. After a few brief introductory remarks he writes:

> I was born on May 6, 1856, at Freiberg in Moravia, a small town in what is now Czecho-Slovakia. My parents were Jews, and I have remained a Jew myself. [2]

To assert that his parents were Jews and also that he remained a Jew himself is not quite as redundant as it may seem. For baptism stood as an invitation and temptation to all Jews who encountered Western civilization. As Heine once put it, baptism was an "admission ticket to European civilization" for the Jew. Baptism held out the promise of the removal of the obstacles that stood in the way of success. "A proof of their [the Jews of Vienna] unfavorable political situation in Austria is afforded by the large number of conversions to Christianity, which amounted to 559 in 1900, and 617 in 1904." [3] That Freud should say he "remained" a Jew is indicative of his position with respect to religious assimilation.

Freud expressed himself very clearly to Max Graf on the matter of conversion. Graf says,

> On the occasion of some of his visits the conversation would touch upon the Jewish question. Freud was proud to belong to the Jewish people which gave the Bible to the world. When my son was born, I wondered whether I should not remove him from the prevailing antisemitic hatred, which at that time was preached in Vienna by a very popular man, Doctor Lueger. [4] I was not certain whether it would not be better to have my son brought up in the Christian faith. Freud advised me not to do this. "If you do not let your son grow up as a Jew," he said, "you will deprive him of those sources of energy which cannot be replaced by anything else. He will have to struggle as a Jew, and you ought to develop in him all the energy he will need for that struggle. Do not deprive him of that advantage." [5]

The idea of Jewishness as a source of energy is one which recurs several times in Freud's writings.

One of his most interesting statements on his Jewish identification occurs in the speech that he prepared for delivery at the B'nai B'rith in Vienna on the occasion of his seventieth birthday. He said that in the years following 1895 [6]

> It seemed to me that I was like a man outlawed, shunned by everyone. In my isolation the longing arose in me for a circle of chosen, high-minded men who, regardless of the audacity

of what I had done, would receive me with friendliness. Your society was pointed out to me as a place where such men were to be found.

That you were Jews only suited me the more, for I myself was a Jew, and it always seemed to me not only shameful but downright senseless to deny it.[7]

Participation in the B'nai B'rith lodge in Vienna was one of the very few recreations that Freud permitted himself—among his recreations was his weekly game of taroc,[8] a popular card game based on Kabbala. It was there that he first presented his ideas on dream interpretation. This was in December 1897, about half a year before he first mentioned writing *The Interpretation of Dreams*. He writes to Fliess about it:

> I gave a lecture on dreams to my Jewish society (an audience of laymen) last Tuesday, and it had an enthusiastic reception. I shall continue it next Tuesday. . . .[9]

It was to this group also that he first expressed himself on his most audacious theme, the theme of God and Satan.[10]

Freud was a member of the Yiddish Scientific Institute (YIVO) in Vilno. In a letter addressed to Dr. Jacob Meitlis in 1938 he writes:

> So you are going to South Africa in order to revive among our people *(Volksgenossen)* there interest in our scientific institute in Vilno. I do not doubt that your mission will be successful.
>
> We Jews have always known how to respect spiritual values. We preserved our unity through ideas, and because of them we have survived to this day. The fact that Rabbi Jochanan ben Zakkai immediately after the destruction of the Temple obtained from the conqueror permission to establish the first

academy for Jewish knowledge in Jabneh was for me always one of the most significant manifestations of our history.*

Once again our people is faced with dark times requiring us to gather all our strength in order to preserve unharmed all culture and science during the present harsh storms. The significance of YIVO of Vilno among our other institutions you know better than I do, and you will be able to pass it on with conviction to our friends in South Africa.[11]

From the article by Meitlis we learn several other things: Freud believed that anti-Semitism was practically ubiquitous in either latent or manifest form; the broad masses in England were anti-Semitic "as everywhere"; he was of the opinion that the book on Moses would anger the Jews; he expressed a love for Hebrew and Yiddish, according to Freud's son; he refused to accept royalties on Hebrew and Yiddish translations of his works; he was sympathetic to Zionism from the first days of the movement and was acquainted with and respected Herzl; [12] he had once sent Herzl a copy of one of his works with a personal dedication; Freud's son was a member of Kadimah, a Zionist organization, and Freud himself was an honorary member of it.

A question of importance is that of the extent of Freud's knowledge of Hebrew and Yiddish. There is a considerable

* We find this idea expressed in *Moses and Monotheism* as follows: "We know that Moses had given the Jews the proud feeling of being God's chosen people; by dematerializing God a new, valuable contribution was made to the secret treasure of the people. The Jews preserved their inclination towards spiritual interests. The political misfortune of the nation taught them to appreciate the only possession they had retained, their written records, at its true value. Immediately after the destruction of the Temple in Jerusalem by Titus, Rabbi Jochanan ben Sakkai asked for permission to open at Jabneh the first school for the study of the Torah. From now on, it was the Holy Book, and the study of it, that kept the scattered people together."—Freud, *Moses and Monotheism*, p. 147.

sprinkling throughout his writings of both Hebrew and Yiddish words. He could not have been around the Jewish quarter of Vienna without running into Yiddish constantly. It is not likely that he would make a collection of Jewish stories without a knowledge of Yiddish. It is indicative that Freud felt some shame or guilt, or at least some desire to conceal the collecting of these stories, since he "confesses" to Fliess that he had made "a collection of deeply significant Jewish stories" in 1897.[13] As far as Hebrew is concerned, Jones says, "He had of course been taught Hebrew." [14] On Freud's thirty-fifth birthday, his father gave him the Bible in which he had read as a boy, inscribed in Hebrew as follows:

> My dear Son,
>   It was in the seventh year of your age that the spirit of God began to move you to learning. I would say the spirit of God speaketh to you: "Read in My book; there will be opened to thee sources of knowledge and of the intellect." It is the Book of Books; it is the well that wise men have digged and from which lawgivers have drawn the waters of their knowledge.
>   Thou hast seen in this Book the vision of the Almighty, thou hast heard willingly, thou hast done and hast tried to fly high upon the wings of the Holy Spirit. Since then I have preserved the same Bible. Now, on your thirty-fifth birthday [15] I have brought it out from its retirement and I send it to you as a token of love from your old father.[16]

The internal evidence of the quotation and the fact that the inscription itself is in Hebrew strongly suggest that Freud himself must have known the language, since, it would seem, Jakob Freud expected his son to understand it. Jones even tells us the name of the man who taught Freud "Scriptures and

Hebrew," a Professor Hammerschlag, with whom, moreover, Freud was on intimate terms. Freud named one of his children after Hammerschlag's daughter and another after Hammerschlag's niece. "Freud said of him, 'He has been touchingly fond of me for years: there is such a secret sympathy between us that we can talk intimately together.' " [17]

In view of this evidence it seems strange indeed that Freud should deny knowledge of these languages in print. In an introductory statement to a Yiddish translation [18] of one of his works he addresses the translator by saying that he was happy to have received a copy of the work and that he took it in his hands with great respect. It is unfortunate, he adds, that he can do no more with it. For, in the days when he was a student, they gave no care to the cultivation of the national tradition. He, therefore, did not learn either Hebrew or Yiddish, which he regrets very much. Nevertheless, he has still become a good Jew, although perhaps, not a believer. [19] He makes a similar denial in the preface to the Hebrew edition of *Totem and Taboo.*

It may well be that although he had learned these languages in his youth, he had forgotten much of them. However, we cannot believe that his knowledge of Hebrew and Yiddish was so slight that it would have been difficult for him to have been influenced by Jewish traditions expressed in these languages—as witness the "deeply significant Jewish stories" * which he collected. We can perhaps speculate that his denial

* Freud, *Origins,* p. 211. It is interesting to speculate whether these "deeply significant Jewish stories" were exclusively of jokes, or whether they were not out of the treasury of Chassidic legends.

may have been motivated, again consciously or unconsciously, by the desire to avoid too close an association of psychoanalysis with Judaism.

Jones tells us that Freud ". . . felt himself to be Jewish to the core, and it evidently meant a great deal to him. He had the common Jewish sensitiveness to the slightest hint of anti-Semitism and he made very few friends who were not Jews." [20] On one occasion he "announced that he was a Jew and neither an Austrian nor a German." [21] He was extremely fond of telling Jewish stories and jokes and sometimes demonstrated an extreme sensitivity about expressing Jewish character publicly, a prudence which appears to be highly relevant to our present thesis. For example, on one occasion, after the publication of one of Theodor Reik's reviews, Freud referred to one of Reik's remarks as "a Jewish joke, too good for those *goyim* † and makes a bad impression." [22] That he felt that there were certain things about Jews which are better concealed is indicated in a letter to his wife-to-be. He writes that George Eliot's *Daniel Deronda* had "amazed him by its knowledge of Jewish intimate ways that 'we speak of only among ourselves.' " [23] When he was in America he sent greetings by cablegram to his family on the High Holidays.[24]

It is important to distinguish between Freud's sense of identity as a Jew and his acceptance of Jewish religious doctrines. The intensity of his feelings on his Jewish identity was matched by his rejection of religious doctrine and practice. His works on religion are *against* the classical Judaeo-Christian religious doctrines. Yet his sense of Jewish identity was so

† Gentiles.

strong that we might consider his *genetic* conception of the Jew, most clearly asserted in his *Moses and Monotheism,* as the theoretical counterpart of his deep feeling of Jewish identity.

NOTES TO CHAPTER 7

1. Freud, *Origins,* p. 281.
2. Freud, *Autobiographical Study,* p. 12.
3. *The Jewish Encyclopedia,* XII, p. 437.
4. Cf. pp. 30-31, above.
5. M. Graf, "Reminiscences of Professor Sigmund Freud," *Psychoanal. Quar.,* 1942, **11**, 465-476, p. 473.
6. The year in which Freud had the dream of Irma's injection and presumably in which *The Interpretation of Dreams* was conceived.
7. Freud, "On Being of the B'nai B'rith," *Commentary,* March, 1946, 23-24, p. 23.
8. "On Saturday evenings I indulge in an orgy of taroc, and I spend every other Tuesday evening among my Jewish brethren."—Freud, *Origins,* p. 312.
9. Freud, *Origins,* p. 238.
10. Sachs, p. 105; cf. pp. 187 ff., below.
11. Jacob Meitlis, "The Last Days of Sigmund Freud," *Jewish Frontier,* September, 1951, **18** (No. 9), 20-22.
12. Theodor Herzl was the founder of the Zionist movement. Cf. pp. 173 ff., below.
13. Freud, *Origins,* p. 211.
14. Jones, I, p. 21.
15. I.e., the beginning of his thirty-sixth year. Cf. pp. 198 ff., below.
16. Jones, I, p. 19.
17. Jones, I, p. 163.
18. Freud, *Arainfir in Psichoanalyz* [Introduction to Psychoanalysis], trans. M. Weinreich (Vilno: YIVO, 1936).

19. Cf. p. 296, below.
20. Jones, I, p. 22.
21. Jones, I, p. 184.
22. Theodor Reik, *The Search Within* (New York: Farrar, Straus and Cudahy, 1956), p. 637.
23. Jones, I, p. 174.
24. Personal communication from Theodor Reik.

8

Freud's Relationship to Fliess and His Other Jewish Associates

Freud spent his whole life in a virtual ghetto, a world made up almost exclusively of Jews. Not, however, that there were no noteworthy exceptions as, for example, Brücke and Jung; and not that his non-Jewish associations were not important to him. Still, the essential part of his cultural experience was with the community of Jews.

Both of Freud's parents came from Galicia, a region whose atmosphere was saturated with Chassidism, a late and socially widespread form of Jewish mysticism. Freud says explicitly, in a letter to Roback, that his father came from a Chassidic milieu,[1] and we know from a paper by Aron that Tysmenitz, the birthplace of Jakob Freud, Freud's father, was filled with Chassidic lore and learning. Aron also reports a conversation between Freud and Chaim Bloch in which they discussed Kabbala, Chassidism, and Judaism in general. Aron remarks, "What it was that moved Freud to interest himself in Kabbala and Chassidism is not hard to understand. He must have felt himself to be spiritually at home in these worlds."[2]

Freud's mother was born in the Galician city of Brody, one of the great centers of Chassidic thought in Eastern Europe. Her ancestry goes back at least to Samuel Charmatz, who died in Brody in 1717.[3]

It is interesting that Freud's parents were married by a rabbi associated with the Jewish Reform movement, Rabbi Noah Mannheimer, who, moreover, in 1841 had engaged in a polemic against Rabbi Isaac Bernays, the grandfather of Martha, Freud's wife,[4] whom we will discuss shortly.

The town of Tysmenitz is significant because of the early efforts of the Jews there to move into Western civilization while maintaining their Jewish identity. In a document[5] written by the Jews of Tysmenitz in the mid-nineteenth century, they openly declared their nationalistic convictions with respect to Poland, and embraced the prevailing revolutionary doctrine of "liberty, equality, and fraternity." The document asserts the conviction that the new political events are indicative of a new life for "the oppressed and deeply bowed Israel." The cleavage between Jews and Christians is attributed to the old system and wholehearted allegiance is given to the new political events of 1848. Some significance may be attached to the fact that Freud was originally named Sigismund and not Sigmund. This is the name that appears on his birth record in Freiberg[6] and the name he kept at least until his thirteenth year as indicated by the *Gymnasium* records.[7] The name Sigismund is one which is traditionally associated with a liberal attitude toward the Jews, the first, second, and third Sigismunds, kings of Poland, each having played the role of protector of the Jews.[8]

Freud's intimate association with the Bernays family may also be significant. Rabbi Isaac Bernays of Hamburg had been called the "leading monarch of mind" for the Jewish world at his time. He is described as "a queer and eccentric personality and his philosophy of Judaism was full of mystic vagaries, some of which were contrary and foreign to the true Jewish spirit." [9] As we shall see later, the mystical mood often spilled over into apostasy. As a possible instance of this trend, it should be noted that Isaac Bernays' son Michael, uncle of Martha, was converted to Christianity.[10] Freud's sister married Martha's brother; and Martha's sister, Minna, lived in the Freud household for many years and evidently provided Freud with assistance in his work and also moral support.

Owing perhaps to ambiguities in Freud's writings about Josef Breuer, the role that Breuer may have played in the development of psychoanalysis is somewhat obscure. For our purposes, it is of particular note that Breuer was, like Freud, a Jew, and thus under similar cultural influences. He was the son of Leopold Breuer, one of the most famous Jewish religious leaders and teachers of his time.[11] In a brief autobiographical statement written as a *curriculum vitæ* for the archives of the *Wiener Akademie der Wissenschaft* in 1923, Breuer tells of studying under his father and of the great significance his father played in his development.[12]

Freud, as we recall, had attributed the original discoveries of psychoanalysis to Breuer. In his Clark University lectures he asserted quite forthrightly that Breuer was the originator of psychoanalysis,[13] although he disclaimed this later.

Furthermore, it may be argued that a cultural readiness for

psychoanalysis existed among the Jews in Vienna from the facts that Freud's first audience for his psychoanalytic ideas was his "Jewish Society," the B'nai B'rith, and that practically all of the early psychoanalysts were Jews. The major non-Jewish figure among them was Jung, who arises from a clearly mystical tradition within Christianity.[14] We recall in this connection the affairs at the Second International Psycho-Analytical Congress at Nuremberg in 1910. Freud had proposed that Jung be made permanent president. A protest meeting was held in a hotel room. Freud appeared on the scene and said,

> "Most of you are Jews, and therefore you are incompetent to win friends for the new teaching. Jews must be content with the modest role of preparing the ground. It is absolutely essential that I should form ties in the world of general science. I am getting on in years, and am weary of being perpetually attacked. We are all in danger." Seizing his coat by the lapels, he said, "They won't even leave me a coat to my back. The Swiss will save us—will save me, and all of you as well." [15]

Perhaps the most noteworthy of Freud's associations was his friendship with Wilhelm Fliess, a Jewish physician living in Berlin, with whom Freud carried on a very extensive correspondence between 1887 and 1902. A substantial portion of Freud's correspondence to Fliess has been made available. Besides letter writing, they arranged for frequent "congresses" at designated cities to spend time discussing each other's ideas. "The letters cover the period from 1887 to 1902, from Freud's thirty-first to forty-sixth year, from when he had just set up in practice as a specialist in nervous and mental diseases until he was engaged in his preliminary studies for *Three Essays on the Theory of Sexuality*. To the years of this correspondence there belong, besides his first essays on the neuroses, the *Studies on Hysteria* (1895 . . .), *The Interpretation of Dreams* (1900 . . .), *The Psychopathology of Everyday Life* (1901 . . .) and *Fragment of an Analysis of a Case of Hysteria* (1905 . . .)." [16]

Fliess is described as follows: "All who knew him emphasize his wealth of biological knowledge, his imaginative grasp of medicine, his fondness for far-reaching speculation, and his impressive personal appearance; they also emphasize his tendency to cling dogmatically to a once-formed opinion." [17]

There are two views of Freud's relationship to Fliess. Kris, in his introduction to the published version of the correspondence, says:

> However, the true motive of the correspondence was not provided by the similarity in the two men's origin, intellectual background and family situation, or, indeed, by anything personal . . . All Freud's letters that have come down to us go to show that the true motive behind the correspondence was the two men's common scientific interests. [18]

On the other hand, Jones advances the view that the relationship was primarily emotional. He refers to this friendship as "the only really extraordinary experience in Freud's life," and indicates that it is to be understood as a "passionate friendship" for someone intellectually his inferior, a "passionate relationship of dependence" [19] from 1895 to 1901. "The extreme dependence he displayed towards Fliess, though diminishing in degree, up to the age of forty-five has almost the appearance of a delayed adolescence." [20]

Jones cites a passage from a letter to Fliess written on New Year's Day of 1896, in which Freud says,

> People like you should not die out, my friend; we others need the like of you too much. How much have I to thank you for in consolation, understanding, stimulation in my loneliness, in the meaning of life you have given to me, and lastly in health which no one else could have brought back to me. It is essentially your example that has enabled me to gain the intellectual strength to trust my own judgment . . . and to face with deliberate resignation, as you do, all the hardships the future may have in store. For all that accept my simple thanks.[21]

What may Fliess have meant to Freud? Fliess was a person who had a deep and wide knowledge of biology, physiology, and the general science of his day. He may well have been to Freud an embodiment of contemporary scientific knowledge, in part symbolic of the scientific materialistic superego of the day, the same superego with which Freud's scientific background had provided him. In these matters, Fliess was more competent than Freud, at least in Freud's opinion, and Freud could look up to him. Thus Fliess could play much the same role as Brücke, Freud's earlier scientific mentor. By virtue of his scientific knowledge Fliess could represent to Freud the authority of science.

Around the autumn of 1895, Freud wrote what the translator calls a "Project for a Scientific Psychology," [22] in immediate response to a "congress" with Fliess. It was written in three parts and sent to Fliess. The first and second parts were begun on the train on the return trip. The manuscript was truly a Project for a Scientific Psychology in the tradition of the science of the day.

Although Fliess may have embodied the scientific superego, yet he permitted himself to be quite wanton with the scientific tradition. In his own work he essentially abandoned the discipline associated with materialistic science. For example, in 1897 Fliess published his book on the relationship between the nose and the female sexual organs.[23] This book, by the scientific standards of 1897 as well as of today, is readily dismissable. Yet when a disparaging review of it appeared in the *Wiener Klinische Rundschau,* Freud demanded redress for Fliess and resigned in protest from his association with this periodical.

In his book Fliess argues for a relationship between menstruation and the turbinate scrolls of the nose, and claims that certain gynecological complaints can be cured by cauterizing the appropriate parts of the nasal apparatus. The book is replete with numerology. There are, he says, two major periods in animal and vegetable species, and all the major events fall on multiples of these numbers. The male period is twenty-three days and the female period is twenty-eight days. On this basis important events are determined. Presumably, the last battle of Napoleon can be explained by such a numerological scheme. Goethe's death was on his 30,156th day, or 1,077 cycles of twenty-eight days; Goethe died "when the 1,077th feminine menstruation had exhausted the last bit of his wonderful organization." [24]

The combination in a single person of great scientific competence with speculative nonconformity must have been extremely important to Freud. For if Fliess, who had so much more scientific knowledge than Freud, was unimpressed by the scientific superego, then Freud too could win license to abandon worship of this image. The fact that he had never quite been able to wear the cloak of the scientist with comfort made discard all the easier when Fliess, who wore it well, could shed it because *it* was not good. The fact that Fliess could abandon the classical scientific image may have meant to Freud that there was more reason than his own possible incompetence for abandoning it.

Whether Fliess was really so eminently competent on scientific matters as Freud may have believed is an open question. All that matters is that Freud regarded him in this way. Kris says that Freud's high opinion of Fliess as a scientist

> ... lends support to the suspicion that his over-rating of Fliess's personality and scientific importance corresponded to an inner need of his own. He made of his friend and confidant an ally in his struggle with official medical science, the science of the high-and-mighty professors and university clinics, though Fliess's contemporary writings show that such a role was remote from his thoughts. Freud, to bind his friend closer to him, tried to elevate him to his own level, and sometimes idealized his picture of his assumed ally into that of a leader in the world of science.[25]

Fliess, in his major thought, combined three important Kabbalistic elements: the notion of bisexuality, the extensive use of numerology, and the doctrine of the predestination of the time of death—the doctrine of "life portions." Thus Fliess may be regarded as an even less secularized Kabbalist than Freud. Freud, as we know, later despaired of Fliess's scientific extravagances. Fliess was further left than Freud ever dared to be. Compared to Fliess, Freud was conservative. And perhaps his contact with Fliess allowed him to liberate his imagination in a way which the orthodox scientific superego could not permit.

Fliess, then, represented the suspended scientific superego.[26] We have no information concerning Fliess on the degree to which he may have been immersed in the Kabbalistic tradition. Certainly his work, both technically and atmospherically, seems to suggest this tradition. And it is evident that Freud found in him someone who was permissive of deviations from the strict scientific spirit. Thus the relationship between them was neither exclusively emotional nor exclusively intellectual. Just as neither Kabbalah nor psychoanalysis separates the intellectual and affective, so these aspects were not separated in the relationships of the two men.

We have pointed out that there was a cultural readiness for psychoanalysis in Fliess, Breuer, and the early psychoanalysts. In our view this cultural readiness is based upon the tradition of Jewish mysticism. In the few instances in which Freud assigns priority to others, they were primarily Jews. To Breuer he ascribes the beginning of psychoanalysis, although he later retracted it. Fliess is the source of the theory of bisexuality. To Börne he ascribes the method of free association. And finally he takes a deep bow in the direction of another Jew, Popper-Lynkeus, this time for the theory of dream interpretation. In "On the History of the Psychoanalytic Movement," he writes,

> I found the essential characteristic and most significant part of my dream theory—the reduction of dream-distortion to an inner conflict, a kind of inward dishonesty—later in a writer who was familiar with philosophy though not with medicine, the en-

gineer J. Popper, who published his *Phantasien eines Realisten* under the name of Lynkeus.[27]

Among Popper's engineering achievements was his work on the transmutation of electrical power and his development of the turbine. He had written on many topics and was interested in the furtherance of the humanitarian ideal and the institution of social reform. In Freud's essay "My Contact with Josef Popper-Lynkeus," he writes that after he had discovered Popper's treatment of dream distortion, he read all of his works. He says, "A special feeling of sympathy drew me to him, since he too had clearly had painful experience of the bitterness of the life of a Jew and of the hollowness of the ideals of present-day civilization." [28]

Most interesting, however, is the final paragraph, in which he identifies Popper as a Jew, identifies him with the scientific tradition, and adds that part of his reluctance to approach him was that Popper was a scientist. He says, in explanation of this reluctance, "And after all Josef Popper had been a physicist: he had been a friend of Ernest Mach. I was anxious that the happy impression of our agreement upon the problem of dream-distortion should not be spoilt." [29] In Popper-Lynkeus we see the same combination of elements that we have seen before: the ascription to a Jew of an essential feature of psychoanalysis, the identification with him as a Jew, and the attraction to a person who combined the psychoanalytic and scientific types of thought; although, as the last quotation would indicate, he was in this case afraid of being rejected by the scientific side of the man. Popper was thus in part identified by Freud as a person sympathetic to his views. Yet Popper could not serve so well as a symbolized suspension of the scientific superego. Freud felt that he was too closely allied to the scientific tradition.

NOTES TO CHAPTER 8

1. A. A. Roback, *Freudiana* (Cambridge, Mass.: Sci-Art Publishers, 1957), p. 27.
2. W. Aron, "Farzeichnungen wegen opshtam fun Sigmund Freud un wegen sein Yiddishkeit" [Notes concerning the genealogy of Sigmund Freud and concerning his Jewishness], *Yivo Bleter,* 40, 166-174, p. 169.
3. Aron, p. 170.
4. Aron, p. 166.
5. Karol Widman, *Franciszek Smolka* (Lwow: 2. Drukarni Instytutu Stauropigianskiego, 1886), pp. 870-873.
6. Adams, p. 361.
7. Susan C. Bernfeld, "Freud and Archaeology," *American Imago,* 1951, 8, 107-128, p. 125.
8. S. M. Dubnow, *History of the Jews in Russia and Poland,* trans. Friedlaender (3 vols., Philadelphia: Jewish Publication Society of America, 1916), I, pp. 71, 83, 93.
9. Meyer Waxman, *A History of Jewish Literature* (3 vols.; New York: Bloch Publishing Co., 1936), III, p. 400.
10. W. Aron, "Professor Dr. Michael Bernays—Renegade," *Jewish Forum,* 1950, 33, 39-40.
11. Grunwald, p. 521.
12. C. P. Oberndorf (ed. and trans.), "Autobiography of Josef Breuer (1842-1925)," *Int. J. Psychoanalysis,* 1953, 34, 64-67. This document is part of the collection at the library of the New York Psychiatric Institute.
13. Freud, "The Origin and Development of Psychoanalysis," *Am. J. of Psychology,* 1910, 21, 181-218, p. 181. Cf. p. 16, above.

14. On the influence of Kabbala on Christianity, see J. L. Blau, *The Christian Interpretation of the Cabala in the Renaissance* (New York: Columbia University Press, 1944).
15. Fritz Wittels, *Sigmund Freud,* trans. Eden and Cedar Paul (New York: Dodd, Mead and Co., 1924), p. 140.
16. Freud, *Origins,* p. 3.
17. Freud, *Origins,* p. 4.
18. Freud, *Origins,* p. 11.
19. Jones, I, p. 287.
20. Jones, I, p. 295.
21. Jones, I, 298-299. This passage is not in the *Origins.* It is our hope that someday the editors might be persuaded to release all of Freud's correspondence with Fliess, Martha Bernays, and others.
22. Freud, *Origins,* pp. 347-445.
23. Wilhelm Fliess, *Die Beziehungen zwischen Nase und weiblichen Geschlechtsorganen, in ihrer biologischen Bedeutung dargestellt* (Wien: Deuticke, 1897).
24. Fliess, p. 210.
25. Freud, *Origins,* p. 14.
26. Cf. pp. 187 ff., below.
27. Freud, *Col. Papers,* I, p. 302.
28. Freud, *Col. Papers,* V, p. 301.
29. Freud, *Col. Papers,* V, p. 301.

Part II

The Milieu of Jewish Mysticism

9

Early Kabbala

Jewish mysticism is an historically evolved tradition. To better appreciate the character of Freud's participation in this tradition, we pause to gain some conception of its evolution. The beginning of an intellectual or spiritual movement cannot be accurately dated. A live school of Jewish mysticism is already evident in the first century A.D. among the pupils of Jochanan ben Zakkai, to whom, it will be recalled, Freud makes reference in his letter to Josef Meitlis and in *Moses and Monotheism*.[1] For the first thousand years of the Christian era the tradition was maintained and continuously developed among small groups of Jews, transmitted largely by word of mouth from generation to generation. The central theme of the early Jewish mystics is Merkabah (throne) mysticism. The central theme of this early mysticism is the image of God sitting on His throne, surrounded by the heavenly beings. The major source for the content of this image is the vision of Ezekiel.[2]

The term Kabbala, as such, appears in written form for the first time in the eleventh century,[3] in the writings of Ibn Gabirol. Among the earliest Kabbalistic texts is the *Sefer*

Yetzirah [The Book of Formation]. Waite refers to it as "the primitive text of accepted Kabbalistic doctrine in Israel." [4] It is referred to in the Talmud. According to legend it was written by Abraham. It may have been available as early as 850 in France.[5] Evidently Gabirol knew of it.[6]

One meaning of the word Kabbala is *tradition* in a way which connotes an oral transmission. Another meaning is *acceptance* as the mystics are accepted before God. A third meaning of the term is *that which is received,* suggesting its revelatory character. The Kabbala is sometimes referred to as the *Secret Wisdom (chochmah nistarah)* to indicate that it is comprehensible only to the initiated and that it is hidden in the Scriptures in ways to be extracted only by those who know its mysteries.[7]

Kabbala has always had about it an aura of danger, perhaps for good reason. In the light of the later psychoanalytical developments, this danger may be best understood as that associated with bringing repressed material to consciousness. The warning in connection with Jewish secret doctrine is expressed as early as the *Book of Sirach,* III, 20-24:

> Neither search the things that are above thy strength,
> But what is commanded thee, think thereon with reverence,
> For it is not needful for thee to see with thine eyes the
>   things that are secret.
> Be not curious in unnecessary matters;
> For more things are showed unto thee than men understand.

We find the same warning in the Talmud tractate *Chagigah,*

> Seek not things that are too hard for thee and search not things that are hidden from thee. The things that have been permitted

thee, think thereupon; thou hast no business with the things that are secret.[8]

In the *Sefer ha-Gematria* of Jehudah ha-Chassid, it is said that "Ben Sira wanted to study the Sefer Yezirah when an heavenly voice came out and said, 'Thou canst not do it alone.' So he went to his father Jeremiah . . . and they studied it." [9] In another version of the same episode "Jeremiah began to study the Sefer Yezirah, when a heavenly voice came forth and said: 'Get thee an associate.' He accordingly went to his son Sira, and they studied the Sefer Yezirah together." [10]

Recalling our earlier discussion of the friendship between Freud and Fliess,[11] Kabbalistic tradition provides a further hint concerning the nature of the relationship. In his psychoanalytical work, which we maintain is Kabbalistic, Freud needed an "associate," because the burden of the Kabbalistic thought is too difficult for anyone to bear in independent study. The breach that took place eventually between Freud and Fliess was perhaps made possible only because Freud found other "associates" in connection with psychoanalysis.

The tradition is one pervaded by a sense of secrecy. The substance of Kabbala was transmitted by word of mouth, because this presumed that a judgment of eligibility was made of the hearer. Even when transmitted by word of mouth, the technique of allusion was used, rather than direct expression, partly to allow the individual to work out his own interpretation, and partly because only those who were ready to receive the tradition would be able to appreciate the allusion.[12]

The Kabbalists were endowed with mystery and power. At various times they have been referred to in different ways, indicating the complexity of mood associated with the tradition. They have been called *Yod'e chen* (those who know the grace of God; the word *chen,* which means "grace," is also an abbreviation of *chochman nistarah,* meaning "secret wisdom"). They have been called *Ba'ale ha-Sod* (bearers or masters of the secret), *Chochme ha-Tushiah* (students of profound knowledge), *Yod'im* (gnostics or knowers), *Anshe maaseh* (men who are able to do things).[13] In the later period of Jewish mysticism, from about the sixteenth century onward, the title *Ba'al Shem* came into use.[14] This means "Master of the (Holy) Name," and refers to the ability of these men to perform miracles by using the varieties of God's name as they are known in Kabbalistic lore.

In a passage of his *Moses and Monotheism,* after Freud has made the identification of Aton with Adonai,[15] he says hesitatingly "Moreover, we shall have to come back to the problems of the divine name," [16] and later he suggests the interpretation that the plurality of God's name is a sign of an earlier polytheism.[17] Perhaps Freud is here betraying a sense of the implicit paganism in the Kabbalistic diffusion of God's name, and its tendency to turn from a strict monotheism.*

---

* The interested reader is referred to Nandor Fodor, "A Personal Analytic Approach to the Problem of the Holy Name," *Psychoanal. Rev.,* 1944, **31**, 165-180. In this paper, which is both psychoanalytic and manifestly Kabbalistic, Fodor says, "The meaning of the four letter word, the Tetragrammaton, is as fresh a challenge to the human mind as it was in remote ages."—p. 165. He ends the paper as follows:

. . . I am used by my dream mind for a lesson in religious mysticism the sweep of which is rather staggering. Zsiga [of the dream which he interprets] is an abbreviation for Zsigmond (Sigmond), a name which I am tempted to resolve into the German *Sieg* (victory) and *Mond* (world). Victory over the world would be secured by any man who possessed the Shem [God's ineffable

NOTES TO CHAPTER 9

1. Cf. pp. 48-49, above.
2. Gershom G. Scholem, *Major Trends in Jewish Mysticism* (3d ed.; New York: Schocken, 1954), pp. 44ff. (also Schocken Paperback, 1961)
3. Ernst Müller, *History of Jewish Mysticism* (Oxford: East and West Library, 1946), p. 61.
4. A. E. Waite, *The Holy Kabbalah* (London: Williams and Norgate, 1929).
5. Waite, p. 43.
6. Isaac Meyer, *Qabbalah* (Philadelphia: MacCalla and Co., 1888), p. 159. *The Jewish Encyclopedia,* XII, p. 605, says "there is nothing to disprove that the book was written in the sixth century."
7. Christian D. Ginsburg, *The Kabbalah* (London: Routledge and Kegan Paul, 1955), p. 86. This book first appeared in 1865.
8. Müller, pp. 62-63.
9. Müller, p. 63.
10. Müller, p. 63.
11. Cf. pp. 58 ff., above.
12. Scholem, pp. 119 ff.
13. Müller, pp. 67-68.
14. The first person to have borne this name was Elijah of Chelm, who lived about 1500. *The Jewish Encyclopedia* lists eleven

---

name]. But the way of Zsiga C. is the way of Satan who showed Jesus the richness of the world from the top of a mountain. [Cf. p. 175] There is a better way. It will be found when we shall no more seek union with the divine in fantasied returns to the womb [Cf. p. 312] in the hope of recapturing the fetal sensation of omnipotence, but when we shall attain the consciousness of the Shem within us and will control the power of the Golem to regenerate the world."—p. 180.

The Golem is a legendary Frankenstein's monster, energized by the Shem, who fought against the enemies of the Jews. He was sometimes referred to as Joseph, and would seem to partake of some of the characteristics of the Messiah ben Joseph. Cf. pp. 171 ff.

such persons, which is an "approximately" complete list.—*The Jewish Encyclopedia,* II, p. 383.

15. Cf. pp. 248-249, below.
16. Freud, *Moses and Monotheism,* p. 28.
17. Freud, *Moses and Monotheism,* p. 47.

10

Modern Kabbala

We may date modern Kabbala from about the year 1200. The "Golden Age of Kabbalism" was at the turn from the thirteenth to the fourteenth centuries.[1] The major document of the Kabbalistic tradition, the *Zohar,* was made known (written or uncovered) by Moses de Leon at about the end of the thirteenth century. "Its place in the history of Kabbalism can be gauged from the fact that alone among the whole post-Talmudic rabbinical literature it became a canonical text, which for a period of several centuries actually ranked with the Bible and the Talmud."[2]

A figure of particular interest in modern Kabbala is Abraham ben Samuel Abulafia. The significance of Abulafia inheres in the fact that he developed a method which is amazingly close to the psychoanalytic method of free association.

Abulafia was born in Spain in 1240. He spent his youth with his father in the study of Torah, commentary, Mishnah, and Talmud. He studied Maimonides' *Guide for the Perplexed,* to which he gave a Kabbalistic interpretation,[3] and immersed himself in the Kabbala, particularly the *Sefer Yetzirah.*

75

At the age of thirty-one, Abulafia was overcome by the prophetic spirit, and is presumed to have obtained knowledge of God's true name. In this period he was accompanied by "Satan to his right," evidently to confuse him. It was not until he was forty years old that he felt himself to be writing distinctly prophetic works.

In the year 1280 Abulafia picked himself up and went to Rome to discuss the problems of the Jews with the Pope. This was evidently motivated by his Messianic tendencies, in confirmation of a widely circulated prediction that when the Messiah would come he would go to the Pope and ask for the liberation of the Jews.[4]

As we will see later, the fortieth year, Rome, Messianism, and the Devil have significance with respect to Freud's biography. For the present, let us simply indicate that this pattern in Abulafia is essentially repeated in Freud.

The psychological objective that Abulafia had was to "unseal the soul, to untie the knots which bind it."[5] This was based on the view that the inner forces of man are bound in as a result of his ordinary, daily activity. In Abulafia's writing there is the view that there is a value in these knots in that they keep the individual from being overwhelmed by the stream of the cosmos. However, if the individual is to make contact with the divine stream, it is necessary that the knots be untied.

As will become increasingly evident in what follows, a theory of repression and the role of the ego in repression are already germinally here. Abulafia has essentially two methods of meditation in order to achieve the desired release of the soul. The first of these is an interpretative method based on taking liberties with the letters of the alphabet. In meditating, the letters are separated and combined; new themes arise by recombining and separating them. Abulafia had a profound sense of the "mystical logic" of letters. The arrangements of the letters were not arbitrary, but were rather in accordance with some higher principles; and from the results of these movements of the letters one could get a greater insight into the nature of the divine realms.[6]

Thus we see in Abulafia the germ of the conviction that this kind of language product is not simply whimsical, but corresponds rather to another "logic"—for Abulafia, the logic of God's real world, which to Freud becomes the "logic" of the unconscious.

The second important method for which the first is but a preparation is called "jumping and skipping." Scholem describes Abulafia's conception as follows:

> . . . the modern reader of these writings will be most astonished to find a detailed description of a method which Abulafia and his followers call *dillug* and *kefitsah,* "jumping" or "skipping" viz., from one conception to another. In fact this is nothing else than a very remarkable method of using associations as a way of meditation. It is not wholly the "free play of association" as known to psychoanalysis; rather it is the way of passing from one association to another determined by certain rules * which are, however, sufficiently lax. Every "jump" opens a new sphere, defined by certain formal, *not* material, characteristics. Within this sphere, the mind may freely associate. The "jumping" unites, therefore, elements of free and guided association and is said to assure quite extraordinary results as

* Freud would probably differ with Scholem's suggestion that free association is without rules. Cf., e.g., *The Int. of Dreams,* p. 101 or pp. 522-523.

far as the "widening of consciousness" of the initiate is concerned. The "jumping" brings to light hidden processes of the mind, "it liberates us from the prison of the natural sphere and leads us to the boundaries of the divine sphere." All the other, more simple methods of meditation serve only as a preparation for this highest grade which contains and supersedes all the others.[7]

Scholem offers in translation a set of instructions from Abulafia:

Be prepared for thy God, oh Israelite! Make thyself ready to direct thy heart to God alone. Cleanse the body and choose a lonely house where none shall hear thy voice. Sit there in thy closet and do not reveal thy secret to any man. If thou canst, do it by day in the house, but it is best if thou completest it during the night. In the hour when thou preparest thyself to speak with the Creator and thou wishest Him to reveal His might to thee, then be careful to abstract all thy thought from the vanities of this world. Cover thyself with thy prayer shawl and put *Tefillin* on thy head and hands that thou mayest be filled with awe of the Shekhinah [8] which is near thee. Cleanse thy clothes, and, if possible, let all thy garments be white, for all this is helpful in leading the heart towards the fear of God and the love of God. If it be night, kindle many lights, until all be bright. Then take ink, pen and a table to thy hand † and remember that thou art about to serve God in joy of the gladness of heart. Now begin to combine a few or many letters, to permute and combine them until thy heart be warm. Then be mindful of their movements and of what thou canst bring forth by moving them. And when thou feelest that thy heart is already warm and when thou seest that by combination of letters thou canst grasp new things which by human tradition or by thyself thou wouldst not be able to know and when thou art thus prepared to receive the influx of divine power which flows

† Freud used writing in his self-analysis.—*The Int. of Dreams*, p. 103.

into thee, then turn all thy true thought to imagine the Name
and His exalted angels in thy heart as if they were human beings sitting or standing about thee. And feel thyself like an
envoy whom the king and his ministers are to send on a mission, and he is waiting to hear something about his mission
from their lips, be it from the king himself, be it from his
servants. Having imagined this very vividly, turn thy whole
mind to understand with thy thoughts the many things which
will come into thy heart through the letters imagined. Ponder
them as a whole and in all their detail, like one to whom a
parable or a dream is being related, or who meditates on a
deep problem in a scientific book, and try thus to interpret
what thou shalt hear that it may as far as possible accord with
thy reason. . . . And all this will happen to thee after having
flung away tablet and quill or after they will have dropped
from thee because of the intensity of thy thought. And know,
the stronger the intellectual influx within thee, the weaker will
become thy outer and thy inner parts. Thy whole body will
be seized by an extremely strong trembling, so that thou wilt
think that surely thou art about to die, because thy soul, over-
joyed with its knowledge, will leave thy body. And be thou
ready at this moment consciously to choose death, and then
thou shalt know that thou hast come far enough to receive the
influx. And then wishing to honor the glorious Name by serving it with the life of body and soul, veil thy face and be afraid
to look at God. Then return to the matters of the body, rise
and eat and drink a little, or refresh thyself with a pleasant
odor, and restore thy spirit to its sheath until another time, and
rejoice at thy lot and know that God loveth thee.[9]

Associated with such meditation is an intellectual ecstasy
identifiable with psychoanalytic insight. This ecstasy, together
with its associated content in terms of cognition of the divine,
is the aim of Abulafia's meditation. Abulafia is careful to
distinguish between this state and wilder states of emotional

excitement. As a matter of fact he believes that these other states, which can be confused with the kind of ecstasy that he is talking about, can actually be quite dangerous. In Abulafia's ecstasy it is the "light of the intellect" which comes in; and for this careful preparation is required.[10]

Furthermore, Abulafia regards the Kabbalistic teacher as extremely important, a harbinger of the idea of the transference. There are required both a mover from the outside and a mover from the inside, and the teacher plays the role of the former. In the state of ecstasy a kind of identification with the teacher takes place, which becomes an identification with God, and paradoxically ends up with a transcendent self-identification. In this state also the man and the Torah have become identified.[11]

Associated with this mode of thought is a tendency (though one which is highly suppressed) to engage in autobiographical and introspective analysis. For example, we have an account of a student of Abulafia translated by Scholem.[12] A noteworthy feature of this account is the described relationship of Kabbala to the natural sciences. This student writes that it is necessary in the Kabbalistic ascent to cleanse oneself from the effects of the naturalistic sciences, since the effect of the sciences is to block the divine stream from entering the soul.[13]

The similarity between this kind of thinking and the method of free association is striking. The question whether Freud could have come in contact with it remains to be answered. As we have already indicated, Freud's family, as well as large numbers of Jews in Vienna, had migrated from Galicia, which had been saturated with Jewish mysticism. A direct scholarly contact may have been made through the figure of Adolf Jellinek.

In the nineteenth century a small group of Jewish European scholars undertook to study the nature of the Kabbala in the tradition of modern Western scholarship. Adolf Jellinek (1821-1898) was one of the outstanding members of this group. Among other achievements in connection with Kabbala, Jellinek published extensively on Abulafia in German.[14]

Jellinek was the most popular Jewish preacher in the city of Vienna of his day. It is said that when Jellinek spoke on the week end the Jews of Vienna would discuss what he said for the whole succeeding week. Jellinek preached in Vienna over several generations from 1856 to 1893. "Through the lips of Jellinek spoke the genius of the Jewish people. The spark of Sinaitic fire seemed to flash from his eyes. Whoever heard him was stirred to enthusiastic recognition of the underlying greatness of Judaism, its spiritual uniqueness and its glorious history," [15] says Grunwald, who was Jellinek's successor and himself personally acquainted with Freud.[16] According to Kurrim, who wrote the article on Jellinek in *The Jewish Encyclopedia,* he was "the greatest, most gifted Jewish preacher that modern Judaism has produced." [17]

It is difficult to imagine that a person whose primary associations were Jewish could have avoided coming into contact with Jellinek either directly or indirectly.

NOTES TO CHAPTER 10

1. Scholem, p. 119.
2. Scholem, p. 156.
3. Cf. Strauss's interpretation of Maimonides, p. 36, above.
4. Scholem, p. 128.
5. Scholem, p. 131.
6. Scholem, p. 134.
7. Scholem, pp. 135-136.
8. See pp. 273 ff., below, on the *Shekinah*.
9. Scholem, pp. 136-137.
10. Scholem, p. 138.
11. Scholem, pp. 139 ff.
12. Scholem, pp. 147-155.
13. Scholem, p. 154.
14. Scholem, p. 124, p. 429.
15. Grunwald, *History of the Jews in Vienna*, pp. 360-361.
16. Grunwald, "Zichronos un Briev," *Yivo Bleter*, 1952, 36, 241-251.
17. *The Jewish Encyclopedia*, VII, p. 93.

11

The Zohar

The most important document in the Kabbalistic tradition is the *Zohar*.[1] It is ostensibly the work of Simeon ben Yohai in the first half of the second century. The major part of the *Zohar* consists of a lengthy commentary on passages from the Torah. Besides, various other writings are included within it. Scholem enumerates the contents of the *Zohar* under twenty headings in addition to the main one.[2] The work was first brought to light by Moses de Leon in the latter years of the thirteenth century. There has been much speculation about the problem of its authorship. Scholem believes that it was written in its entirety by Moses de Leon.[3] For about two centuries the work remained relatively obscure, but then its influence flowered. It became one of the most significant writings in Jewish thought, an expression of the deepest currents in the history of Judaism. Not only was it an expression of the thought and emotions of the Jewish community, but it became the supporting document for some of the most far-reaching social developments among the Jews of Eastern Europe.

The spirit of the *Zohar* is markedly different from the writings of Abulafia. The *Zohar* lacks the intense personalism and emphasis on individual mystical experience which is present in Abulafia. Instead, the *Zohar* casts its religious messages in terms of the intimate idiom of family and sexual relationships. Scholem contrasts Abulafia's Kabbalism with Kabbala as represented by the *Zohar*. The former, he declares, is more aristocratic. The latter was closer to the normal emotions and fears of the people, and as a consequence, was more successful as an expression of the people.[4]

Besides its singular emphasis on sexual and family relationships, the *Zohar* shares with Freud's psychoanalytic writings the following characteristics: views on anti-Semitism, the conception of man as bisexual, a theory of sexual-social development, and, perhaps most important, a set of techniques for the interpretation of linguistic productions. The latter, in the pattern of the Midrash, but quite exaggerated, is used in the *Zohar* on Biblical quotations, and in Freud on human expressions.

We will postpone further consideration of the content of the *Zohar*[5] to make room for a discussion of the social consequences which it supported since it came to be both an intellectual tradition and a social-revolutionary force.

NOTES TO CHAPTER II

1. *The Zohar,* trans. H. Sperling, M. Simon, and P. P. Levertoff (5 vols.; London: Soncino Press, 1931-1934).
2. Scholem, pp: 160-162.
3. Scholem, Fifth Lecture, particularly pp. 190 ff.
4. Scholem, p. 205.
5. Cf. pp. 246 ff.

12

The Chmielnicki Period

In the year 1492 the Jews were expelled from Spain. From that time onward we see a growth in the concern with exile and redemption in the thought of the Jews. Owing largely to the influence of Isaac Luria (1522-1570) and his follower Hayim Vital (1543-1620), the Kabbalistic doctrines played an important role in the development of these ideas. After about 1630 the Lurianic doctrine spread widely. It was strongly supernaturalistic and superstitious in content. It promised redemption soon, and the coming of the Messiah. It became integrated into the thought, feeling, and religious rituals of practically all the Jews living in the diaspora.

The blackest part of the history of the Jews in Spain was the last decade of the fifteenth century. In the year 1648 the worst persecution of the Jews in history, excepting only that under Hitler in our own century, took place in eastern Europe. The mood of the Jew of the last three hundred years may be largely traced to the middle decade of the seventeenth century, the period of the Cossack pogroms under the leadership of the eminently talented and ruthless Bogdan Chmielnicki.[1] The

85

atrocities which were committed, facilitated by an ostensibly righteous cause, can only be matched by those committed under Hitler. We read, for example, of the Cossacks opening up Jewish women and sewing in live cats. Estimates of the number of Jewish deaths in the years 1648 and 1649 run to about 300,000. It is ironic that the Kabbala had predicted the coming of the Messiah in 1648.[2]

In the period prior to 1648, many Jews played the role of agents, administrators, and tax collectors for the Polish nobility. During those years a number of colonies composed of runaway serfs, criminals, and adventurers had been founded along the lower Dnieper River and the northern shore of the Black Sea. One of these groups was the Cossacks, which means "warriors" or "light riders." They lived on the great steppes where the Dnieper and the Dniester Rivers empty into the Black Sea, and existed almost exclusively by plunder and hunting. They would attack the Tartars or go by small boat and pillage Turkish towns along the Black Sea. Actually, the Cossacks served as a kind of "border patrol" for the Polish nobility against the Turks and the Tartars. In return for this service they were freed from many responsibilities, particularly in connection with taxation.

The Polish nobility were Catholics. The Cossacks and the other colonists were Greek Orthodox. Under the influence of the Jesuits, efforts were made to bring these people into the Catholic Church, and failing this, to have them at least recognize the spiritual leadership of the Pope. The hostility between the Poles and Jesuits on the one hand and the Greek Orthodox on the other grew in acuity for both religious and economic reasons.

The Jews, as agents for the Polish nobility, were obviously the most ready object for the hostility of the non-Catholic groups. Irksome devices had been established, such as having the Jewish tax collector keep the keys of the church and the official garments of the Greek Orthodox clergymen, in order to enforce the collection of taxes.

Under the leadership of Bogdan Chmielnicki, the Cossacks rebelled. Chmielnicki was an intelligent, well-educated, and wealthy man, who was schooled in the art of warfare. His personal venom had been stimulated by an event in which his son had been mortally wounded by flogging and his wife seized and carried away, presumably at the instigation of a Jew in the employ of a Polish nobleman. Chmielnicki organized the Cossacks, made an alliance with the Khan of Crimea, which gave him protection on the east as well as large numbers of auxiliary Tartar troops, and attacked many of the Polish and Jewish communities. He cut a path of violence and destruction the like of which had never been seen in Poland. Jews were massacred by the thousands. It is estimated, for example, that a substantial portion of the 10,000 Jews in Nemirov were killed. Approximately 200 Jewish communities were destroyed.

In the years following the massacres of 1648 there continued to be sporadic attacks. It is estimated that another 100,000 Jews were killed in the succeeding decade. Following this period a black cloud of fear and anguish settled upon the Jews of Europe.

The Poles, having suffered at the hands of the Cossacks, for psychological reasons which are readily understandable now, turned their hostility towards the Jews, applying the lessons in Jew-killing they had learned from the Cossacks. Although there was some attempt on the part of the higher Polish nobility to rectify the wrongs done to the Jews, there were many counterforces, in which the Jesuits played no small role. It was not unusual for groups of students of the Christian colleges to riot and invade the Jewish quarters and cause many deaths. Thus in 1664 the students of the Cathedral School and Jesuit Academy of Lemberg stormed the Jewish quarter, killed about 100 Jews, demolished a number of houses, and desecrated the synagogues. Charges were regularly brought against Jews for killing Christian children to obtain their blood for ritual purposes. The executions which ensued were barbarous. In one instance it was decreed that an Italian-born Jewish apothecary living in Cracow by the name of Mattathiah Calahara be executed for having committed blasphemy. He was killed by cutting off first his lips, then his hands and then his tongue; finally his body was burned at the stake, and the ashes loaded into a cannon and discharged into the air.

We have recited some of these events because they occasioned among the Jews of Eastern Europe a readiness to accept the Kabbalistic spirit, especially the ideas of the significance of the exile and redemption through the Messiah. The persecutions from the outside forced a weakening of the social structure within, and stimulated among the Jews some gross social movements in the direction of self-modification.

NOTES TO CHAPTER 12

1. The Chmielnicki episode constituted one of the great shocks for the Jews of eastern Europe. Details are recounted in general Jewish histories, and detailed documentation is not given here.
2. *The Zohar,* III, p. 29.

13

Jewish Self-Government

In our attempt to understand Freud we will show that a substantial part of his work, particularly his writings on religion,
participate in the ideological and social struggles which began
to take place following the Chmielnicki period. Prior to the
devastations which began in 1648, the Jews vigorously pursued
the ways of life associated with the Torah, the Talmud, and the
highly detailed and legalistic interpretations thereof. With
the seemingly endless persecution from the outside, the hold
of the Talmudic way of life weakened, and the people turned
to Kabbala, with its Messianic spirit, as a source of hope.

Two major currents run through the history of the Jews.
One, which we have been discussing, is the mystical. The
other, associated with the characteristic pattern of Jewish self-
government, is the rabbinic. In terms of written documents,
the *Zohar* was the most important support of the mystical current, and the Talmud was the most important support for the
rabbinic current. The mystical mood has tended to verge on
apostasy and heresy especially in face of persecution. Among
other things, by making the relationship between man and God

more intimate, it fostered some threat to the theocratic form of government and encouraged more personal liberty than was usual under rabbinic administration. Further, it later advocated or implied a doctrine of the value of evil as part of God's world, and held out an exaggerated hope for the coming of the Messiah and the redemption.

Up to the seventeenth century Judaism was sufficiently strong and elastic to contain these contradictory forces without any great threat to the social structure. The rabbinic temper was the dominant one, and certainly the Kabbalists did not interpret their doctrines in terms of any political consequences. Frequently the same persons were both Talmudists and Kabbalists. There is reason to believe that the esoteric quality of the doctrines of Kabbala was partly motivated by the faith of the earlier Kabbalists in the Talmud and its associated way of life, and their concern with its protection.

But as life grew darker for the Jews of Eastern Europe in the seventeenth century, the conflict between mysticism and rabbinism grew. The doctrines might be interpreted as two strategies for coping with the prevailing political problems and with God. Ideologically, both accepted the essential idea of the Covenant between God and Israel. The critical question was, of course, why God should so abuse His chosen people. The rabbinic answer to this question was that the Jews had defected from the Law and were being punished. The ideological and social strategy was to close ranks and redouble the communal effort to follow the commandments and their proper interpretation as laid out in the Talmud. It led to the most critical self-examination of acts and thoughts to make sure that the Covenant would be carried out to the last letter of the fine print of the Torah.

Although the mystics agreed that the Jews had defected from the Covenant, they felt that it was not because of lack of conscientiousness, but rather because of lack of appropriate understanding. The Torah was but the outward form of the Covenant, and deeper forms of interpretation were required. Thus Kabbala, and in particular the *Zohar,* showed the way by which the underlying meaning of the Torah could be understood. The Torah was taken as a grand cryptogram to be deciphered by a variety of semi-rationalistic and mystical-intuitive devices.

The Jews in Poland had early been organized as a separate estate, conducting their own affairs under the authority of the rabbinic Kahals. The pattern of Jewish government and its relations to the state were well established by the middle of the sixteenth century. According to a charter issued by King Sigismund Augustus in 1551, the Jews were entitled to elect their own leaders. They were not under the jurisdiction of the civil law courts as far as their internal affairs were concerned. The rabbinical Kahal administration was the legal authority under which the Jews lived as well as the agency responsible to the government. The authority which the Kahal exercised was inordinately large, extending to every act in which the Jew engaged. The permission of the Kahal was required to live in the community, to own land, or to borrow money from non-Jews, and it was the exclusive agency for collecting taxes among the Jews.

Leadership and prestige in the Jewish community was based primarily on scholarship in the Talmud and rabbinical literature, though considerations of family and wealth also entered. Education was an inalienable right and responsibility for every Jewish child. Friedlaender says,

> The authority of the official religious leader, profoundly revered though he was, was frequently assisted, equalled, and even surpassed by the influence of the *Lamden*, or lay-scholar. Perhaps one might say, employing the phraseology of Carlyle, that Polish Jewry was a 'heroarchy,' a government by the Hero who dominated the ideals and aspirations of his fellow-men, the Hero being represented by the Man of Letters, clad in the robe of the Polish-Jewish *Lamden*.[1]

The lower classes had little influence in the selection of the members of the Kahal, and sometimes the actions of the Kahal were in the service of the upper classes rather than the community at large. With the massacres of 1648 the hold of the rabbis on the community in the old tradition began to deteriorate. In 1676, for example, the leaders of the community found it necessary to issue the following appeal:

> Gravely have we sinned before the Lord. The unrest grows from day to day. It becomes more and more difficult to live. Our people has no standing whatsoever among the nations. Indeed it is a miracle that in spite of all misfortunes we are still alive. The only thing left for us to do is to unite ourselves in one league, held together by the spirit of strict obedience to the commandments of God and to the precepts of our pious teachers and leaders.[2]

NOTES TO CHAPTER 13

1. Israel Friedlaender, *The Jews of Russia and Poland* (New York: G. P. Putnam's Sons, 1915), p. 181.
2. Dubnow, Vol. I, p. 188.

14

The Sabbatian Episode

From time to time events occur in which a vast variety of social forces come to a focal point, and the meaning and implications of these events are active for centuries afterward. The appearance of Sabbatai Zevi was such an event. The set of events which surrounded the personality and acts of Sabbatai Zevi, the "false Messiah," was of the deepest moment for the psychological and emotional patterns of the Jews in the modern period. Sabbatai Zevi may have been psychotic, as Scholem suggests.[1] He may have been a homosexual and a confirmed egoist as is suggested by Kastein.[2] The fact remains that to the Jews of the world, he was for a time the Messiah.

The Kabbala, it will be recalled, had prophesied that the year 1648 would begin the Messianic era. It was also the year of the great Chmielnicki pogrom. With the pre-existence among the Jews of a strong Kabbalistic ideology, particularly of the Lurianic type with its intense Messianism, the suffering and the devastation of that year were interpreted paradoxically as confirmation of the coming of the Messiah. The pogroms were, presumably, the cleansing in preparation. Towards the end of

1648, Sabbatai Zevi carried out the single action which would draw attention to him as the Messiah. Rising in the synagogue, he uttered the mystical full name of God. Presumably only the Messiah would have so dared.

Sabbatai Zevi was a descendant of the Spanish Jews who had been expelled in 1492. He lived in the Jewish community of Smyrna in Turkey. Evidently, he was talented enough to have been given the title Chakam when he was still quite young. By the time he was eighteen he was teaching Kabbala to groups of young men and was given a certain amount of recognition for his evident profundity and knowledge. He had immersed himself in the study of Kabbala and manifested an extraordinary imagination in providing interpretations along Kabbalistic lines. From the very beginning of his career the charismatic features of his personality were evident. The possibility of some sexual aberration in him is evidenced by the fact that he suffered two marriage annulments because of his inability or lack of desire to engage in sexual consummation of the marriages. His third wife, Sarah, was a prostitute who traveled about the world in search of the Messiah, whose bride she had declared herself destined to be. Although Jewish, she had been raised in a Christian convent. She openly declared that since she could not marry until she had been received by the Messiah, God had authorized her to satisfy her passions as she could until the Messiah arrived. Sabbatai Zevi married her after she had thus presented herself to him, and presumably she continued to have sexual relations after the marriage with various of his youthful followers.[3]

Following his utterance of God's name in the synagogue, a

ban was pronounced against Sabbatai Zevi by the rabbis of Smyrna. The ban was partly motivated by his large popularity among the lower classes and the fact that his presence seemed to lead them to acts of insubordination. He left Smyrna and traveled very widely: Constantinople, Salonika, Cairo, Gaza, Aleppo, and Jerusalem. He struck poses of various kinds which were consistent with his conception of himself as the Messiah. In Salonika he requested that his marriage with the Torah be celebrated. In Constantinople he carried a fish in a baby basket and indicated that the redemption would come under the zodiacal sign of Pisces. Wherever he went his charismatic personality attracted people and convinced them that he was indeed the Messiah.

In the years from 1648 to 1665 various rumors and legends grew up around his personality. When he returned to Smyrna in 1665, he was received by large numbers of people with great demonstration. Masses fell into religious ecstasies. By and large, the Jews of Smyrna were now ready to receive him as the Messiah. During the Chmielnicki episode many Jews had surrendered to the Tartars to avoid falling prey to the Cossacks. The Tartars had sold them for ransom to the Turkish Jews. Kabbalism had always had its adherents in Turkey. But now, news of their coreligionists in Poland caused a swelling of the Messianic mood among them. The Jews in the diaspora had always maintained an amazing homogeneity of spirit and culture. Communications of some kind were always kept up. Thus news of Sabbatai Zevi and the spirit generated by him traveled through Europe as a fire across a plain. Since the year 1648 had failed to produce the redemption, Sabbatai Zevi placed his faith on another year which, paradoxically, had a source quite different from Jewish Kabbala. Sabbatai Zevi had heard from his father, who was an agent for an English firm, that some Christian calculation, based on the Book of Revelation, had assigned 1666 as the beginning of the Millennium. The year 1666 was now the redemption year.

The Jews of Poland responded with great hope, especially after the great persecutions to which they had been subjected.

> The Jews—says the contemporary Ukrainian writer Galatovski —triumphed. Some abandoned their houses and property, refusing to do any work and claiming that the Messiah would soon arrive and carry them on a cloud to Jerusalem. Others fasted for days, denying food even to their little ones, and during that severe winter bathed in ice-holes, at the same time reciting a recently-composed prayer. Faint-hearted and destitute Christians, hearing the stories of the miracles performed by the false Messiah and beholding the boundless arrogance of the Jews, began to doubt Christ.[4]

Sabbatai Zevi was to begin his work of redemption by dethroning the Sultan of Turkey, who at that time ruled over the Holy Land. Two days before the beginning of the year 1666 he departed for Constantinople where he was to do his Messianic work. On his arrival there he was imprisoned and then sent to the fortress of Abydos in Gallipoli. But the strength of his support was so great that the prison was transformed into a royal residence to which Jews from all over the world flocked bearing gifts. He had become the spiritual leader of hundreds of thousands of people.

The Turks struck on a plan, suggested, interestingly enough, by a Jewish advisor to the Sultan, to make the Sabbatian movement ineffective. They confronted Sabbatai Zevi with the option of death or public conversion to Islam. He was told he could go through the motions of conversion as a pretense, but the action must be public. In November 1666, towards the end of the year for which the redemption was scheduled, Sabbatai Zevi became a Moslem in full pomp and ceremony. He was given a Moslem name, Mehmet Effendi, and appointed a chamberlain to the Sultan with a handsome salary.

The immensity of this spiritual upheaval, which lasted from 1665 to 1666, cannot be overestimated. It manifested itself in the most extreme forms of penance. The Messiah was about to arrive and one had to be ready to receive him. The people were overcome with emotion. The long-awaited redemption was about to come. What had been a hope and a dream was about to become a reality. The proof that the thousands of years of suffering which the Jews had experienced had not been in vain was soon to be revealed.[5]

Sabbatianism did not pass away with the conversion of Sabbatai Zevi, however. Among some it led to a kind of spiritual nausea that persisted for centuries, based on the sense of having been trifled with and betrayed. Other groups followed the lead of Sabbatai Zevi and became Moslems. Large numbers of Jews sought the traditional safety of orthodox Judaism, redoubling their efforts to satisfy every demand to the last letter in the rabbinic mood. But most important, it represented a turn of the mystical impulse from an esoteric study to a large scale movement, with important political, social, and economic consequences. There is little doubt but that it was revolutionary, that it made cracks in the old system of rabbinical rule, and that the disruption which was experienced had to be countered by the Jewish community for centuries afterward. According to Scholem, Sabbatianism was largely responsible for the creation of the atmosphere which eventually led to the Jewish reform movement in the nineteenth century.[6]

Sabbatianism continued to propagate itself as a sect in spite of strenuous efforts to blot it out. The orthodox rabbis persecuted the Sabbatians and invoked the *herem* (excommunication) against them. Groups of Jews clung to the idea that Sabbatai Zevi was the Messiah and continued to worship him. A Lithuanian Jew by the name of Zadok prophesied that 1695 would be the date of the coming of the Messiah. A Kabbalist, Hayim Malakh, preached that Sabbatai Zevi was really the Messiah, but as with Moses who kept the Jews from entering the Holy Land for forty years, forty years would have to elapse between 1666 and 1706 before the redemption would come. In 1700 Hayim Malakh together with Judah Hasid led a trek of about 1300 people to the Holy Land to be ready for the appearance of the Messiah in 1706. About a thousand survived the arduous journey. In their disillusioned wait, some became Christians, some Moslems, some returned to Poland to spread fantastic mystical tales, while others stayed and developed strange rites among which, it is alleged, was a dance about a wooden image of Sabbatai Zevi.

Sabbatianism presented the first translation of Kabbalistic doctrines into a major social movement. Its failure produced a deep distrust of Messianism, and profound shame. With eminent conscientiousness all forms of Sabbatian literature and

Sabbatian associations were destroyed. It became characteristic to say that the movement had been only a minor one, and that only a small number of people were involved. It also became characteristic to overlook the degree to which Sabbatianism had taken hold even among the most orthodox. People who had descended from Sabbatian families took pains to conceal this fact.[7]

Scholem advances an interesting hypothesis which is particularly relevant to our interest in Freud. Scholem holds that *Sabbatianism, encountering the emancipation of the Jews in the nineteenth century, passes into a rationalism which tends to conceal its Sabbatian origins.*[8] After the French Revolution, it was the Sabbatian groups still within the Jewish fold that fostered the movements toward reform, liberalism, and the enlightenment.[9] Sabbatianism articulated with rationalism in several ways. For one thing, although Sabbatianism had its own collection of myths, it was opposed to the myths of orthodoxy. For another, the Sabbatians held to a doctrine of the necessity of the descent into evil in order to attain spiritual liberation, a doctrine which was to be endowed with specific sexual reference by the Frankists, discussed below. The "holiness" of participating in all things, evil or non-evil, already contains a harbinger of the more enlightened view of pursuing truth no matter where it might lead, with full confidence that "truth" must lead to good. But perhaps most important is the fact that Sabbatianism, as a form of mysticism, shares with rationalism the conviction that the world of reality, all reality, may be apprehended by, and encompassed in, thought. And as for our relating this to Freud, Sabbatianism encouraged concern with the forbidden areas of human experience.

In such a movement toward the world of Western civilization, Sabbatianism lent itself as a rationalization of apostasy. Although the failure of a Messianic prediction may have the effect of disillusionment, it may also act paradoxically to make the original conviction even stronger. This is what took place in the instance of Sabbatianism.

One of the more important supports to Sabbatianism came from the Marrano Jews who had migrated from Spain into other parts of Europe. During the great persecution of the Spanish Jews in the fifteenth century, many permitted themselves to be baptized, behaving outwardly as Christians. In secret, they managed to maintain their Jewish identity and some of the Jewish practices. It is a phenomenal fact that they were able to work out a system of religious duplicity which could be maintained for generations. In the seventeenth century many of these Jews fled from Spain to other parts of Europe and quickly reasserted their Judaism. Nevertheless, guilt feeling over their apostasy was still very strong, and this made the figure of Sabbatai Zevi extremely attractive, especially and paradoxically because of his apostasy.

The fact that the Messiah should have been an apostate served to reinforce the Marrano acceptance of him. They themselves had been apostates and suffered guilt because of it. The image of a Messiah who had, like themselves, been forced into the violation of the critical commandment not to worship strange gods, served the function of relieving them from their deep sense of guilt. Scholem believes that this psychological condition was one of the important factors associated with the disintegration of the ghetto.[10]

It should be evident that the movement of the Jew from the world of the ghetto to the larger world of Western civilization cannot be conceived of as a simple instance of cultural diffusion. The usual idea is that the Jews migrated into Western civilization at large, the children were sent to Western schools, and thus the larger culture simply placed its stamp on them. Sometimes, in discussions of this kind, it is added that the Jews had a long tradition of scholarship, and they transferred their attitudes toward the Torah to secular studies. This view, though not in itself false, is extremely oversimplified. It would be more correct to say that Western enlightenment was seized upon by the Jews as an ally to one party of the desperate struggle within Judaism between Sabbatianism and orthodoxy. The entrance of the Jews into Western civilization is complex and dynamic, and the motives must be sought among the many strands of history, and particularly in the religious life of the participants.

NOTES TO CHAPTER 14

1. Scholem, p. 290.
2. J. Kastein, *History and Destiny of the Jews,* trans. H. Paterson (New York: Viking Press, 1933), pp. 334-335.
3. J. Kastein, *The Messiah of Ismir: Sabatai Zevi,* trans. H. Paterson (New York: Viking Press, 1931), p. 117.
4. Dubnow, I, p. 205.
5. Cf. the fictionized account of the events in one Jewish village: Isaac Bashevis Singer, *Satan in Goray,* trans. Jacob Sloan (New York: Noonday Press, 1955).

6. Scholem, p. 299.
7. Scholem, pp. 300-301.
8. Scholem, p. 301.
9. Scholem, p. 304.
10. Scholem, pp. 309-310.

15

The Frankist Episode

It is one of the more important characteristics of psychoanalysis that it views evil as a distortion of love. This paradoxical identification of good with evil pervades all of Freud's
writings so that their classical polarity is virtually obliterated.

In order to appreciate the historical antecedents of this aspect of Freud, we turn to a development which took place
within the Sabbatian movement under the leadership of Jacob
Frank, and the doctrines which came into prominence with
it, in particular, the doctrine of the Holiness of Sin.

Jacob Frank was born in 1726 in Korolovka on the frontiers
of Podolia and Wallachia. His father was a Sabbatian who
had been expelled from the community where he had been a
rabbi or a preacher. He was raised in an atmosphere filled with
the Sabbatian ideas, fancies, and superstitions. Although he
was a man of little learning, an *am-haoretz,* an ignoramus, as
far as rabbinic studies were concerned, he evidently spent a
considerable amount of time dipping into the Kabbalistic literature, particularly the *Zohar*. He was gifted with great physical strength and a rich fantasy.

The tales which have come down to us indicate that he was what we would today call a psychopathic personality, a person without any strong superego formation. He wandered about as an itinerant salesman, preaching Kabbala, posing as a healer, and ministering mystical and medical aid. He is said to have engaged in highway robbery with his followers, to have cut up the parchment of a Torah for footgear for his friends, and to have stolen a shofar from a synagogue, which he taught a group of Gentile boys to blow. He peddled silks and trinkets to the harems of the Turkish pashas and boasted of having intimate relations with the Turkish women.[1]

He regarded himself as the incarnation of Sabbatai Zevi, and restimulated the Sabbatian movement. In 1755 Frank appeared in Podolia and reorganized and reawakened the disintegrating Sabbatian groups. In his new Sabbatian doctrine he asserted the idea of the Holy Trinity. He distinguished between God as having become incarnate in Sabbatai Zevi, and a female counterpart, the Shekinah[2] or Matronita, and assigned the role of Messiah to himself. He cast aside the Talmudic injunctions and declared that only the *Zohar* was sacred. The idea of a male-female God became the occasion for sexual religious practices. The Law, he declared, was dead. The yoke of the old Torah had been broken. The yoke of the Law was valid only for a world which was not yet redeemed, to which the Messiah had not yet come. The new redemption, and the revelation that came with it, were such that *everything,* including evil, was now sanctified.

As Scholem puts it in his general characterization of Jewish mysticism,

> . . . the mystic does not even recoil before the inference that in a higher sense there is a root of evil even in God. . . . Every attribute [of the Divine realm] represents a given stage, including the attribute of severity and stern judgment, which mystical speculation has connected with the source of evil in God.[3]

The doctrine of evil was given support by the thesis that the Holy Sparks had been scattered, and it was necessary for men to hand themselves into sin in order to regather them. The idea of the Holy Sin became prominent. Through sin, salvation would come. From the great sinning would emerge a world in which there would no longer be sin. Frank had declared, "I have come to rid the world of all the laws and statutes which have been in existence hitherto."

The doctrine is expressed by Buber with respect to the Messiah:

> . . . the conception of the Messiah as he who must enter completely into the "Klipah," the daemonic power of the shells, that he may liberate the holiness there held fast, and who in doing thus fulfills the purpose of the exile of Israel, and redeems Israel and the world in one. But even that is not enough. The holy sin becomes a pattern, men must hurl themselves into sin in order to tear from it the holy sparks; and soon there is no sin any longer, with the fulfilment of the meaning of the new, messianic aeon the yoke of the old Torah has been broken; it was only valid for the unredeemed world, and now the new revelation has come; the revelation which allows all and sanctifies all is here.[4]

Sexuality as the locus for the expression of personal freedom has, of course, deep roots. In the *Zohar* the sexual metaphor is used very freely. The orthodox tradition sharply restricted sexual expression, perhaps, as has been suggested by some writers,* as a result of the effort of the Jews to dissociate themselves from religious practices involving sexual rites. The sexual is also a temptation which is ever-present and sometimes pressingly so; and it offers the most accessible sins. Perhaps the most important reason for the sexual excesses among the Frankists is to be found in the contribution of Freud himself, that sexuality is at the core of human personality.

Jacob Frank followed the lead of Sabbatai Zevi into the paradox of apostasy. The movement grew into a violent political threat to the orthodox theocracy, and measures and countermeasures were taken by both sides. The Frankists were placed under the *herem* (excommunication), and the Frankists replied by an attack upon the Talmud, arguing that it was false and harmful. The Frankists even charged that the Talmud made the use of Christian blood obligatory, and they lent testimony that the Jews engaged in ritual murder. The climax of Frank's career came when he and all of his followers were converted to Catholicism with great pomp and ceremony. The members of the Polish nobility acted as sponsors, and the newly baptized Jews assumed their family names. Numbers of them thus came into the Polish nobility. Jacob Frank himself had King Augustus III as his godfather and became a Catholic in the presence of the royal family and the court dignitaries in November 1759, less than one hundred years after the apostasy

---

* Cf. e.g. A. C. Kinsey et al., *Sexual Behavior in the Human Female* (Philadelphia: W. B. Saunders Co., 1953). "Many of the Talmudic condemnations were based on the fact that such [sexually perverse] activities represented the way of the Canaanite, the way of the Chaldean, the way of the pagan, and they were originally condemned as a form of idolatry rather than sexual crime"—p. 482.

of Sabbatai Zevi and less than one hundred years before the birth of Sigmund Freud. It is of interest that Frank took Joseph as his baptismal name. The Messianic associations of the name Joseph we will discuss later when we deal with Freud and the significance of this name to him.[5]

NOTES TO CHAPTER 15

1. G. Bader, *Dreisig doros Yiddin in Polin* [Thirty generations of the Jews in Poland] (New York: Oriom Press, 1927), pp. 251 ff.
2. Cf. pp. 273 ff., below.
3. Scholem, p 13.
4. Martin Buber, *Hasidism* (New York: Philosophical Library), pp. 7-8.
5. Cf. pp. 171 ff., and footnote on p. 153, below.

16

Chassidism

In Chassidism we find the dialectical synthesis of Sabbatianism and rabbinic Judaism. It integrated the deep emotional quickening of the Sabbatian movement with the law and discipline of orthodoxy. The founder of Chassidism was Israel Baal Shem Tov, sometimes referred to as the Baal Shem Tov (the good Master of the Name [of God]), or the Baal Shem, or simply Besht, an abbreviation based on the first letters of Baal, Shem, and Tov.

The Baal Shem Tov was born about 1700—like Jacob Frank, on the border between Podolia and Wallachia. The legends of his birth contain the usual involvements. In one version,[1] his parents are an old lonely couple who are attacked by robbers. Since they have no money or possessions, the robbers take them captive. The old woman escapes but Reb Elieser, the Baal Shem Tov's father, is sold as a slave in a faraway country. There the story seems to take off from the Biblical Joseph story. He lives an inordinately righteous life, pleases his master greatly, and wins certain privileges such as the opportunity to observe the Sabbath. He soon finds his way into the service of the king, is made the chief commander of the king's armies, and is provided with a wife by the king. The woman whom he thus marries is passionately in love with him, but he remains pure and stays aloof. She becomes ill with her unrequited love. He finally takes her into his confidence and tells her that he is really a Jew. Upon discovering this, she is almost maddened by anguish at the thought that her relationship with him will never be consummated. Nevertheless, her love for him overpowers everything and she helps him to return. On the way home he is met by Elijah the prophet, who tells him that he will have a son who will enlighten the eyes of the congregation of Israel. He returns to his home and finds his old wife. Then, reminiscent of the Abraham and Sarah story, when they are both almost a hundred years old, their son Israel, the Baal Shem Tov, is born.

Israel soon becomes an orphan. The Jewish community sends him to *cheder,* the Jewish school, to study. But he would rather play truant. He spends his time wandering about in the woods lost in thought. When he is grown, he works in seemingly desultory fashion as a synagogue beadle and as a *behelfer,* an assistant at the school for the children. To the world he presents the picture of an unambitious, lazy, dull, and harmless kind of person. In the dead of night, however, when everyone else is asleep, he arises to pray and read Kabbalistic books.

For years, the Baal Shem Tov is in all eyes simply a boorish, uneducated, *am-haoretz,* an ignoramus. We find him engaging in miscellaneous occupations. Now he is an operator of an inn, now he digs clay in the mountains, etc.

In his thirty-sixth year, which is the mystical number, the Baal Shem Tov throws off the shabby cloak in which he has wandered up to that time and reveals himself to the world in all his splendor.

He is a Baal Shem, master of the Name (of God), performing miracles through its uses. The practice of healing by the appropriate use of the name of God had become fairly widespread. Somewhere around the year 1700 the class of Baale' Shem wonder workers became relatively numerous. They are healers, using quack remedies, medicines, amulets, and the name of God. They are in serious competition with physicians, and hostility between the two groups prevails. They use whatever medical knowledge they can acquire besides the Kabbalistic tools. The following is a prayer of one of these Masters of the Name:

> Preserve me from enmity and quarrels; and may envy between me and others disappear. Let, on the contrary, friendship, peace and harmony prevail between me and the physicians, . . . that I may be respected in their opinion, . . . that they may not speak evil of me or of my actions.[2]

Israel Baal Shem Tov lives a life of great personal piety and saintliness. He performs miracles of healing and telepathy, and foretells the future. He opens the *Zohar* at random and on the basis of what he sees there utters truths and advice that fill the listeners with awe and ecstasy. Chassidim * gather around him. The masses fall in love with him and his fame spreads far and wide.

A new synthesis between rabbinism and mysticism begins

* As the Chassidic followers are called.

to emerge. The rabbinic forms are accepted, but are infused with a glorified emotionality. If in his acts the individual is completely pious, he can study Kabbala, protected, as it were, from the commission of outrage by the actual purity and piety of his real life. Thus, Kabbala would be characteristically delayed until the man had reached maturity, usually some time after his thirtieth birthday. For a young person to study Kabbala was regarded as dangerous and treacherous. He might die, and his soul might then wander homelessly in an eternal *galuth,* exile.† Particularly was it desirable that the passions be somewhat abated before the study of Kabbala was undertaken, because of its emotionally releasing content.

The Baal Shem Tov tempered the extravagances of the Sabbatians but yet achieved a loosening of the severe and rigid bonds imposed by the rabbinic stream of thought in Judaism. He achieved what is perhaps one of the profoundest revolutions in the history of Judaism. Chassidism was, in a sense, a new form of Judaism. It did not move into apostasy, as had Sabbatai Zevi and Jacob Frank. Yet it overhauled Jewish thought and life so as to make it possible for the Jews to catch up with the great developments which were taking place in the rest of the world.

According to Waxman, the Modern Period in Jewish history can be regarded as being about two hundred and fifty years behind the development of the analogous modern period in

† This is the idea of the *Dybbuk,* which has received magnificent dramatic rendering in S. Ansky, *The Dybbuk: A Play in Four Acts,* trans. H. G. Alsberg and W. Katzin (New York: Liveright Publishing Corp., 1926). The *Dybbuk,* as a spirit that wanders and can find no home anywhere, is very likely a projection of the general homeless feeling of the diaspora Jew. Cf. Freud's dream after seeing Herzl's *Das neue Ghetto,* discussed on pp. 173 ff.

general history.[3] In a sense, then, the Jews of the eighteenth and nineteenth centuries entering the main stream of Western civilization had to transcend a relatively medieval culture. Chassidism served as a religious bridge between medievalism and modern times in the same way that the Haskalah * served as a cultural bridge between the Jews and other peoples of the world.

Chassidism provided historical continuity for the mystical movement within Judaism from the middle of the eighteenth century to the very end of the nineteenth century. The early Sabbatianism which became transformed into the Jewish reform movement and liberalism [4] opened the way for early passage of Jews from the ghetto and shtetl world into the wider currents of Western civilization. This early passage was made, following our metaphor, without baggage. It was achieved by a rapid and dramatic severance of Jews from their ancient traditions and from their Jewish identification. With Chassidism the passage was slower and more even and permitted integration of the Jewish tradition with Western civilization. Chassidism emphasized the pleasurable aspects of life, albeit in a religious context. Joy in life was regarded as an ultimate blessing. Chassidism thawed the medieval Jewish mind by opening new possibilities for happiness and satisfaction as contrasted with the old resignation and deprivation. Thus the Baal Shem Tov violated the sensibilities of the community by encouraging school children to sing on the way to school. It is perhaps not a mere coincidence that Freud's surname may be translated as *Simchah,* a not uncommon Jewish name which

* The Jewish enlightenment.

means "joy." Chassidism runs a close parallel to Romanticism as a way of bringing medieval Man into the modern world. As legend depicts, the Baal Shem Tov seeks freedom from the restrictions of the community and wanders about the woods and fields in a Rousseauan fashion. The Reformation, by separating man from the central medieval institution, the Catholic Church, led to severe self-discipline. Personal freedom found its ideological reaffirmation eventually in Romanticism, which involved the same idealization of sexual expressiveness as the Jewish mystical movements.

The Chassidic concept of personal freedom is illustrated in the following parable, presumably told by the Baal Shem Tov: Once there was a great king. Not wanting to be disturbed, the king built for himself a great magical palace filled with many misleading magical illusions. At the entrances the king placed pots of gold, silver, and precious stones to make the people tarry there and not try to enter. But one of the king's ministers, who felt that it was wrong that the king should so deny himself to his people, could no longer contain the secret within himself, and he addressed the people: "You cannot enter only because you are blinded by the king's magic. Walk straight through and be not afraid. The walls are only magical illusions. If you would but decide to enter there is nothing that can prevent you from coming into His Presence."

Freud, we believe, participated in the historical continuity provided by Chassidism. However, the Sabbatian elements were still present in Chassidism, even if in latent form. The encounter of the Jews with Western civilization tended to re-arouse these dim Sabbatian elements. As we will see, Freud had strong heretical tendencies, yet he would not relinquish his self-identification as a Jew. His quarrel with religion was with the older orthodox forms of Judaism. He felt he could still maintain his Jewish identity, despite the violation of orthodoxy.

We will close this section with two quotations from modern thinkers on the significance of mysticism. Sperling, to whom we are indebted for his part in the translation of the *Zohar,* writes:

> . . . the law regulates life, and keeps it in proper balance. Mysticism, on the other hand, is a free lance, it possesses inordinate inquisitiveness; the bare and natural sense of the scriptural text does not suffice it; it delves and digs and pierces into the inner and most hidden sense. The Law, indeed, gains thereby in reverence and awe, since it is seen to be founded not upon simple human considerations, but upon eternal verities. Nevertheless, the mystic is exposed to the two-fold danger of lawless mysticism and rigid rationalism; since in the mind there is no clear-cut division between religious meditation and philosophical speculation. The mystic, in trying tracks unbeaten and ways untrodden, acquires a mental independence, either on the side of pure feeling and emotion, or on that of pure reason.[5]

In an essay entitled "The Two Centres of the Jewish Soul," Martin Buber, one of the outstanding modern representatives of Jewish mysticism, writes:

> My point of view with regard to this subject [the Law] diverges widely from that which has been handed down to us; it is not without its basis of law, but neither is it entirely based on law. For this reason I should neither attempt to present tradition, nor substitute my own personal standpoint for the information you have desired of me. Besides the problem of

the Law does not seem to belong at all to the subject with which I have to deal. It would be a different matter were it my duty to present to you the teaching of Judaism. For the teaching of Judaism comes from Sinai; it is a teaching of Moses. But the *soul* of Judaism was before Sinai, and there received what it did receive; it is older than Moses; it is of the patriarchs, a soul of Abraham, or, more truly, as it concerns the *product* of a primordial age, it is a soul of Jacob. The Law joined itself to it, and it cannot henceforth ever again be understood outside of it, but it itself is not of the Law. If one wants to speak of it, one must consider all its transformations down the ages until this day, but never forget that on all its stages, it is still always it itself which is on its way.[6]

NOTES TO CHAPTER 16

1. S. H. Setzer, *Reb Israel Baal-Shem-Tov* (In Yiddish; New York: Verlag Feierberg, 1919).
2. *The Jewish Encyclopedia,* II, p. 383. From *Toledot Adam* (Zolkiev, 1720).
3. Waxman, III, p. 9.
4. Scholem, p. 304.
5. H. Sperling, "Jewish Mysticism," in L. Simon (ed.), *Aspects of the Hebrew Genius* (London: George Routledge and Sons, 1910), Chap. VI, pp. 145-176.
6. Martin Buber, *Mamre: Essays in Religion,* trans. Greta Hort (Melbourne: Melbourne University Press, 1946), pp. 18-19.

Part III

The Moses Theme in the Thought of Freud

17

The Moses of Michelangelo

Earlier in this essay, some considerations were set forth
pointing to an identification of Freud's thought with the developments in Jewish mysticism. We have sketched some
features of Jewish history which we believe can help us to illuminate Freud's contributions. The line-up within Jewish
history was that of the mystical versus the orthodox, the former advancing varieties of approaches against the domination
of thought and life associated with the classical disciplined approach of the latter. We believe that viewing Freud's works in
the light of this classical struggle increases their intelligibility.
We hope, in addition, to illuminate some of the seemingly
more bizarre aspects of Freud's productions by drawing upon
this history.

We believe that the primary key to the understanding of
Freud is contained in his concern with Moses. In his autobiography Freud tells us, "My early familiarity with the Bible
story (at a time almost before I had learnt the art of reading)
had, as I recognized much later, an enduring effect upon the
direction of my interest." [1] We have two essays on Moses by

Freud. One of these is "The Moses of Michelangelo," [2] a discussion of Michelangelo's famous statue, and the other the book, *Moses and Monotheism*. That there may be something especially significant in connection with these two essays is indicated by the fact that in both instances Freud hesitated to reveal his identity as their author.[3] "The Moses of Michelangelo" was published anonymously. It appeared in *Imago* in 1914 and contained the strange editorial note which we have previously cited.*

After writing it in the days between the Christmas of 1913 and New Year's Day of 1914, he decided against its publication. He finally allowed it to appear, but anonymously, saying, "Why disgrace Moses by putting my name to it? It is a joke, but perhaps not a bad one." He offered three reasons for publishing the essay anonymously, which, says Jones, seem rather thin. These were that it was a joke, that he was ashamed of its anti-Jewish character, and "Lastly because my doubt about my conclusion is stronger than usual; it is only because of editorial pressure (Rank and Sachs) that I have consented to publish at all." [4]

Jones points out that the essay was written at the time of Freud's deep concern with Jung's defection. Jung, as we have seen,[5] was extremely important to Freud, for in Jung he saw a bridge to the Gentile world. Jung was the only important member of the early group of psychoanalysts whom Freud regarded as being able to command respect from the outside world, in view of the fact that he was a Gentile. In "On the History of the Psychoanalytic Movement," which he wrote at

* See p. 39, above.

about the same time as "The Moses of Michelangelo," he writes bitterly of Jung that he "seemed ready to enter into a friendly relationship with me and for my sake to give up certain prejudices in regard to race which he had previously permitted himself." [6] It is clear that "The Moses of Michelangelo" was written at a time when Freud was in the throes of considerations regarding the lot of the Jews.

Jones is well aware of the significance of the essay. He says, "This essay is of special interest to students of Freud's personality. The fact alone that this statue moved him more deeply than any other of the many works of art with which he was familiar gives his essay on it a peculiar significance." [7] In it Freud writes:

> For no piece of statuary has ever made a stronger impression on me than this. How often have I mounted the steep steps of the unlovely Corso Cavour to the lonely place where the deserted church stands, and have essayed to support the angry scorn of the hero's glance! Sometimes I have crept cautiously out of the half-gloom of the interior as though I myself belonged to the mob upon whom his eye is turned—the mob which can hold fast no conviction, which has neither faith nor patience and which rejoices when it has regained its illusory idols.
>
> But why do I call this statue inscrutable? There is not the slightest doubt that it represents Moses, the Law-giver of the Jews, holding the Tables of the Ten Commandments. That much is certain, but that is all. . . . [8]

Those who knew Freud were evidently aware of his deep feeling regarding Moses. Jones says:

> There is every reason to suppose that the grand figure of Moses himself, from Freud's early Biblical studies to the last book he

ever wrote, was one of tremendous significance to him. Did he represent the formidable Father-Image or did Freud identify himself with him? Apparently both, at different periods.[9]

And Sachs writes:

It is as if Freud walked intuitively and unknowingly in the footsteps of his ancestors, and followed one of the oldest Jewish traditions: this is the belief that all Jews, born and unborn alike, were present on Mount Sinai and have there taken on themselves "the yoke of the Law." [10]

Some measure of the significance of the essay and the statue to Freud is indicated by his letter to its Italian translator.

My feeling for this piece of work is rather like that towards a love-child. For three lonely September weeks in 1913 I stood every day in the church in front of the statue, studied it, measured it, sketched it, until I captured the understanding for it which I ventured to express in the essay only anonymously. Only much later did I legitimatize this non-analytical child.[11]

The essay itself is, in a sense, hardly the kind that one might ordinarily expect from Freud. It is not a psychoanalytic investigation of the mind of Michelangelo, the creator of the statue. Instead, the essay gives its attention to the statue itself and to the Moses figure it represents. It attempts only a superficial analysis of Michelangelo to determine what he may have intended by the statue. At the close of the essay, Freud indicates that he may, after all, have just been projecting. He writes:

But what if we both [Freud and a critic, Lloyd] strayed on to a wrong path? What if we have taken too serious and profound a view of details which were nothing to the artist, details which he had introduced quite arbitrarily or for some purely formal reasons with no hidden intention behind? What if we have shared the fate of so many interpreters who have sought to see quite clearly things which the artist did not intend either consciously or unconsciously? I cannot tell.[12]

This is hardly the Freud who argued so cogently that no human production is whimsical or arbitrary. He does not plumb the nature of Michelangelo's motivation. Rather, he simply uses the statue as an occasion for the clarification of his own problem with respect to Moses.

Freud engages in laborious analysis of the statue. He concludes that the statue does not represent Moses about to rise in anger. Instead, he argues, what is represented is restrained anger, anger which will never materialize in a hostile action.

> The figure of Moses, therefore, cannot be supposed to be springing to his feet; he must be allowed to remain as he is in sublime repose like the other figures and like the proposed statue of the Pope (which was not, however, executed by Michelangelo himself). But then the statue we see before us cannot be that of a man filled with wrath, of Moses when he came down from Mount Sinai and found his people faithless and threw down the Holy Tables so that they were broken. And, indeed, I can recollect my own disillusionment when, during my first visits to the church, I used to sit down in front of the statue in the expectation that I should now see how it would start up on its raised foot, hurl the Tables of the Law to the ground and let fly its wrath. Nothing of the kind happened. Instead, the stone image became more and more transfixed, an almost oppressively solemn calm emanated from it, and I was obliged to realize that something was represented here that could stay without change; that this Moses would remain sitting like this in his wrath for ever.[13]

The picture we get is that of Freud sitting for weeks at the tomb of Pope Julius II in Rome gazing at the statue of Moses.

He sits in fear of the wrath of Moses, feeling this statue to be Moses himself, about to strike at the Jews for their defection. Slowly the image is converted into one of restrained anger. In his initial reaction to the statue he identifies with the "mob which can hold fast no conviction," with those who danced about the golden calf, who returned to pagan forms of worship when Moses was gone, and, we might add, forms of worship rekindled in the Sabbatian period. But his fear exerts itself as the creation of a counterimage.

> What we see before us is not the inception of a violent action but the remains of a movement that has already taken place. In his first transport of fury, Moses desired to act, to spring up and take vengeance and forget the Tables; but he has overcome the temptation, and he will now remain seated and still in his frozen wrath and in his pain mingled with contempt.[14]

In the essay Freud quotes the relevant passage from the Bible (Exodus 32:7-35). However, in doing this *he leaves out verses* 21-29. These deleted passages describe how Moses ground up the golden calf and forced the children of Israel to drink of it, and how the sons of Levi went through the camp killing the defectors. That Freud deletes these passages is indeed another way of making his point: the punishment for defection will not ensue. He writes:

> But Michelangelo has placed a different Moses on the tomb of the Pope, one superior to the historical or traditional Moses. He has modified the theme of the broken Tables; he does not let Moses break them in his wrath, but makes him be influenced by the danger that they will be broken and calm that wrath, or at any rate prevent it from becoming an act. In this way he has added something new and more than human to the

figure of Moses; so that the giant frame with its tremendous physical power becomes only a concrete expression of the highest mental achievement that is possible in a man, that of struggling successfully against an inward passion for the sake of a cause to which he has devoted himself.[15]

Jones provides an interpretation of this essay in terms of Freud's positive identification with Moses. Jung had defected, and Freud had to find a way to control the deep anger that this defection produced in him. We would certainly agree with Jones regarding this identification, but we believe that its significance is hardly probed. If Freud conceives of himself as the new Lawgiver, then the new Lawgiver must at one and the same time be like unto Moses, the previous Lawgiver, whose place he must preempt, and must be destructive of Moses. The new Lawgiver must revoke the older Law. The identification with Moses turns into its opposite, the destruction of Moses. Therefore Freud is also part of the mob, upon whom Moses' "eye is turned—the mob which can hold fast no conviction, which has neither faith nor patience and which rejoices when it has regained its illusory idols."

Freud suggests in the essay that his view of a tempered, restrained Moses is perhaps a reproach against the strong-mindedness of Pope Julius II, who

> . . . attempted to realize great and mighty ends, especially designs on a large scale. He was a man of action and he had a definite purpose, which was to unite Italy under the Papal supremacy. He desired to bring about single-handed what was not to happen for several centuries, and then only through the conjunction of many alien forces; and he worked alone, with impatience, in the short span of sovereignty allowed him, and used violent means.[16]

In *Moses and Monotheism,* Freud characterizes Moses in much the same way.[17] The reproach against the Pope which he attributes to Michelangelo may be interpreted as the reproach of Freud against Moses also.

Moses' most important characteristic is as the Lawgiver of the Jews. It was Moses who imposed the "yoke of the Law" upon the Jews. Moses is the image which embodies the whole brunt of Jewish orthodoxy. The Talmud and the other rabbinical writings constitute an elaboration of dicta of the Mosaic code, which the orthodox Jew takes upon himself to guide his life at every moment and in connection with every action. In a word, Moses is representative of the superego, the force generated within the individual to keep him from "instinctual gratification." The force which maintains renunciation of instinctual gratification is the fear of punishment. *In the allegory of the discussion of a statue Freud is saying that the feared punishment will never eventuate.* The superego is restrained. The superego will withhold its wrath, and will not strike. In this new view of Moses, Freud has turned him into a stone image, one which will not kill those who dance around the golden calf, those who do not accept, but violate the commandments upheld by the rabbinic tradition. Freud's essay on Moses is a symbolic Sabbatian assertion of freedom against the severe restrictions of thought and action which had been the life strategy of the Eastern European Jews.

Yet Freud was never quite able to extricate himself from the Mosaic dicta. This is exemplified by the thesis which he advanced in *Totem and Taboo* and reaffirmed in *Moses and Monotheism,* that the acquired sense of guilt is transmitted

128

hereditarily. This "peculiarity" of Freud, as it has been regarded by many, is made clear by his involvement with the Mosaic dicta. His supposition "that the sense of guilt for an action has persisted for many thousands of years and has remained operative in generations which can have no knowledge of that action" [18] is a simple version of the Mosaic threat that God visits "the iniquity of the fathers upon the children, and upon the children's children, unto the third and to the fourth generation." [19] That Freud should have permitted himself to accept an essentially bizarre hypothesis, despite his awareness of its peculiarity, lends weight to our hypothesis that he was consciously or unconsciously obscuring the cultural origins of the problems with which he was coping.

We may summarize our addition to Jones's interpretation of the significance of Freud's essay as follows: *Moses is the symbol of orthodoxy, the author of the Law, the figure responsible for imposing its heavy yoke.* In the Sabbatian tradition Freud opposed himself to the Law. In his interpretation the excess of the Mosaic-type Law made for neurosis and was generally inappropriate for modern living. He was echoing the message of Jacob Frank, who had asserted that the Law was useful only for an unredeemed world. The devices for living adopted earlier by the Jews, the stern and forbidding adherence to every detail of the Law, was rendered inappropriate by the enlightenment and the new freedom of the Western world.

Freud then goes to Rome, which has its own significance in the tradition of Messianic Judaism, [20] and sits for weeks before the imposing statue of Moses. He is filled with guilt for the defection from orthodoxy and expects the drastic punishment which the Mosaic dicta threaten. He identifies himself with the mob as the object of Moses' wrath. By a tortuous analysis of the statue, hardly differentiating Moses from the statue, he finds small details for making a case that Moses will not punish. He takes advantage of the fact that Moses is cast in stone, and, paradoxically, "worships" a graven image in the citadel of Christianity. He paralyzes the Mosaic image, asserting that Moses "will now remain seated and still in his frozen wrath," [21] "that this Moses would remain sitting like this in his wrath for ever." [22]

NOTES TO CHAPTER 17

1. Freud, *Autobiographical Study,* p. 13.
2. Freud, *Col. Papers,* IV, pp. 251-287.
3. Cf. his reluctance to publish *Totem and Taboo,* p. 295, below.
4. Cf. the discussion of this essay, Jones, II, pp. 363-367.
5. Cf. p. 58, above.
6. Freud, *Col. Papers,* I, p. 329.
7. Jones, II, pp. 363-364.
8. Freud, *Col. Papers,* IV, 259-260.
9. Jones, II, 364-365.
10. Sachs, p. 152.
11. Jones, II, p. 367.
12. Freud, *Col. Papers,* IV, p. 286.
13. Freud, *Col. Papers,* IV, p. 269.
14. Freud, *Col. Papers,* IV, p. 279.
15. Freud, *Col. Papers,* IV, p. 283.
16. Freud, *Col. Papers,* IV, p. 284.
17. Cf. pp. 154-155, below.
18. Freud, *Totem and Taboo,* trans. James Strachey (London: Routledge and Kegan Paul, 1950), p. 158.

19. Exodus 34:7.
20. Cf. pp. 173 ff., below
21. Freud, *Col. Papers,* IV, p. 279.
22. Freud, *Col. Papers,* IV, p. 269.

18

Some Relevant Biographical Items

We might at this point pause briefly to consider two items in Freud's biography which seems to be relevant here as substantiation of our thesis concerning Freud's Sabbatian tendencies. There is, of course, a sense in which these items are trifles in the life of an eminently great man. And yet in view of what Freud has taught us about the significance of trifles, we are pressed to bring them to bear in our analysis for the weight that they lend to the argument.

The first of these has to do with the nature of Freud's interest in law. In the Jewish tradition, law and orthodoxy were practically identical. It is not an exaggeration to say that the rabbi was essentially a teacher of Jewish law and a judge. Leadership in the Jewish community was based primarily on the person's knowledge and wisdom with respect to law. The rabbi governed the community; he rendered decisions in connection with civil disputes; he was consulted in all matters where there was a question of whether a given act was or was not permitted according to the law.

We know that Freud's own initial intellectual interest was

law.* If he had followed this initial pursuit, one could regard him as having fulfilled, in secular form, the traditional young Jewish scholar's quest of becoming a rabbi in the orthodox community.†

Jones relates an event in Freud's life which cannot, perhaps, be regarded as trivial in this connection. Jones tells us, "It is a curious fact that the only examination in his life at which he failed was in medical jurisprudence," upon which Jones comments that "deep impulses were driving him in another direction." [1] What Jones calls a "curious fact" is quite comprehensible if we accept the idea that Freud was manifesting in his abandonment of legal interests and failure in medical jurisprudence his impulses against orthodox Judaism with its strong legalistic orientation.

It might be pointed out, parenthetically, that this attitude concerning law was not unique with Freud among the young Jewish men in Vienna. The fact that Freud had discovered an acceptable secular way of reacting to the orthodox Jewish tradition was probably one of the reasons he was able to find adherents among the Jews of Vienna. We see the same phenomenon in Hanns Sachs, who describes himself before he had read Freud's *Interpretation of Dreams* as "a young man who was supposedly studying law but not living up to the supposi-

---

* Freud, *Autobiographical Study*, p. 13. It is of interest, in terms of our thesis, that he tells us this immediately after he tells us of the effect of the Bible on him: "My early familiarity with the Bible story (at a time almost before I had learnt the art of reading) had, as I recognized much later, an enduring effect upon the direction of my interest. Under the influence of a school friendship with a boy rather my senior who grew up to be a well-known politician I developed a wish to study law like him and to engage in social activities" (pp. 13-14).

† Is the commonly expressed wish of the Jewish mother that her son might become "a doctor or a lawyer" a reflection of the traditional roles of healer and rabbi?

tion—a type common enough among the middle class in Vienna at the turn of the century." [2]

The second item of note in this connection is Freud's penchant for collecting idols. The commandment reads:

> Thou shalt have no other gods before Me. Thou shalt not make unto thee a graven image, nor any manner of likeness, of any thing that is in heaven above, or that is in the earth beneath, or that is in the water under the earth; thou shalt not bow down unto them, nor serve them; for I the Lord thy God am a jealous God, visiting the iniquity of the fathers upon the children unto the third and fourth generation of them that hate Me; and showing mercy unto the thousandth generation of them that love Me and keep My commandments. [3]

An enlightened person in the nineteenth and twentieth centuries could hardly violate this commandment in its literal sense. We have seen, however, that the violation of this commandment was characteristic of the Sabbatians, who went so far as to worship a wooden image of Sabbatai Zevi. Opposition to a god who can be identified with an actual thing was basic to the Jewish religion associated with the image of Moses. Freud's deep emotional involvement with God in the statue of Moses is itself a sign of his tendency to violate the commandment, and the fact that it took place in a Catholic Church only adds to the irony.

In his rooms Freud surrounded himself with every heathen god he could find. As if in sheer spite * he pursued "idols" and their associated trappings with a deep fascination. His study and consulting room bulged with them. Sachs tells of the early meetings at Freud's quarters, how "under the silent

---

* A common Yiddish expression is *meshamed uf tselochos*, "an apostate out of spite."

stare of idols and animal-shaped gods, we listened to some new article by Freud or read and discussed our own products or just talked about things that interested us." [4] He tells us how "Freud had the habit of taking one or another piece of his collection from its place, and of examining it by sight and touch while he was talking." [5] In a letter to Fliess, Freud writes, "The ancient gods still exist, for I have bought one or two lately, among them a stone Janus, who looks down on me with his two faces in very superior fashion"; [6] and a few days later he writes, "My grubby old gods, of whom you think so little, take part in my work as paper-weights." [7] Susan Bernfeld describes his collection:

> First he had chosen some bronze statuettes and terra cotta figurines from Rome and Greece, with an occasional Egyptian piece. . . . The little statues found a place on his desk, until his treatment room and the adjoining library were filled with the large collection. Glass cases held innumerable vases, bowls and statuettes from Pompeian and Etruscan tombs, and iridescent glasses, occhiales and earthen lamps from Rome. The permanently open doors to the library were flanked by Egyptian stone reliefs that stood on the floor. On the small table that was before his eyes when he sat in the large chair behind the couch was the Chinese jade bowl that he had bought in America, at Tiffany's in 1909. On one wall hung the portrait of an Egyptian female mummy—'with a nice Jewish face,' as Freud occasionally commented. Over the couch hung an etching of the great temple of Karnak, and next to it a plaster copy of the marble relief of Gradiva, on the ledge of which he kept for many years a bundle of dry papyrus leaves.[8]

Susan Bernfeld interprets this interest of Freud as follows: "He fell in love with archaeology and therefore gained the strength to live in mental security without religion."[9] This interpretation can be given further specification: The hostility which he had towards religion was not to religion as such. It has, for example, been quite appropriately argued that Freud's whole psychoanalytic contribution shares many of the characteristics which we generally subsume under the rubric of religion. Rather, what Freud opposes is religion in the Mosaic tradition, most fully expressed in Jewish orthodoxy. His resistance to law and his tendency towards the violation of the commandment against idolatry, as manifested in his jocular yet passionate "having of other gods before" the Mosaic God, expressed his rebellion against orthodox Jewish religion. The "grubby old gods" lessened Moses' magic power.

NOTES TO CHAPTER 18

1. Jones, I, p. 27.
2. Sachs, p. 3.
3. Exodus, 20:3-7. The version is that of *The Holy Scripture, According to the Masoretic Text* (Philadelphia: The Jewish Publication Society of America, 2 vols., 1955).
4. Sachs, p. 82.
5. Sachs, pp. 101-102.
6. Freud, *Origins,* p. 286.
7. Freud, *Origins,* p. 288.
8. Susan C. Bernfeld, pp. 109-110.
9. Susan C. Bernfeld, p. 123.

19

Moses and Monotheism — A Book of Double Content

We turn now to what we consider Freud's most revelatory work with respect to our hypothesis. This is his book, *Moses and Monotheism*. It was the last book Freud wrote and, in our opinion, expresses some of his deepest impulses, impulses which were operative throughout his life. The book is the only one written by Freud which directs itself avowedly to the problem of Judaism and the meaning of being Jewish.

Let us first consider this book, so to speak, on the face of it. It is, by any of the usual criteria used to evaluate books, incredibly bad. Some of the followers of Freud have tended to dismiss it; and by some, it is regarded as the product of senility, with the suggestion, perhaps, that respect to Freud's genius is best paid by ignoring it. If this book had not come from the hand of Sigmund Freud, one would seriously doubt whether it would ever have seen the light of day. Morris Raphael Cohen, who was, we know, more interested in Talmud than the Jewish mystical currents, wrote of it:

If anyone else had written this book, we should have been justified in dismissing it as the work of an opinionated crank who is more interested in his tortuous speculation than in getting at the verifiable facts. Freud, however, is the discoverer of an extensively used method of mental therapeutics and the inventor of what is claimed to be the science of psychoanalysis, which has swept over our popular literature and the conversation of those who call themselves sophisticated. A very large number thus regard him as the infallible source of profound and even scientific truth. Morever, he not only possesses an extraordinary gift for making the most fanciful hypotheses seem plausible, but admits the inadequacy of the evidence to support his conclusion. Nevertheless, he does claim certainty for propositions for which there is no evidence at all—for instance, that Moses introduced circumcision. He unhesitatingly dismisses the identification of the Habiru of the Amarna tablets with the Hebrew invaders of Palestine and also waves aside the sole known Egyptian reference to Israel, because they do not fit into his chronologic scheme. He is certain that the Priestly Code did not adopt any new tendencies, that religion is a neurosis and only thus can it be understood, that all children and primitive people are neurotic, and (contrary to all experience) that tradition is less subject to distortion in time than a written text. While, therefore, no careful student of the subject is likely to be misled by a work which has so little sound foundation, the general public is likely to get the impression that a new and substantial contribution to the understanding of Jewish history has been made on the basis of psychoanalysis.[1]

The evidence which Freud cites for his assertions are dubious and do not support his conclusions. His argument, for example, that Moses was an Egyptian and not a Jew resides in part on dubious etymological evidence concerning Moses' name, which Freud himself does not consider decisive, and on com-

parison between the Moses legend and other legends. Freud
is actually his own most severe critic on the idea that Moses
was an Egyptian. After making the assertion he says,

> We have seen that the first argument, that of his name, has not
> been considered decisive. We have to be prepared for the new
> reasoning—the analysis of the exposure myth—not faring any
> better. The objection is likely to be that the circumstances of
> the origin and transformation of legends are too obscure to
> allow of such a conclusion as the preceding one, and that all
> efforts to extract the kernel of historical truth must be doomed
> to failure in the face of the incoherence and contradictions
> clustering around the heroic person of Moses and the unmis
> takable signs of tendentious distortion and stratification accu-
> mulated through many centuries. I myself do not share this
> negative attitude, but I am not in a position to confute it.[2]

Besides the general weakness of the argument the book man-
ifests other striking characteristics. As we have seen, there is
the evident hesitation and ambivalence with respect to its publication; and throughout the book there is repetition in various
ways that the book should not be taken too seriously.

Towards the end of the first section of the book, immediately
after the passage quoted above, he writes,

> If there was no more certainty than this to be attained, why
> have I brought this inquiry to the notice of a wider public?
> I regret that even my justification has to restrict itself to hints.[3]

At the very end of the first section he again expresses the
same sentiment:

> Even if one were to accept it as historical that Moses was Egyp-
> tian, we should want at least one other fixed point so as to
> protect the many emerging possibilities from the reproach of

their being products of imagination and too far removed from reality. An objective proof of the period into which the life of Moses, and with it the exodus from Egypt, fall would perhaps have sufficed. But this has not been forthcoming, and therefore it will be better to suppress any inferences that might follow our view that Moses was an Egyptian.[4]

Yet the very next words in the book, the title of the second part, are "If Moses Was an Egyptian . . ."[5] Early in this section he repeats his hesitation to publish,

At the end of my essay I said that important and far-reaching conclusions could be drawn from the suggestion that Moses was an Egyptian; but I was not prepared to uphold them publicly, since they were based only on psychological probabilities and lacked objective proof. The more significant the possibilities thus discerned, the more cautious is one about exposing them to the critical attack of the outside world without any secure foundation—like an iron monument with feet of clay. No probability, however seductive, can protect us from error; even if all parts of a problem seem to fit together like the pieces of a jigsaw puzzle, one has to remember that the probable need not necessarily be the truth, and the truth not always probable. And lastly, it is not attractive to be classed with the scholastics and Talmudists who are satisfied to exercise their ingenuity, unconcerned how far removed their conclusions may be from the truth.[6]

Besides his remark about not wanting to be classed with the Talmudists, in this passage Freud criticizes the work which he is presenting in a fundamental way. The last sentence, interesting in its own right because of what it says regarding the Talmudists, suggests Cohen's criticism.

Later on Freud says,

I am quite prepared to hear anew the reproach that I have put forward my reconstruction of the early history of the tribe of Israel with undue and unjustified certitude. I shall not feel this criticism to be too harsh, since it finds an echo in my own judgment.[7]

He has two prefaces to the third part of the essay. The first one indicates that because he is living in a "Catholic country under the protection of that Church" he will withhold it from publication.[8] Yet ambivalence is clearly present, because this preface, which ends with an assertion that he will not publish the essay, begins with

With the audacity of one who has little or nothing to lose I propose to break a well-founded resolution for the second time and to follow up my two essays on Moses . . . [contained as the first two parts of the book] with the final part, till now withheld.[9]

He makes the point that he is an old man and old men lose their creative faculties. He even enters into a minor quarrel with George Bernard Shaw on the question of the value of contributions by old men.[10]

The second preface, written in London, asserts that he had had "inner misgivings as well as external hindrances"[11] in connection with the essay. Because of changed political conditions, he says, "I dare now to make public the last part of my essay."[12] Towards the end of this second preface he writes, "To my critical faculties this treatise, proceeding from a study of the man Moses, seems like a dancer balancing on one toe."[13] He protests his right to be arbitrary with the work of others in a discussion of the work of Robertson Smith. "Above all, however," he says, "I am not an ethnologist, but a psychoanalyst. It was my good right to select from ethnological data what would serve me for my analytic work." [14]

Remarks such as these in the essay indeed make us wonder whether this work by Freud is meant to be taken at its face value. We can bring to bear upon this essay the consideration which Leo Strauss makes about books written under conditions of persecution. Strauss says,

> If a master of the art of writing commits such blunders as would shame an intelligent high school boy, it is reasonable to assume that they are intentional, especially if the author discusses, however incidentally, the possibility of intentional blunders in writing.[15]

Freud was certainly a "master of the art of writing," the book is a bad book, and no one has told us more about the intent of blunders than he has. The book is replete with indications of hesitancy, with indications that what is really being said is but hinted at, and with arguments which are cuttingly criticized by the author himself.

To what conclusions do these considerations lead us? The most parsimonious and the most cogent is that the book must be considered in a typically Freudian manner, *as having a manifest and a latent content;* and Freud himself has told us something of the ways by which to determine the latent from the manifest content. Making this assumption, an assumption strongly suggested in various ways by the book itself, let us attempt to win an understanding of this book, a book that cannot, under any circumstances, be considered, as Cohen suggested, the work of an "opinionated crank."

As psychologists are aware, it is easier to determine the nature of a motive than it is to decide whether the motive is conscious or unconscious. Since our culture associates consciouness with responsibility, and Freud was evidently aware of the hostility the book might generate, we can suspect that part of his motivation was to generate the impression of unconscious intent. As his communications with Meitlis showed, he was afraid that the book would anger the Jews,[16] and he opens the book with a sentence which strongly suggests that the book was in some sense hostile to the Jews—in our interpretation, the orthodox Jews. The first sentence of the book reads "To deny a people the man whom it praises as the greatest of its sons is not a deed to be undertaken lightheartedly—especially by one belonging to that people." [17] He also sensed that the book would elicit hostility from the Catholics. Thus, that the book should have been written with a certain amount of deliberate obscurity is, at the very least, a real possibility.

The option that we have is either to dismiss the book or to find a way of understanding it which will do justice to Freud's genius. In the suggestion that the book is one which is perhaps deliberately obscure, and that it has a double content, we can reconcile our knowledge of Freud's profundity with the fact that he did write the *Moses and Monotheism*. If the book is one which is in the Kabbalistic tradition, and if it was written under the sense of persecution, that it should be deliberately obscure is completely understandable.

NOTES TO CHAPTER 19

1. Morris R. Cohen, *Reflections of a Wondering Jew* (Boston: Beacon Press, 1950), pp. 139-140. Chapter 15, pp. 139-146, is a review of Freud's *Moses and Monotheism*.
2. Freud, *Moses and Monotheism*, p. 14.
3. Freud, *Moses and Monotheism*, p. 14.
4. Freud, *Moses and Monotheism*, p. 15.
5. Freud, *Moses and Monotheism*, p. 16.
6. Freud, *Moses and Monotheism*, pp. 16-17.
7. Freud, *Moses and Monotheism*, pp. 49-50.
8. Cf. pp. 39 ff., above.
9. Freud, *Moses and Monotheism*, p. 66.
10. Freud, *Moses and Monotheism*, p. 66.
11. Freud, *Moses and Monotheism*, p. 69.
12. Freud, *Moses and Monotheism*, p. 70.
13. Freud, *Moses and Monotheism*, p. 71.
14. Freud, *Moses and Monotheism*, p. 169.
15. Strauss, p. 30.
16. Cf. p. 49, above.
17. Freud, *Moses and Monotheism*, p. 3.

20

Moses as an Egyptian

What significance shall we ascribe to Freud's thesis that Moses was an Egyptian? From the point of view of all evident tradition Moses was both an Egyptian and a Jew. The well-known Biblical story has it that he was born a Jew, but was taken into and brought up in the royal household of Egypt. Josephus, the historian, tells us that Moses was a general for Egypt who fought against the Ethiopians, as Freud knew.[1]

The *Zohar,* too, asserts that Moses was an Egyptian, (although not in a way to exclude his Jewishness) on the basis of the Biblical passage which relates that when Moses ran away from Egypt in fear of being apprehended for having killed an Egyptian, the daughters of Reuel reported to their father "An Egyptian delivered us. . . ."[2] The *Zohar* even suggests the relationship between the sun (in Freud, Aton) and Moses which Freud asserts. "Moses is dead, and the sun is gathered in and the time has come for the moon to rule."[3]

But the fact remains that in spite of all Egyptian associations, Moses is still taken as a Jew. Freud's point is that Moses was *genetically* an Egyptian. Actually, whether Freud's thesis is valid is a question of little moment for our purposes.

As we have already seen, Freud starts his book with a "denial" of Moses; that is, if Moses is genetically a Gentile, he is thereby necessarily "denied." It is interesting to note a psychoanalyst, M. Wulff, quite astutely pointing out that "the whole question as to the national origin of Moses does not appear to be of decisive importance for Freud's main problem, the origin and development of monotheism." [4] It is actually quite conceivable that the whole book, as an essay on the psychology of the Jews, could have been written without imputing genetic Gentilism to Moses. On the presumption of a Gentile Moses, Freud argues an association of Moses with the Egyptian Aton religion, a point that he could easily have made simply on the basis of the Biblical story that Moses was raised in the royal household.

As the internal evidence of Freud's book indicates, he regards the idea of Moses-as-a-Gentile as critically important. Yet the logic of his manifest presentation does not require it. As we have seen, he recognizes that his arguments for the assertion are tenuous and that his "justification has to restrict itself to hints." Thus we are indeed pressed to plumb the latent psychological significance of the Moses-as-a-Gentile theme. On the basis of Freudian theory, turning Moses into a Gentile-Egyptian would seem to be a wish-fulfillment on Freud's part.

In the same paragraph in which Freud says "it is not attractive to be classed with the scholastics and Talmudists," he writes "Moses was an Egyptian whom a people needed to make into a Jew." [5]

In *The Interpretation of Dreams* Freud describes the process

by which dream-thoughts may be turned into their opposites.
He writes:

> There is yet another alternative way in which the dream-work
> can deal with affects in the dream-thoughts, in addition to al-
> lowing them through or reducing them to nothing. It can *turn
> them into their opposite*. We have already become acquainted
> with the interpretative rule according to which every element
> in a dream can, for purposes of interpretation, stand for its
> opposite just as easily as for itself. . . . We can never tell before-
> hand whether it stands for the one or for the other; only the
> context can decide.[6]

Nor does Freud limit these considerations to dreams. In the
same paragraph he goes on to tell how this technique of resolving elements into their opposites is also used in social dissimulation![7]

If, following Freud, the context tends to bear out the
interpretation by opposites, as it seems to in this instance, then
Freud's assertion that "Moses . . . was an Egyptian whom a people needed to make into a Jew" can more meaningfully be
formulated as *Moses was a Jew whom Freud needed to make
into a Gentile.*

Several mutually clarifying interpretations suggest themselves as to why Freud should be thus motivated, beyond the
requirements of logic, to show Moses to be a Gentile.

A. THE SABBATIAN FULFILLMENT

We have already indicated the role of Sabbatianism in the
movement of the Jews into the main streams of Western civilization. Sabbatianism sometimes reached out greedily and des-

perately to catch at some kind of positive identification with the non-Jewish elements in Western culture. We have seen that even the apostasy of Sabbatai Zevi and Jacob Frank had paradoxically supported the hold of Sabbatianism in certain groups.

In *Moses and Monotheism,* Freud brings the Sabbatian impulse to its dramatic climax. Sabbatai Zevi *became* a Gentile. Jacob Frank *became* a Gentile. The ultimate fulfillment of the theme of Sabbatianism, is to have Moses, the most profound Messianic figure of Judaism and the image of all other Messiahs, already *be* a Gentile.

For Freud, a modern product of the enlightenment, an avowed and ritualistic act of conversion was essentially too trivial to have any deep emotional significance. By converting Moses into a Gentile, Freud committed his psychological act of apostasy. If, as we have seen, Freud strongly identified himself with Moses, then his preoccupation with the Moses of Michelangelo, *who sits petrified in a church in Rome and graces the tomb of a Pope,* and his turning Moses into a Gentile, can be understood as Freud's own realization of the Sabbatian act of apostasy. Through the image of Moses, as he develops it in his *Moses and Monotheism,* Freud becomes a Gentile psychologically as he makes a Gentile of Moses.

B. THE FANTASY OF THE "FAMILY ROMANCE"

In his attempt to demonstrate that Moses was an Egyptian, Freud draws upon the idea of the family romance,[8] which he had developed in a paper bearing the title *Family Romances.*[9]

He cites Rank's book, *Der Mythus von der Geburt des Helden,* to confirm his point. Freud writes,

> [Rank's book] . . . deals with the fact "that almost all important civilized peoples have early woven myths around and glorified in poetry their heroes, mythical kings and princes, founders of religions, of dynasties, empires and cities—in short, their national heroes. Especially the history of their birth and of their early years is furnished with phantastic traits. . . ." [10]

He argues that in the "average myth," the hero is born into a noble and royal family, but grows up in a humble and degraded family. Then he points out that the myth of Moses is quite different. Moses is born of the Jewish Levites but is raised in the royal house. On the basis of this divergence, Freud infers that Moses was an Egyptian by birth.

That Freud, who was well aware of the tendentious character of myth, should attempt to go back to the actual *facts* associated with Moses through myth is most strange. If he had limited himself to inferences concerning an original myth of which the Biblical myth is a distortion, he would be on sounder ground. But inferences as to presumptive facts on the basis of the logic of myth cannot be made.

Freud says clearly in *Moses and Monotheism* that the idea of a person born into nobility is mythical and grounded in psychological needs.

> The inner source of the myth is the so-called 'family romance' of the child, in which the son reacts to the change in his inner relationship to his parents, especially that to his father. The child's first years are governed by grandiose over-estimation of his father; kings and queens in dreams and fairytales always represent, accordingly, the parents. Later on, under the influ-

149

ence of rivalry and real disappointments, the release from the parents and a critical attitude towards the father set in.[11]

And then Freud tells us:

> The Moses myth as we know it today lags sadly behind its secret motives. If Moses is not of royal lineage our legend cannot make him into a hero; if he remains a Jew it has done nothing to raise his status.[12]

By conceiving of Moses as an Egyptian nobleman Freud is, in effect, completing the Moses myth in a way which had never been done in the history of the Jews. The Jews have "lagged behind" because they have not added the critical element to the myth, that Moses was born of nobility, and this Freud is doing by writing this book. Cogent evidence that such is indeed the case is provided by Freud's use of the term "family romance." For in his essay on the family romance Freud points out that the child develops the idea that he is "a step-child or an adopted child." But the theme of the Jews having been *adopted* by Moses is exactly what Freud's book is about!

Freud tells us that the family romance myth is due to the child's discovery that his father is not what he had previously conceived him to be. The disillusionment from his infantile overestimation of him expresses itself as the family romance fantasy, that he was adopted. Freud, similarly, disillusioned from his infantile overestimation of Moses, creates the family romance fantasy that the Jews were adopted.

We now see the significance of the genetic emphasis for Freud. It is, in part, self-aggrandizing. By creating a Gentile Moses of high position and royal lineage, he overcomes his sense of the Jew as a person of low social status. Freud, as we

150

know from various biographical items, felt very sensitive about the low social position to which his Jewishness held him. Freud's myth that the Jews were *adopted* by a Gentile of high nobility overcomes the sense of degradation associated with his feelings of being a Jew. And in this he repeats in thought what the Sabbatians did in action: Sabbatai Zevi was taken into the Sultan's court; Jacob Frank was sponsored by King Augustus III when he was baptized; and the Frankists as a group were sponsored by the Polish nobility in their baptism.

By developing the myth of Moses as a member of the Egyptian royal household, Freud is reforming it to fit the pattern of the usual myth. Thus it becomes a candidate for the kind of psychoanalytic scrutiny Rank engaged in in his book. It was necessary for Freud to refashion the myth, so that its merely mythical character would be revealed. This brings us to our next point, the Moses-as-a-Gentile image as a device for coping with anti-Semitism.

C. MOSES AND ANTI-SEMITISM

We know that throughout his life Freud suffered from a deep sense of being discriminated against as a Jew. The Moses-as-a-Gentile fantasy may be understood as a desperate and brilliant attempt to ward off anti-Semitism. The book was written in the throes of the greatest anti-Semitic disaster the Jews had ever experienced. Part of it was written in Vienna when the shadow of Hitler loomed over all of Austria, and part of it in London, where Freud had been displaced by Hitler. There can be little doubt that this book, which is Freud's most intense expression of his concern with the problem of Judaism, must in some sense have been a response to the outward events of his life. To say that Freud wrote this book as a reaction to his experience of the force of anti-Semitism must hit at the truth in some way.

The book contains among other contributions, a most interesting set of ideas concerning anti-Semitism. One of these ideas which Freud voices, with the announcement that it will appear incredible, is indeed a reflection of a theory of anti-Semitism which appears in the *Zohar*. Freud writes:

> The deeper motives of anti-Semitism have their roots in times long past; they come from the unconscious, and I am quite prepared to hear that what I am going to say will at first appear incredible. I venture to assert that the jealousy which the Jews evoked in other peoples by maintaining that they were the first-born, favourite child of God the Father has not yet been overcome by those others, just as if the latter had given credence to the assumption.[13]

This "incredible" theory of anti-Semitism is set out in the *Zohar* as follows:

> And it is because God holds Israel in affection and draws them near to himself that all the idolatrous nations hate Israel; for they see themselves kept at a distance whilst Israel are brought near. Similarly it was by reason of the love that Jacob showed towards Joseph above all his other sons that they conspired to slay him, though he was their own brother. How much greater, then, must be the enmity of the idolatrous nations toward Israel! Observe the consequences that followed the excessive love shown to Joseph by his father: he was exiled from his father, and his father joined him in exile, and along with them . . . the Shekinah also went into exile. It is true that the exile was

really the consequence of a divine decree; yet the proximate cause was the coat of many colours which he made for him specially.*

Now how does the idea of a Gentile Moses work to soften the force of anti-Semitism? Freud says explicitly that it is to Moses that the Jewish people owes "much of the hostility which it has met and is meeting still." [14] As we have just seen, Freud believed that the basis of anti-Semitism is to be found in the Jewish idea of the "chosen people." To this Freud counterposes the thesis that the Jews are not God's "chosen people," but rather the "chosen people" of Moses. He says,

> Sometimes, it is true, we hear of a people adopting another god, but never of a god choosing a new people. Perhaps we approach an understanding of this unique happening when we reflect on the connection between Moses and the Jewish people. Moses had stooped to the Jews, had made them his people; they were his "chosen people." [15]

The characteristics that make the Jew obnoxious to the Gentile are, according to Freud, not at all uniquely Jewish, but rather of Gentile origins. He writes

> that . . . the man Moses created their character by giving to them a religion which heightened their self-confidence to such a degree that they believed themselves to be superior to all other peoples. They survived by keeping aloof from the others.[16]

---

* *Zohar*, II, p. 198. It should be noted, parenthetically, that this passage in the *Zohar* occurs in the discussion of Joseph as an interpreter of dreams. We know that Freud, the dream interpreter, identified with the Biblical Joseph: "It will be noticed that the name Josef plays a great part in my dreams. . . . My own ego finds it very easy to hide itself behind people of that name, since Joseph was the name of a man famous in the Bible as an interpreter of dreams"—*Int. of Dreams*, p. 484. Had Freud read the *Zohar* these passages would have been of particular interest to him. Or, if associates were to have pointed out the *Zohar* to him, they would very likely have pointed out the Joseph passages.

The circumcision, which in the Jewish tradition is taken as the sign of the Covenant—the word for the circumcision ceremony, *b'rith,* means Covenant—is, according to Freud, merely an Egyptian custom imposed on the Jews, and the Jews have been the objects of anti-Semitic attack because of it.

> The possibility that the Jews in Egypt adopted the usage of circumcision in any other way than in connection with the religion Moses gave them may be rejected as quite untenable.[17]

But,

> . . . among the customs through which the Jews marked off their aloof position, that of circumcision made a disagreeable, uncanny impression on others.*

The idea of Moses-as-Gentile makes the Jews the buffoons of history! As buffoons they are of course to be laughed at and scorned but not attacked. In Freud's account, Moses is presented as a man of great knowledge and extremely strong personality, who could take advantage of the innocence of the children of Israel living under tyranny.

> Without doubt it must have been a tremendous father imago that stooped in the person of Moses to tell the poor Jewish labourers that they were his dear children. And the conception of a unique, eternal, omnipotent God could not have been less overwhelming for them; he who thought them worthy to make a bond with him promised to take care of them if only they remained faithful to his worship. Probably they did not find it easy to separate the image of the man Moses from that of his

---

* Freud, *Moses and Monotheism,* p. 116. Freud's emphasis on the castration fear may be given a somewhat Kabbalistic interpretation as a fear that the sign of the Covenant, worn on the penis in the form of the mark of cimcumcision, will be taken away; i.e., fear that God will break the Covenant, that love will be withdrawn and punishment will ensue.

God, and their instinct was right in this, since Moses might very well have incorporated into the character of his God some of his own traits, such as his irascibility and implacability.[18]

At times, when faced with persecution, the Jews have been brought into doubt about the genuineness of the Covenant. In Sabbatianism particularly we have seen the tendency of the Jews to abandon their faith in this God, to regard the religion which they received from Moses as appropriate for an earlier day, but contemporarily inappropriate. We recall in this connection Jacob Frank's assertion that the Law, the Torah, was dead. Freud renews the breach of faith in the Mosaic God, by the identification of this God with the all-human image of Moses, who had thus seduced the Jews into several thousands of years of deception. This Moses, *who was not even a Jew himself,* turned their heads with a glamorous idea of having a special relationship to God; and they, rather than face up to the humiliation of the seduction, retain only this grand image of themselves painted by their seducer.

If, as Jacques Barzun says, the modern mind fears most being wrong, being ridiculous, and being taken in,[19] then Freud, were he fulfilling the Sabbatian mood in modern dress, could not have expressed himself better. For what he is essentially saying is that the Jews believed Moses was a Jew and he was not; they have been made ridiculous and have persisted in being ridiculous; all of the pain they have suffered over the centuries because they have embraced the Torah was due to an historical imposition by a Gentile-Egyptian. That he was Egyptian, the classical enemy and the classical oppressor, makes the situation so ironic, that Freud's message, if taken seriously, should produce a most anguished burst of tears and laughter. And most important, Freud's assertions make the Jews the butt of the greatest joke in history; and thereby achieve for them also the greatest gain in history, freedom from persecution. It converts them from threatening to comical and stupid characters.

D. THE DISSOCIATION OF MOSES FROM THE JEWS

Freud clung to the Lamarckian idea of genetic transmission of cultural characteristics throughout his life. He makes the point in *Totem and Taboo,* and reaffirms it in *Moses and Monotheism.* When challenged by Joseph Wortis on the concept of the inheritance of acquired characteristics to the effect that it was inconsistent with what most biologists believed, he said, "But we can't bother with the biologists. We have our own science." And then he added, "We must go our own way." [20]

The idea of the cultural continuity of a people through genetic transmission sharpens the significance of Freud's assertion that Moses was genetically a Gentile. If the set of beliefs associated with Moses are the reasons for anti-Semitism, and if Moses was not a Jew, then anti-Semitism is properly directed against Moses, not the Jews.

It is characteristically maintained that the Jewish contribution to Western civilization is its strong ethical orientation, and this is reaffirmed by Freud. The effect of Moses was to make the Jews accept "instinctual renunciation." The Jews took upon themselves the "yoke of the Law," and through them it was transmitted to Christianity. Freud indicates that one of the reasons for anti-Semitism is exactly this, that the Jew is symbolic of the superego. Anti-Semitism, says Freud, is most acute in those people who have newly taken upon themselves the burden of Mosaic morality.

> We must not forget that all the peoples who now excel in the practice of anti-Semitism became Christians only in relatively recent times, sometimes forced to it by bloody compulsion. One might say they all are "badly christened"; under the thin veneer of Christianity they have remained what their ancestors were, barbarically polytheistic. They have not yet overcome their grudge against the new religion which was forced on them, and they have projected it on to the source from which Christianity came to them. The facts that the Gospels tell a story which is enacted among Jews, and in truth treats only of Jews, has facilitated such a projection. The hatred for Judaism is at bottom hatred for Christianity, and it is not surprising that in the German National Socialist revolution this close connection of the two monotheistic religions finds such clear expression in the hostile treatment of both.[21]

This theme of Freud's, that anti-Semitism is at bottom an attack upon the Mosaic superego, has been taken up and developed by other psychoanalysts. Thus Ernst Simmel writes that the "anti-Semitic crowd man" is one who finds in the mechanism of anti-Semitism

> . . . a temporary solution of his latent ambivalent conflict with the parent. Through participation in the collective ego of the crowd, he can split in two the re-externalized parental power: into the leader whom he loves and into the Jew whom he hates.
> . . . in choosing the Jew as the object of his hatred, his ego takes upon itself the privilege of attacking this super-ego, to punish it, instead of being punished by it. It will therefore not

evoke surprise if we assert that the Jew, as the object of anti-Semitism, represents the bad conscience of Christian civilization.[22]

As the evidence indicates, Freud was aware of these dynamics of anti-Semitism, as a reaction of the "badly christened" to the repressive forces of the Mosaic code. To ward off anti-Semitism, he would wish to *separate the Mosaic characteristics from the image of the Jew*. Moses, he therefore says, was not a Jew and hence the Jews should not be blamed for the Mosaic "yoke." In effect, he casts Moses from the Jewish fold, and says to the world, "Why do you blame me for the impositions of the superego when the one who was responsible for it was not even a Jew?"

It is appropriate at this point to show in what sense the whole burden of psychoanalysis may be regarded as a fulfillment of the Sabbatian ethos. For a variety of reasons the modern ego has been forced to surrender the various devices for coping with guilt that have been developed historically in association with a set of supernaturalistic religious ideas. In our century it has often been pointed out that modern science and psychoanalysis have seemed to "take the place of" religion. Modern psychoanalysis plays a "religious" role in people's lives, especially with respect to their "sins" as sins are defined by the Mosaic code. The deepest violations of the Mosaic code—aggression, murder, sexuality, incest, etc.—are the very subject matter of psychoanalysis. The psychoanalyst stands first as a representative of the superego, as Freud so well recognized when he discussed the transference relationship; and second as a *nonpunishing* superego. In the course of psychoanalysis the patient learns that the expected punishment will not materialize. The transference is essential; for unless the patient identifies the figure of the psychoanalyst with the superego, then the permissiveness is essentially ineffectual. The psychoanalyst listens to the patient's discussion of his deepest "sins" and does not blame. As a matter of fact, if there is any blame which is implicitly or explicitly contained within the psychoanalytic mood, it is directed against the parents of the patient in their treatment of him when he was an infant and a child. The psychoanalyst presents himself as a better—a more indulgent and more forgiving—parent, in the patient's struggle with the "other" parent.

Freud's repeated affirmation of his Jewish identity becomes illuminated through the *Moses and Monotheism*. If it is the Jew who carries the burden of the historical superego, then it it only a Jew who can really remove the sense of sin. We recall in this connection Freud's assertion that psychoanalysis could only have been created by a Jew;[23] and that in a letter to Oskar Pfister he wrote, ". . . by the way, how comes it that none of the godly ever devised psychoanalysis and that one had to wait for a godless Jew?"[24] If the Jews represent the authority of the Law, only a Jew can declare the Law is dead. Psychoanalysis, in this larger cultural sense, may be viewed as a fundamental effort to modify the classical image of the Jew. The Jew no longer stands in the shadow of Moses insisting upon rigid adherence to the letter of the Law, for example, Shakespeare's Shylock, but rather as a father figure, patient and forgiving, tolerant and understanding of violations of the Mosaic code. Such a role can be accomplished by Freud only through his full identification of himself as a Jew who is, moreover, dissociated from the figure of Moses. In his presumptive position of authority he can *rescind* the Law, declare the Law invalid. Thus Freud plays the role of a new Moses who comes down with a new Law dedicated to personal psychological liberty.

NOTES TO CHAPTER 20

1. Freud, *Moses and Monotheism*, p. 32.
2. *Zohar*, I, p. 27; Exodus 2:19.
3. *Zohar*, II, p. 368.
4. M. Wulff (ed.), *Max Eitingon: In Memoriam* (Jerusalem: Israel Psycho-Analytical Society, 1950). M. Wulff, An appreciation of Freud's *Moses and Monotheism*, pp. 124-142.
5. Freud, *Moses and Monotheism*, p. 16.
6. Freud, *The Int. of Dreams*, p. 471.
7. Freud, *The Int. of Dreams*, p. 471.
8. Freud, *Moses and Monotheism*, p. 9.
9. Freud, *Col. Papers*, V, pp. 74-78.
10. Freud, *Moses and Monotheism*, p. 7.
11. Freud, *Moses and Monotheism*, pp. 9-10.
12. Freud, *Moses and Monotheism*, p. 12.
13. Freud, *Moses and Monotheism*, p. 116.
14. Freud, *Moses and Monotheism*, p. 136.
15. Freud, *Moses and Monotheism*, p. 55.
16. Freud, *Moses and Monotheism*, p. 158.
17. Freud, *Moses and Monotheism*, p. 30.
18. Freud, *Moses and Monotheism*, pp. 140-141.
19. Jacques Barzun, *Romanticism and the Modern Ego*, (Boston: Little, Brown and Co., 1944), p. 163.
20. Joseph Wortis, *Fragments of an Analysis with Freud* (New York: Simon and Schuster, 1954), p. 84.
21. Freud, *Moses and Monotheism*, pp. 115-117.

22. Ernst Simmel (ed.), *Anti-Semitism: a Social Disease* (New York: International Press, 1946), Chap. III, Anti-Semitism and Mass Psychopathology, pp. 33-78, p. 50.

23. Cf. pp. 42-43.

24. Jones, II, p. 458.

21

Moses Was Killed By the Jews

We have suggested that in *Moses and Monotheism* Freud is fashioning a myth which would be more appropriate for the Jews of the modern world. In so doing he was fulfilling a force in the history of the Jews that may be traced to Kabbala and the Sabbatian episode. We turn our attention now to another major element in this myth, Freud's supposition that the Jews killed Moses.

If the theme of Moses-as-Gentile invites a deeper interpretation, so must the theme of the murder of Moses. Freud's arguments on this point are less tortuous than those he uses in connection with the Moses-as-Gentile idea. The murdered father theme was already present in his *Totem and Taboo* in the notion of the totem feast; and he uncritically accepts the idea of a murdered Moses from Sellin's Biblical analysis. Even with respect to Sellin's work, however, Freud admits that he has chosen what suits him.

> Sellin thinks that Shittim in the land east of the Jordan is indicated as the scene of the violent deed. We shall see, however, that the choice of this locality does not accord with our argument.[1]

Later, when he discusses the refutation of Robertson Smith's theories by other ethnologists he blithely announces his right to be arbitrary.[2]

In the section immediately following his introduction of the Moses-murder idea, Freud includes a passage which appears to deal with the way in which historical distortion takes place. This passage invites a reflexive interpretation, that is, an interpretation of the passage by its own message.

Freud is discussing the writing of Biblical text:

> The text, however, as we find it today tells us enough about its own history. Two distinct forces, diametrically opposed to each other, have left their traces on it. On the one hand, certain transformations got to work on it, falsifying the text in accord with secret tendencies, maiming and extending it until it was turned into its opposite. On the other hand, an indulgent piety reigned over it; anxious to keep everything as it stood, indifferent to whether the details fitted together or nullified one another. Thus almost everywhere there can be found striking omissions, disturbing repetitions, palpable contradictions, signs of things the communication of which was never intended. *The distortion of a text is not unlike a murder.** The difficulty lies not in the execution of the deed but in doing away with the traces. One could wish to give the word "distortion" the double meaning to which it has a right, although it is no longer used in this sense. It should mean not only "to change the appearance of," but also "to wrench apart," "to put in another place." That is why in so many textual distortions we may count on finding the suppressed and abnegated material hidden away somewhere, though in an altered shape and torn out of its original connection. Only it is not always easy to recognize it.[3]

* Our italics.

The passage applies, presumably, to the processes involved in bringing the Bible to its present form. But let us suppose that it is a kind of verbal ambiguity, such as Freud compared to dreams, and discussed in *The Interpretation of Dreams,* in which the "indefatigable" dream-work or "joke work"[4] has succeeded in making the same assertion not only about the Bible, but about Freud's *Moses and Monotheism* itself. Thus, for example, the italicized sentence in particular could well have been written as a pointed description of *Moses and Monotheism* itself. Freud's book is itself *about* a murder, the murder of Moses, and constitutes just such a distortion of text as he describes here in detail.

What is really of moment, however, is that the murder of Moses is Freud's own doing! *Moses and Monotheism* is indeed one of the grossest distortions of the Biblical text committed in modern times by a reputable scholar. The fantasy of the murder of Moses is a current one, one that Freud engages in at the very moment of writing. The actual evidence for the murder of Moses is very tenuous, but the murder of Moses is something which Freud must assert as fact. What he is doing is projecting a current fantasy onto a past situation, which is what is done in all mythmaking. *It is Freud who wishes that Moses were murdered;* and by this, of course, we must mean he wishes that the current repressive and oppressive forces associated with the Mosaic image would be killed. What Jacob Frank did literally when he cut up the Torah to make shoes of the parchment for his friends, Freud does in his own way through myth. And Jacob Frank's assertion that the Torah was dead, Freud repeats with psychoanalytic sophistication. In *The Interpretation of Dreams* Freud writes,

> The sanctity which we attribute to the rules laid down in the Decalogue has, I think, blunted our powers of perceiving the real facts. We seem scarcely to venture to observe that the majority of mankind disobey the Fifth Commandment.[5]

In the *Moses and Monotheism,* he refers to the murder of Moses as "the murder of the Father."[6] To say, however, that the theme of the Moses murder is but an expression of Freud's own Oedipus complex is to treat Freud much too lightly.

In his writing, Freud frequently did refer to the significance of his own Oedipus complex. Furthermore, he made the infantile relationship of the child to his parents the critical feature in the analysis of human personality. Besides this we find frequent identifications in Freud's writings of father and God, father and Moses, and father and superego. He refers to Oedipus as *that mythical law-breaker.*[7] Evidently Freud conceives of the Oedipal crime as prototypal of all law breaking.*

The technical problem presented to us by Freud's writings is whether to consider as primary the infantile experiences with his actual father, or the larger social forces captured in the idiom of the psychology of the child. We hesitate to answer this question too quickly because of the disparity between the information which we have concerning Freud's actual

---

* Freud's concept has an interesting parallel in the Talmud. In discussing the sins that were committed by the idolatrous Amon, "R. Johanan and R. Eleazor [dispute therein]: One maintained, He burnt the Torah; the other, he dishonoured his mother. His mother remonstrated with him: 'Hast thou then any pleasure in the place whence thou didst issue?' He replied: 'Do I do this for any other purpose than to provoke my Creator!'"—*The Babylonian Talmud. Sanhedrin II (Seder Nezikin)* (Soncino, 1935), p. 703.

father and the image of the father in Freud's paradigm. Freud's actual father does not seem to have been the strong-minded, stern, quick to wrath, deeply emotional, castration-threatening personality of Freud's paradigmatic father. Indeed, in *The Interpretation of Dreams,* Freud writes of his disappointment in his father for having yielded without a struggle after being accosted by a Gentile. Jones tells us that Jakob Freud was of gentle disposition and that Freud described his father in "rather Micawber-like terms as being 'always hopefully expecting something to turn up.'" [8] We hear about his father's illness and get an impression of a gentle and ineffectual personality, one which is at considerable variance with the father image of Freud's discussions. *This suggests that it is the social-religious father who is projected upon the real father, rather than the reverse.*

Under any circumstances we believe that the murder of Moses is Freud's allegorical attempt to destroy the restrictive hold of rabbinism on the Jews and on himself, as well as the parallels to such rabbinism in Western civilization at large. In the details of the processes by which children are acculturated, and particularly in the prescriptions and prohibitions with respect to sexuality, he recognized the significance of the Mosaic code. In *Moses and Monotheism* he implicitly defends his characteristic identification of the development of the neurosis of the individual with the development of society. The figure of Moses is the link between the prevailing conditions of contemporary society and history, for the moral ethos of the whole Judaeo-Christian tradition, in its restrictive aspects at least, may be traced to the Moses image. Moses plays a double role as an historical figure and contemporary image of the variety of forces which Freud asserted to be the root of neurotic conflict. In Freud's avowal and acceptance of the Oedipus complex he attempted to rewrite the Law of Moses in a way which would be more compatible with the prevailing spirit of liberty. He was trying to remake and rework our conceptions of morality in a way which would make it possible for the individual to live a richer and less hampered existence, freed from the taboos which Judaism had imposed upon itself for its survival and which had been accepted by the Christian world as a way of life.

Hence it is necessary for Freud to kill Moses. Not that the real Moses has not been dead for several thousands of years, and not that the real Moses would not have been dead whether killed or not. But the Moses of Freud's murder is the Moses each person carries about with him. And in this too Freud identifies himself with all Jewry. For in his fantasy he is not alone in the murder. The myth he fashions is not of one person murdering Moses. It is a murder which is committed collectively by all the Jews.

There is one final point to be made in connection with the theme of the murder of Moses, bringing into consideration again the Moses-as-Gentile theme. The commission of heresy, which Freud allegorically portrays as a murder, must necessarily invoke the guilt associated with the Oepidal crime. Indeed Freud saw the murder of Moses by the Jews as a necessary explanation of their genetic burden of guilt, which he as a Jew consciously felt. If it is necessary to kill Moses, however, then the idea that Moses was an Egyptian serves to take some of the edge off the guilt. In a sense, the Moses-as-an-Egyptian myth is a countermyth to that of the murdered Moses. By making Moses an Egyptian, Freud absolves himself and the Jews of the guilt associated with the murder-thought. Killing Moses-as-an-Egyptian is simply killing a member of the group which first persecuted the Jews.* Killing an Egyptian Moses is not the complete patricide it seems to be. Freud is killing the classical enemy of the Jew, and moreover, a stepfather at best. In the myth Freud fashions he kills someone in the belief that he is his father, which in "reality" he is not, but rather, in this metaphorical sense, the enemy of his father, an Egyptian.

Thus by writing this book, Freud becomes a Jewish hero in the history of the Jews. He performs the traditional Messianic function of relieving guilt, the very same function he ascribes to Jesus. The full role of positive Messianism in Freud's development is indicated in the next chapter.

NOTES TO CHAPTER 21

1. Freud, *Moses and Monotheism*, p. 43.
2. Cf. pp. 141-142, above.
3. Freud, *Moses and Monotheism*, pp. 51-52.
4. Freud, *The Int. of Dreams*, p. 356.
5. "Honor thy father and thy mother . . ."; Freud, *The Int. of Dreams*, p. 256.
6. Freud, *Moses and Monotheism*, p. 109.
7. Freud, *Col. Papers*, IV, p. 383.
8. Jones, I, p. 2. The pattern of the dominant mother–submissive father family constellation was not at all uncommon among Eastern European Jews.

* This is, paradoxically, also in imitation of the Moses-as-a-Jew who had killed an Egyptian for smiting a Hebrew.—Exodus 2:12.

22

Freud's Messianic Identification

We recall Jones's query about the significance of the Moses image to Freud:

> There is every reason to suppose that the grand figure of Moses himself, from Freud's early Biblical studies to the last book he ever wrote, was one of tremendous significance to him. Did he represent the formidable Father-image or did Freud identify himself with him? Apparently both, at different periods.[1]

We have learned from Freud that the hostility of the child to the father is due to the child's desire to preempt the father's place, to *be* the father. Indeed Freud's idea of the totem contains a *literal* urge to incorporate the father.

> That is to say, they not merely hated and feared their father, but also honoured him as an example to follow; in fact, each son wanted to place himself in his father's position. The cannibalistic act thus becomes comprehensible as an attempt to assure one's identification with the father by incorporating a part of him.[2]

Furthermore, Freud maintains that the image of Moses is the prototypal image of the Messiah. In his discussion of Jesus Christ he says,

> If Moses was this first Messiah, Christ became his substitute and successor. . . . There is some historical truth in the rebirth of Christ, for he was the resurrected Moses and the returned primeval father of the primitive horde as well—only transfigured, and as a Son in the place of his Father.[3]

Moses and Monotheism is an attack upon the Moses figure as embodying the stern wrath and harsh judgment and restrictions of personal liberty in our culture. But an Oedipal attack on Moses must be a preemption, in Freud's own terms, of the Messianic role. One of the critical features of Messianism is its goal of leading people out of slavery and oppression. Thus Freud's whole effort at the creation of psychoanalysis may be viewed as Messianic in this respect. The aim of psychoanalytic thought is the production of greater freedom for the individual, releasing him from the tyranny of the unconscious, which is, in Freud's view, the result of social oppression.

That psychoanalysis should have grown up in the context of the healing of the sick who were incurable by orthodox medical means accords with the Messianic quality of the psychoanalytic movement. For Messianism characteristically proves itself first by miraculously healing the sick. Thereafter it reaches out to large-scale social reform. So Freud's psychoanalysis reached out from the healing of individuals to the healing of society.

The view that Freud conceived of himself as a Messiah in the spirit of Jewish mysticism is supported by otherwise puzzling biographical facts in Freud's life. It is important to note in this connection that in the course of Jewish history, there arose not one, but two, conceptions of the Messiah. On the one hand we find the idea of a *spiritual* Messiah. The spiritual Messiah does not actively engage in producing a new way of life for the people. This Messiah is the one who will rule after the redemption has taken place. He is characteristically referred to as the *Messiah-ben-David*.* On the other hand, there also developed in Jewish history the idea of a Messiah who would be a *warrior*, a *military* hero in the fullest sense,[4] and who would eventually be killed. This Messiah, when he arose, would with great might vanquish all enemies and prepare the way for the *Messiah-ben-David*. The concept of a military Messiah was evidently a reaction to the Roman persecution. "The unhappy people, robbed of freedom, persecuted and afflicted to the point of death by the Romans, longed for vengeance on their enemies and for political independence."[5] In the Jewish tradition three names are associated with him: *Messiah-ben-Joseph, Messiah-ben-Ephraim,* and *Messiah-ben-Manasseh,* Ephraim and Manasseh having been the sons of Joseph.

The military cast of this Messiah stems from the interpretation of the following Biblical passage, the blessing Moses gave before his death:

> And for the precious things of the earth and the fullness thereof,
> And the good will of him that dwelt in the bush;
> Let the blessing come upon the head of Joseph,
> And upon the crown of the head of him that is prince among his brethren.
> His firstling bullock, majesty is his;
> And his horns are the horns of the wild-ox;
> With them he shall gore the peoples all of them, even the ends of the earth;

* *Ben* means "son of."

And they are the ten thousands of Ephraim,
And they are the thousands of Manasseh.[6]

Tradition equips this military Messiah with horns (Michelangelo's Moses is horned!) with which he will strike in all directions and slay the enemy.

If Freud identified himself with the Messiah, it was, we believe, primarily with this military Messiah. Freud once wrote,

> I have often felt as if I had inherited all the passion of our ancestors when they defended their Temple, as if I could joyfully cast away my life in a great cause.[7]

And Jones writes of Freud,

> In his letters there is an account of how he bravely stood up to a crowd of anti-Semitic opponents on his return journey from Leipzig.[8]

In his youth, Jones tells us,

> Freud went through an unmistakable militaristic phase. . . . One of the first books that fell into his childish hands after he had learned to read was Thiers' *Consulate and Empire*. He tells us how he pasted onto the backs of his wooden soldiers little labels bearing the names of Napoleon's marshals. His favorite one was Massena, usually believed to be a Jew; he was aided in his hero worship by the circumstance that they were both born on the same date, a hundred years apart. The Franco-Prussian War, which broke out when he was fourteen, aroused his keen interest. His sister relates how he kept a large map on his writing desk and followed the campaign in detail by means of small flags. He would discourse to his sisters about the war in general and the importance of the various moves of the combatants. His dreams of becoming a great general himself, however, gradually faded. . . .[9]

172

We might hesitate to identify the name Massena with the Messiah-ben-Manasseh, and to assert that this is evidence of Freud's identification, had Freud not himself made the transition for us. In *The Interpretation of Dreams,* where Freud discusses his military interest, he writes,

> And at the time my declared favourite was already Massena (or to give the name its Jewish form, Manasseh).[10]

Freud, as we know, identified himself with the name of Joseph.[11] He certainly followed in the footsteps of Joseph as an interpreter of dreams. In addition, however, we believe that he followed the fuller significance attached to the name of Joseph as the warrior Messiah who would redeem the Jews.

But perhaps the most cogent evidence for our hypothesis regarding Freud's Messianic feeling is to be found in his preoccupation with Rome. According to Jewish tradition, Rome is the legendary dwelling place of the Messiah, and the place where the Messiah will reveal himself.[12] The Messiah is supposed to dwell in concealment at the gates of Rome. We recall in this connection Abulafia's strange visit to the Pope to discuss the problem of the Jews.[13]

In *The Interpretation of Dreams* Freud tells us of one of his dreams in which he actually sees a gateway in association with Rome:

> On account of certain events which had occurred in the city of Rome, it had become necessary to remove the children to safety, and this was done. The scene was then in front of a gateway, double doors in the ancient style (the "Porta Romana" at Siena, as I was aware during the dream itself). I was sitting on the edge of a fountain and was greatly depressed and almost in

tears. A female figure—an attendant or a nun—brought two boys out and handed them over to their father, who was not myself. The elder of the two was clearly my eldest son; I did not see the other one's face. The woman who brought out the boy asked him to kiss her good-bye. She was noticeable for having a red nose. The boy refused to kiss her, but holding out his hand in farewell, said *"Auf Geseres"* to her, and then *"Auf Ungeseres"* to the two of us (or to one of us). I had a notion that this last phrase denoted a preference.

He then goes on to tell us the association with anti-Semitism which is involved:

This dream was constructed on a tangle of thoughts provoked by a play which I had seen, called *Das neue Ghetto* [The New Ghetto].[14] The Jewish problem, concern about the future of one's children, *to whom one cannot give a country of their own, concern about educating them in such a way that they can move freely across frontiers* [our italics]—all of this was easily recognizable among the relevant dream thoughts.

"By the waters of Babylon we sat down and wept." * Siena, like Rome, is famous for its beautiful fountains. If Rome occurred in one of my dreams it was necessary for me to find a

---

* Doubtless a reference to the 137th Psalm:

By the rivers of Babylon,
There we sat down, yea, we wept,
When we remembered Zion.
Upon the willows in the midst thereof
We hanged up our harps.
For there they that led us captive asked us words of song,
And our tormentors asked of us mirth:
'Sing us one of the songs of Zion.'
How shall we sing the Lord's song
In a foreign land?
If I forget thee, O Jerusalem,
Let my right hand forget her cunning.
Let my tongue cleave to the roof of my mouth,
If I remember thee not;
If I set not Jerusalem
Above my chiefest joy. . . .

substitute for it from some locality known to me. . . . Near the Porta Romana in Siena we had seen a large and brightly lighted building. We learned that it was the *Manicomio,* the insane asylum. Shortly before I had the dream I had heard that a man of the same religious persuasion as myself had been obliged to resign the position which he had painfully achieved in a State asylum.[15]

He tells us that *Geseres* and *Ungeseres* are not German words, but come from the Hebrew meaning "imposed suffering" or "doom," that also it suggests "leavened–unleavened" [*gesäuert–ungesäuert*] and that,

> In their flight out of Egypt the Children of Israel had not time to allow their dough to rise and in memory of this, they eat unleavened bread to this day at Easter.[16]

In the following dream that Freud reports, Messianism is clearly evident:

> Another time someone led me to the top of a hill and showed me Rome half-shrouded in mist; it was so far away that I was surprised at my view of it being so clear. *There was more in the content of this dream than I feel prepared to detail; but the theme of 'the promised land from afar' was obvious in it.**

The following footnotes that Freud added in later editions indicate that he had to overcome great resistance to visit Rome, and that it was a deeply cherished wish:

* Freud, *The Int. of Dreams,* p. 194, with our italics. "And Moses went up from the plains of Moab unto mount Nebo, to the top of Pisgah, that is over against Jericho. And the Lord showed him all the land, even Gilead as far as Dan; and all Naphtali, and the land of Ephraim and the Plain, even the valley of Jericho the city of palm-trees, as far as Zoar. And the Lord said unto him: 'This is the land which I swore unto Abraham, unto Isaac, and unto Jacob, saying: I will give it unto thy seed; I have caused thee to see it with thine eyes, but thou shalt not go over thither.'"—Deuteronomy 34:1-5.

175

[*Footnote added* 1909] I discovered long since that it only needs a little courage to fulfill wishes which till then have been regarded as unattainable; [*added* 1925] and thereafter became a constant pilgrim to Rome.[17]

He says of a dream which he cites as "warding off a threatened interruption of my sleep. . . ."

> One morning at the height of summer, while I was staying at a mountain resort in the Tyrol, I woke up knowing I had had a dream that *the Pope was dead*.† I failed to interpret this dream —a non-visual one—and only remembered as part of its basis that I had read in a newspaper a short time before that his Holiness was suffering from a slight indisposition. ‡

Several significant references to his strong emotional involvement with Rome are found in his letters to Fliess. In spite of his evident involvement, he does not mention Rome until November 1897,[18] ten years after the inception of his correspondence with Fliess.* One tradition has it that the days of the Messiah will be forty years, to correspond to the forty years that the Jews spent in the desert.[19] It may well be that only with the passage of Freud's fortieth year, which occurred on May 6, 1896, could he bring himself to talk openly of his feelings about Rome. It is also of interest in this connection that he carefully dates the revelation of the "secret of dreams," as two months into his fortieth year. He writes to Fliess,

> Do you suppose that some day a marble tablet will be placed on the house, inscribed with these words: 'In this house on July

† Freud's italics.

‡ Freud, *The Int. of Dreams,* p. 232. When Abulafia came to Rome to confer with the Pope, "in the name of Jewry," he learned, as he entered the city gate, that the Pope, Nicholas III, had died suddenly during the night.—Scholem, p. 128.

* There is, of course, the possibility that he may have mentioned Rome earlier in the unpublished parts of the letters.

24th, 1895, the Secret of Dreams was revealed to Dr. Sigmund Freud.' [20]

The dream that occurred that night, the one of Irma's injection, is the only dream which he dates in *The Interpretation of Dreams*.[21] Also it was in his thirty-ninth or fortieth year that he made his Jewish identification a public and social thing by joining the B'nai B'rith in Vienna.[22]

He writes to Fliess on November 5, 1897,

> Not long ago I was treated to a stimulating evening by my friend Emanuel Löwy, who is professor of archaeology in Rome. He has a fine and penetrating mind and is an excellent fellow. He pays me a visit every year and keeps me up till three o'clock in the morning. He spends his autumn holiday in Vienna, where his family lives. He tells me about Rome. . . .[23]

In December of that year he tells that he dreamt he was in Rome, and

> Incidentally my longing for Rome is deeply neurotic. It is connected with my schoolboy hero-worship of the Semitic Hannibal, and in fact this year I have no more reached Rome than he did from Lake Trasimene.[24]

That Hannibal represented the Jewish opposition to Rome is clearly indicated in his discussion in *The Interpretation of Dreams*,[25] where he says,

> To my youthful mind Hannibal and Rome symbolized the conflict between the tenacity of Jewry and the organization of the Catholic church. And the increasing importance of the effects of the anti-Semitic movement upon our emotional life helped fix the thoughts and feelings of those early days. Thus the wish to go to Rome had become in my dream life a cloak and symbol for a number of other passionate wishes.[26]

177

In beginning a discussion of some of his problems in connection with his "dream book" he writes,

> In any case I am not in a state to do anything else, except study the topography of Rome, my longing for which becomes more and more acute.[27]
>
> The secret dossier is getting thicker and thicker, as if it were really looking forward to being opened at Easter. I am curious myself about when Easter in Rome will be possible.[28]

Discussing a possible change of occupation and residence, he says, "It is a pity that these plans are just as fantastic as 'Easter in Rome.' " [29] "Rome is still far away; you know my Roman dreams." [30]

Discussing giving up of his lectures, he says

> Also I have a secondary motive; the realization of a secret wish which might mature at the same time as Rome, so, when Rome becomes possible I shall throw up the lectureship. But, as I have said, we are not in Rome yet.[31]
>
> What would you think of ten days in Rome at Easter (the two of us, of course) if all goes well, if I can afford it and have not been locked up, lynched or boycotted on account of the Egyptian dream book? I have looked forward to it for so long. Learning the eternal laws of life in the Eternal City would be no bad combination.[32]
>
> On the whole I am further away from Rome than at any time since we met, and the freshness of youth is notably declining. The journey is long, the stations at which one can be thrown out are very numerous, and it is still a matter of "if I can last out." *
>
> If I closed with "Next Easter in Rome," I should feel like a pious Jew.[33]

---

* Freud, *Origins*, p. 310. Doubtless a reference to a joke about a Jew who tried to get to Karlsbad without paying his fare, and who is treated severely each time the tickets are inspected. He tells a friend that he will get to Karlsbad "if my constitution can stand it." Cf. *The Int. of Dreams*, p. 195.

The association of Jerusalem with Rome is here quite evident, since this is a play on "Next year in Jerusalem" with which the Passover service is closed.

> In the midst of this mental and material depression I am haunted by the thought of spending Easter week in Rome this year.[34]

"I shall no more get to Rome this Easter than you will," he writes, and then refers to a promise that Fliess made. about holding a "congress" with him on classical soil.[35]

In September 1901, after he finally succeeded in reaching Rome, he writes to Fliess,

> I ought to write to you about Rome, but it is difficult. It was an overwhelming experience for me, and, as you know, the fulfillment of a long-cherished wish. It was slightly disappointing, as all such fulfillments are *when one has waited for them too long,* † but it was a high-spot in my life all the same. But, while I contemplated ancient Rome undisturbed (I could have worshipped the humble and mutilated remnant of the Temple of Minerva near the forum of Nerval),[36] *I found I could not freely enjoy the second Rome* [medieval Rome]; *I was disturbed by its meaning, and, being incapable of putting out of my mind my own misery and all the other misery which I know to exist, I found almost intolerable the lie of the salvation of mankind which rears its head so proudly to heaven* [our italics].[37]

In March 1902 he writes to Fliess,

> When I got back from Rome, my zest for life and work had somewhat grown and my zest for martyrdom somewhat diminished.[38]

---

† Our italics. "Too long" because more than five years after his fortieth birthday?

This implies, evidently, an earlier wish to martyr himself.

The idea that Freud had of himself as a military hero who would die as a martyr, a fighter against anti-Semitism, an interpreter of dreams, a dweller in Rome where he would realize his deepest wish, all become intelligible if we assume that Freud conceived of himself, at least to some degree, as the military Messiah of the Jews, the Messiah-ben-Joseph, the Messiah-ben-Ephraim, the Messiah-ben-Manasseh.

Freud's emotional identification with the military Messiah of the Jews catches in metaphor several critical aspects of Freud's personality. The military Messiah, blessed by Moses,[39] can violate one of the strongest taboos among the Jews, the commandment against killing, and the derivative taboo against thoughts of aggression which might involve bloodshed. Thus by participating in this image, Freud could feel free to indulge in thoughts of killing oppressors in a way which would have been otherwise traditionally closed. His ego could tolerate murderous thoughts. We need only remind ourselves of the great significance in Freud's writings of death wishes directed against others, particularly the father, and its formulation in the fundamental paradigm of the Oedipus complex. Furthermore, the military ethos may well have been one of the primary sources of his enormous energy.

Combining what we have already said about Freud's Sabbatianism with the information we have concerning his identification with the military Messiah, Freud's personality emerges as militant-Sabbatian. Evidently Freud was prone to seize upon the classical and supernatural figures as metaphorical expressions of his own inclinations.

Freud tended to see himself as protagonist in a grand historical myth-drama, and not merely as a scientist or physician, as the latter were understood in his culture. He early identified himself with Hannibal, the Semitic hero who fought against Roman culture in ancient times. He had the Jewish Messianic élan of participating in the process by which the redemption would come to pass. The medieval "Messiahs" had thus seen themselves as playing the role of Messiah-ben-Joseph, regarding the anguish that they experienced and witnessed as the birth pangs of the creation of a new era.

As we might almost expect, the Devil also had his role to play in Freud's development. The Devil is an extremely complex image. He is a Christian-legendary figure who can satisfy the Sabbatian tendencies toward apostasy. When Satan appears in Jewish legend, his function is largely to tempt the Jew to apostasy. The Devil stands opposed to the Mosaic features incorporated in Christianity.

Freud once remarked to his associates,

> Do you not know that I am the Devil? All my life I have had to play the Devil, in order that others would be able to build the most beautiful cathedral with the materials that I produced.[40]

NOTES TO CHAPTER 22

1. Jones, II, pp. 364-365.
2. Freud, *Moses and Monotheism,* p. 103.
3. Freud, *Moses and Monotheism,* p. 114.
4. Joseph Klausner, *The Messianic Idea in Israel,* trans. from Hebrew W. F. Stinespring (New York: Macmillan, 1955), pp. 483 ff.

5. Klausner, *The Messianic Idea in Israel,* p. 494.
6. Deuteronomy, 33:16-17.
7. Jones, I, p. 197.
8. Jones, I, p. 197.
9. Jones, I, p. 23.
10. Freud, *The Int. of Dreams,* p. 197.
11. Cf. p. 153, above.
12. Cf. Sanhedrin, folio 98b.
13. Cf. p. 176, above.
14. Written by Theodor Herzl, the founder of Zionism. It is of some interest that Jewish opponents of Herzl in Vienna sometimes derogatorily referred to him as the new Sabbatai Zevi.
15. Freud, *The Int. of Dreams,* pp. 441-442.
16. Freud, *The Int. of Dreams,* p. 443.
17. Freud, *The Int. of Dreams,* p. 194.
18. Freud, *Origins,* p. 229.
19. Sanhedrin II, p. 669. Soncino.
20. Freud, *Origins,* p. 322.
21. Freud, *The Int. of Dreams,* p. 107.
22. Jones, I, pp. 329-330. Jones simply says that Freud joined the B'nai B'rith Society in 1895, and not whether it was before or after May 6, since May 6, 1895, marked the end of his 39th year and beginning of his 40th.
23. Freud, *Origins,* p. 229. The remainder of this is deleted in the published edition.
24. Freud, *Origins,* p. 236.
25. Freud, *The Int. of Dreams,* pp. 195-198.
26. Freud, *The Int. of Dreams,* pp. 196-197.
27. Freud, *Origins,* p. 269.
28. Freud, *Origins,* p. 276.
29. Freud, *Origins,* p. 276.
30. Freud, *Origins,* p. 279.
31. Freud, *Origins,* p. 280.
32. Freud, *Origins,* p. 294.
33. Freud, *Origins,* p. 317.
34. Freud, *Origins,* p. 327.

35. Freud, *Origins,* p. 328.
36. Cf. pp. 134 ff., above.
37. Freud, *Origins,* pp. 335-336.
38. Freud, *Origins,* p. 342.
39. Cf. pp. 171-172, above.
40. R. Laforgue, "Persönliche Erinnerungen an Freud," *Lindauer Psychotherapiewoche* (1954), pp. 42-56: "Wissen Sie nicht, dass ich der Teufel bin? Mein ganzes Leben habe ich den Teufel spielen müssen, damit andere mit den Materielen die ich herbeibrachte, die schönsten Dome werden bauen können"— p. 49.

Part IV

The Devil as Suspended Superego

23

Introduction

In spite of the fact that we are centuries beyond the Middle Ages when the Devil loomed as a critical figure in both thought and social organization, the name *Devil* still carries an uncanny association. As we shall see, the significance of this image to Freud was extremely complex. If Freud played the Devil, he yet conceived this role as being in the service of the good, as the quotation cited at the end of Chapter 22 indicates. There was enough precedent for this in the tradition of Jewish mysticism. We recall the Frankists in this connection, who glorified sin as a way toward the redemption. In the mystical dialectic the opposition of evil to good would result in a world in which sin would no longer exist; and a conception of evil as a manifestation of the Divine was never to be completely rejected.

A metaphor which illuminates and yet only hints is perhaps the best that one can hope for in trying to catch the temper of the mind which created psychoanalysis. In Part III an attempt was made to understand the mind of Freud through the inspection of one metaphor, that of the Jewish hero Moses. Here we will try to do the same with another metaphor, that of the Devil. As we hope we can demonstrate, in the same way that the image of Moses was for Freud both a reality and a fiction, so was the image of the Devil.

Before we embark on this task, an important methodological consideration ought to be set out: One of the most important contributions which Freud made to our understanding of human beings was explicating and rationalizing the bizarre, syncretic, illogical, and seemingly accidental features of human thought and behavior. From an historical point of view it should be recognized that it was in the very opposition to such modes of thought and behavior that modern science came into being. The emerging science sought to eradicate these modes of thought and to substitute system, logic, and discipline. In a very fundamental sense, the developing scientific temper recognized that if *objectivity* was to be realized, then a science in which the immediate life concerns of the investigator do not obtrude themselves would be required.

It was by virtue of such a position that classical science was able to make the tremendous progress that it did, the fruits of which we so eminently possess today. But the cost to classical science of this advantage was that it had to put aside—today we can add "temporarily"—whatever truths lay, however distorted and veiled and misformulated, in the mumbo jumbo of magic and religion.

The twist Freud gave to this situation was to point out that mumbo jumbo did not tell us about the environmental world, but about the psychological world; that, for example, though a dream seemed to be about some state of affairs in the environmental world, its deeper meaning was in relation to the mind which fashioned the dream. He turned his attention to the by-products of human behavior: dreams, jokes, slips of the tongue. As he once put it, psychoanalysis ". . . is accustomed to divine secret and concealed things from unconsidered and unnoticed details, from the rubbish heap, as it were, of our observations." [1]

In order to achieve this it was necessary for him to do strange things with his own mind. In some sense he had to let himself descend into chaotic depths, to absorb them and fully appreciate them. He had, so to speak, to enter into the madness of man's thoughts and to re-enact imaginatively the syncretism involved in their generation, in order to apprehend their nature rationally. Every psychological act which Freud described as taking place unconsciously called for the conscious duplication of what ordinarily took place unconsciously. Thus it was necessary for him to deliberately repeat the violations of logic and good sense and morality which he discovered in the unconscious, to consciously consider opposites as the same, to disregard logical and empirical objections, to overlook distinctions, to hold actively in mind an image of incest, etc. And although frequently Freud was able to check himself in the light of modern sobriety, there were times when the necessity for fully appreciating the nature of this double role escaped him.

It is in this way that the notion of the Devil played a role in Freud's thought. Of course Freud did not believe in the Devil superstitiously as a real personage. He believed in the

Devil rather in the profound way in which a great mind might become immersed in metaphor.

Let us now consider one of the important problems with which Freud's biography presents us, the transition from the role of neurophysiologist to psychoanalyst towards the end of the fourth decade of his life.

NOTES TO CHAPTER 23

1. Freud, *Col. Papers,* IV, p. 271.

24

The Transition

We have indicated earlier that the psychoanalytic contribution comes as a magnificent burst in a very short period of time upon a life that, as Freud himself tells us when he discusses his medical education and activities, was essentially prepared for other types of things. The hypothesis which we have suggested, and which can be made more explicit now, is that in the transition, Freud, so to speak, made contact with the Jewish mystical tradition as it was part and parcel of his personality and culture.

The problem of how the transition was effected, what the dynamics involved were, is still an open one. It is of course axiomatic that each person draws upon his culture for the determination of his social role. But in the case of an individual who has one foot in one culture and the other foot in another culture, the problem of why he should put his weight on one foot rather than the other does not submit to solution very readily. And even if we accept a simpler idea of cultural determination, we have still to decide on the factors which make for the particular adaptation of the cultural elements.

In terms of the facts, the following is a summary of some of the main events in his professional career in the years which preceded the shift to psychoanalysis. In 1882 when he was twenty-six years old, he was advised to leave the physiology laboratory by Brücke and he entered the general hospital. Jones tells us that he imparted to Martha "what a wrench the 'separation from science' had been," and "cheerfully added 'but perhaps it is not a final one.' " [1] About his experiences in this new course, Jones says,

> He found no more interest in treating sick patients in the wards than in studying their diseases. By now he must have been more convinced than ever that he was not born to be a doctor.
>
> What this aversion really signified is hard to determine. It was assuredly no lack of respect for the profession of medicine, as might perhaps be thought. On the contrary, there are signs that he regarded it as a Promised Land—or, to be more accurate, a Forbidden Land—into which for some reason he was not destined to enter. Only a few years later, in August, 1888, in reply to a friend's advice to become a regular physician, he wrote: "I entirely agree with you, but nevertheless I cannot do what you recommend. . . . I have not learned enough to be a physician. In my medical development there is a rift which was later painstakingly bridged. I could only learn enough to become a neuropathologist. And now I lack, not youth, but time and independence to make up for what I missed. Last winter I was pretty busy; so I could just make ends meet with my big family and had no time left for study." In other words, there was some sense of inferiority in the matter, which he ascribes— not at all plausibly—to insufficient knowledge or even an incapacity to learn: he who could acquire knowledge so swiftly and easily. Plainly it was a matter of inhibition rather than incapacity. Perhaps from his remark, quoted earlier, about tormenting human beings, one should infer some inhibition in

dealing with physical suffering and, as a doctor, sometimes even having to add to it.[2]

Jones's evidence of inhibition is certainly cogent, although evidence for his explanation about Freud not being able to witness physical suffering is wanting even if this is partially true. Freud transferred to Meynert's psychiatric clinic on May 1, 1883. The five months he stayed there essentially constituted his only purely psychiatric experience. In October 1883 he moved into the department of dermatology. On January 1, 1884, he entered the department of nervous diseases, "but as often as not there were no nerve cases there." [3] The superintendent was not interested in such cases and released them as soon as possible.

In September 1885 Freud was appointed *Privatdocent* in neuropathology, almost exclusively on the basis of his "microscopical-anatomical papers" as Brücke referred to them. Brücke, in his report and recommendation, discussed Freud's papers on "The Posterior Roots in Petromyzon" (1877-1878), "The Nerve Cells in Crayfish" (1882), "A New Method for Anatomical Preparations of the Central Nervous System" (1879), "A Histological Method for the Study of Brain Tracts" (1884), "A Case of Cerebral Hemmorrhage" (1884), and "On Coca" (1884). He also mentioned the zoological paper on eels (1877) and "Structure of the Elements of the Nervous System" (1884).[4] Freud's trial lecture, which he had to deliver as part of the proceedings, was "The Medullary Tracts of the Brain." [5]

Because the superintendent did not want him in the department of nervous diseases, he was transferred to the opthalmological department in March 1885. On June 1, 1885, he transferred to the dermatological department, but went to a private mental hospital on June 7, evidently on leave from the general hospital. Freud was in the meantime awarded a traveling grant, and he severed his connection with the general hospital at the end of August 1885. From October 13, 1885, till February 28, 1886, Freud was visiting Charcot in Paris.

Just prior to his trip to Paris, Freud completed a series of neurological papers on the medulla oblongata and the roots and connections of the acoustic nerve, making observations on the brains of kittens, puppies, embryos, and infants. In Paris, Freud persisted in his neurological research, Charcot and Guignon having provided him with infantile brains for the purpose.

It was in Paris that Freud began to think seriously about leaving the field of neurology.

> Freud found the laboratory conditions in the Salpêtrière, which were doubtless very different from what he had been accustomed to, increasingly unsatisfactory, and on December 3 [1885] he announced he had decided to abandon them. It was almost the end of his work with the microscope; henceforth he was to become a pure clinician. In the next letter he gave seven convincing reasons for his decision, pleading, however, his intention to resume anatomical researches in Vienna. This *multiplicity usually denotes the suppression of the fundamental reason* [our italics], and it might be assumed that this was a fascination for psychopathology that Charcot had implanted in him. But there was a more personal one besides. Within a year of his engagement he had already felt a certain conflict between being engrossed in his "scientific work," by which he always meant laboratory work, and his love for Martha; he said that at times

he felt the former was a dream and the latter a reality. Later he assured her that anatomy of the brain was the only serious rival she had ever had or was likely to have. Then from Paris he wrote: "I have long known that my life cannot be entirely given up to neuropathology, but that one can surrender it altogether for a dear girl has only become clear to me here in Paris"; this was the week before he withdrew from the Salpêtrière laboratory. When announcing this decision he added, "You may be sure that I have overcome my love for science in so far as it came between us." All of this had, of course, its practical aspects as well as the emotional ones. Freud knew very well that a married life could only mean clinical work.[6]

Earlier in this essay we recounted the conditions of anti-Semitism in Vienna, especially around the time Freud was separated from his institutional connection as a neurophysiologist.[7] If, as has been indicated by psychoanalysts in line with Freud's approach, the individual enters a "social contract" to accept the values of his culture in return for acceptance by that culture, then Freud was, in a sense, freed from his part of the bargain with science and the Gentile world. He was told by Brücke that his hoped-for rewards would not be forthcoming. Perhaps in Freud's mind he was rejected by the scientific and Gentile worlds. With a definite rejection because he was a Jew, he was thrown back upon his original cultural identity. Freud himself frequently felt that his Judaism provided him with energy in the face of social rejection. But even here he could not call upon classical Judaism, because, perhaps, he was already too secular. The mystical current in Judaism contained, however, a system of thought which provided opportunities of intellectual advance in psychology which, perhaps, Freud was one of the first to sense, consciously or unconsciously.

The role of his fiancée, Martha, in connection with the transition may also be quite critical. It is of particular interest that Martha, as we recall, came from a family with mystical tendencies. Her grandfather was the mystically inclined Chief Rabbi Isaac Bernays of Hamburg.[8] Isaac Bernays was related to Heine, and Heine refers to him in his letters repeatedly. Heine, it will be recalled, referred to baptism as the "admission ticket" to European civilization. Martha's uncle Michael had actually been baptized and had thus achieved the position of Professor of German at the University of Munich and *Lehr-Konsul* to King Ludwig of Bavaria, a pattern which we have already seen to be associated with Sabbatianism. That Martha herself was a participant in the developing Romanticism of the period is indicated by the fact that she had withdrawn from an engagement into which she had almost entered because she was not in love, having on this ground been persuaded against the marriage by her brother Eli (who had married Freud's sister in 1883).

It may well be that Freud's remark that "I have overcome my love for science in so far as it came between us" has a deeper significance in their relationship than the reason, given by Jones, that only as a clinician could he make enough money for them to marry and live on. From additional material provided by Jones, we know that Freud felt that the scientific role was less attractive to Martha than the artistic. Freud was extremely jealous of two other suitors for Martha. One was a musician and the other an artist, "disquieting facts in themselves," Jones adds.[9] Freud writes,

> I think there is a general enmity between artists and those engaged in the details of scientific work. We know that they possess in their art a master key to open with ease all female hearts, whereas we stand helpless at the strange design of the lock and have first to torment ourselves to discover a suitable key to it.[10]

There is a sense in which sex, Sabbatianism, Romanticism, and art, when put in the same dimension, are at the opposite pole from science and restrictive religion. In the former, personal freedom and individualism are important; in the latter the stern discipline of the kind which we have discussed in connection with Mosaism and rabbinism are important. Freud's engagement to Martha may have been psychologically intertwined with the changes which were taking place in his intellectual interests.

After returning to Vienna from Paris, Freud did very little creative work. For five years, from 1886 to 1891, he published no researches, with the exception of two slight papers.[11] Presumably he was kept busy with his private practice and the support of his growing family. He also busied himself with translations of Charcot and Bernheim. In that period he was evidently working on his essay, "On Aphasia," which came out in 1891. Early in this relatively uncreative five-year period, in October 1886, he gave a paper "On Male Hysteria" which involved an account of Charcot's ideas. It was, he felt, badly received.[12] He was challenged to produce an appropriate case, and he did so the next month. Freud's account of this incident indicates his bitterness.

> This time I was applauded, but no further interest was taken in me. The impression that the high authorities had rejected my innovations remained unshaken; and, with my hysteria in men and my production of hysterical paralyses by suggestion, I found myself forced into the Opposition. As I was soon afterwards excluded from the laboratory of cerebral anatomy and for a whole session had nowhere to deliver my lectures, I withdrew from academic life and ceased to attend the learned societies. It is a whole generation since I have visited the "Gesellschaft der Aerzte." [13]

That this last assertion is not exactly true, as Jones points out, only indicates all the more sharply the sense of rejection Freud felt in this period, which preceded the development of psychoanalysis.

For whatever weight it lends to our general argument, Freud's age at this period should be noted. The Jewish mystical tradition has always maintained that mystical concerns are properly reserved for later life. The reason for this is that if the person is too young he will misunderstand what he learns and will fall into infidelity. Maimonides says,

> I compare such a person to an infant fed with wheaten bread, meat and wine; it will undoubtedly die, not because such food is naturally unfit for the human body, but because of the weakness of the child, who is unable to digest the food, and cannot derive benefit from it.[14]

In further discussing the teaching of the mysteries, Maimonides says,

Therefore it was considered inadvisable to teach it to young men; nay, it is impossible for them to comprehend it, on account of the heat of their blood and the flame of youth, which confuses their minds; that heat, which causes all the disorder, must first disappear; they must have become moderate and settled, humble in their hearts, and subdued in their temperament; only then will they be able to arrive at the highest degree of the perception of God, i.e., the study of Metaphysics, which is called *Ma'aseh Mercabah.**

Further on he says,

. . . we also read the following passage: R. Jochanan said to R. Elasar, "Come, I will teach you *Ma'aseh Mercabah.*" The reply was, "I am not yet old," or in other words, I have not yet become old, I still perceive in myself the hot blood and the rashness of youth. You learn from this that, in addition to the above named good qualities, a certain age is also required.[15]

There is some tradition that the year of transition is thirty-six.† It was in his thirty-sixth year that the Baal Shem Tov is said to have revealed himself to the world. And it is about this time that Freud begins to show himself to the world, emerging from the "latency" of his previous years. Freud completed his thirty-sixth year on May 6, 1892. Jones says,

Although he had a swift enough intuition, one which functioned freely in his mature years, there is good reason to think that in the years we have so far been considering, particularly between 1875 and 1892, his development was slow and laborious. . . . The nineties, it is true, once he got well under way,

---

* Maimonides, p. 48. The *Ma'aseh Mercabah,* the work of the chariot of Ezekiel, was the main Kabbalistic concern from the first to the tenth centuries. Cf. Scholem, Second Lecture, pp. 40-79.

† This number has other special mystical significance. According to legend there are thirty-six men in the world at any given time for whose sake God does not destroy the world.

were otherwise, and one piece of insight after another followed in rapid succession in what was his most creative period. There moods and intuitions were added to arduous work and hard thinking, and they even became more important than these. A change in his personality, one of several in his life, seems to have come over him in the early nineties, and in the summer of 1895, three months after the *Studies* were published, we find Breuer writing to their friend Fliess: "Freud's intellect is soaring at its highest. I gaze after him as a hen at a hawk!" [16]

That the significance of the thirty-sixth year may not have been completely lost to Freud is indicated by the gift his father gave him on his thirty-fifth birthday, i.e., the beginning of his thirty-sixth year—the Bible Freud had studied in his youth.[17]

NOTES TO CHAPTER 24

1. Jones, I, p. 62.
2. Jones, I, p. 64.
3. Jones, I, p. 68.
4. Jones, I, p. 72.
5. Jones, I, p. 73.
6. Jones, I, p. 211.
7. Cf. pp. 26 ff., above.
8. Cf. p. 57, above.
9. Jones, I, p. 111.
10. Jones, I, p. 111.
11. Jones, I, p. 227.
12. Jones, I, p. 230.
13. Freud, *Autobiographical Study,* p. 26.
14. Maimonides, *The Guide for the Perplexed,* p. 44.
15. Maimonides, p. 48.
16. Jones, I, pp. 241-242.
17. Cf. p. 50, above.

25

The Hypnosis and Cocaine Episodes

During this transition period Freud seems to have moved very quickly in his medical practice from the role of physician to "healer." He soon abandoned the traditional methods of the physician and turned to the time-honored devices of the "healer," suggestion and hypnosis. Jones tells us that for the eighteen months following December 1887, Freud used hypnotic suggestion extensively, and "this often brought gratifying successes and replaced the feeling of helplessness by the satisfaction of being admired as a magician." [1]

In 1892, at the end of what we have called the "latency" period, Freud published a paper entitled "A Case of Successful Treatment by Hypnotism," [2] which gives some interesting evidence about what may be called the magician-healer motif in Freud's thought. Freud tells of a woman who could not nurse her infants and who had difficulty in taking food herself. Freud used hypnosis and direct suggestion when she had her second child, and again when she had her third. The paper is essentially lacking in any of the deep psychological insight of Freud's succeeding works. He argues for "antithetic ideas" or a "counter-will" which serves to inhibit the volitional idea in the person. Following the occasion of his first successful treatment of the woman, he says, he found it "annoying that no reference was ever made to my remarkable achievement." [3] Besides this view of himself as able to do "remarkable" things, this paper also indicates that he was concerned with such matters as casting out evil spirits. Thus, characterizing the nature of such difficulties as the one he had cured, he says, "This emergence of a counterwill is chiefly responsible for the characteristic which often gives to hysterics the appearance almost of being possessed by an evil spirit. . . ." [4]

Additional evidence for the existence of this magician-healer motif is to be found in the set of events Jones dubs the "Cocaine Episode." Freud had ordered a quantity of cocaine and took some himself. He was impressed with the effect that it had upon his mood. He quickly gave some to his friend Fleischl, who was already addicted to morphine—an action which resulted, by the way, in hastening his friend's death. Cocaine was for him a "magical drug." In a letter that mentions writing an essay about it, he says,

> I take very small doses of it regularly against indigestion, and with the most brilliant success.[5]

Jones says,

> He sent some to Martha "to make her strong and give her cheeks a red color," he pressed it on his friends and colleagues, both for themselves and their patients, he gave it to his sisters. In short, looked at from the vantage point of our present knowledge, he was rapidly becoming a public menace.[6]

202

In his essay on cocaine he gave an account of the religious practices associated with it among South American Indians.

> He even gave an account of the religious observances connected with its use, and mentioned the mythical saga of how Manco Capac, the Royal Son of the Sun-God, had sent it as "a gift from the gods to satisfy the hungry, fortify the weary, and make the unfortunate forget their sorrows."
> He . . . narrated a number of self-observations in which he had studied the effects on hunger, sleep, and fatigue. He wrote of the "exhilaration and lasting euphoria, which in no way differs from the normal euphoria of the healthy person. . . . You perceive an increase of self-control and possess more vitality and capacity for work. . . . In other words, you are simply normal, and it is soon hard to believe that you are under the influence of any drug. . . . Long intensive mental or physical work is performed without any fatigue. . . . This result is enjoyed without any of the unpleasant after-effects that follow exhilaration brought about by alcohol. . . . Absolutely no craving for the further use of cocaine appears after the first, or even repeated, taking of the drug; one feels rather a certain curious aversion to it." [7]

These rather irresponsible activities in the quest for a "magical drug," to achieve mood modification, are reminiscent of the whole history of magic. As we shall see when we discuss his essay on demoniacal possession,[8] Freud cites overcoming incapacity for work as a major motive for entering a pact with the Devil. Thus his evident concern with finding a means for increasing "vitality and capacity for work" may be taken as indicative of a predilection for the sort of thing that such a pact may represent, psychologically. It is also interesting that he believed that his Jewishness was a source of energy.

Indeed, perhaps, one of the important reasons for the aversion to "magical drugs" is that they are reminiscent of black magic. A major psychological feature of black magic is that it provides *immediate gains without immediate payment*. The payment is feared as "really" *both deferred and excessive*. Thus deferred and excessive payment for immediate gain is characteristically associated with pacts with the Devil. The aversion towards usury, in current times as well as throughout the history of Christianity, is not completely coincidental. For usury is exactly a social expression of the essential features of the Satanic Pact, immediate gains and excessive deferred payment.*

NOTES TO CHAPTER 25

1. Jones, I, p. 235.
2. Freud, *Col. Papers,* V, pp. 33-46.
3. Freud, *Col. Papers,* V, p. 37.
4. Freud, *Col. Papers,* V, p. 44.
5. Jones, I, p. 81.
6. Jones, I, p. 81.
7. Jones, I, pp. 82-83.
8. Cf. pp. 214 ff., below.

* This is not, of course, the place to discuss the various psychological phenomena associated with the use of drugs, but we believe that the historical demoniacal associations, such as that suggested, constitute important elements in this connection. Freud's later aversion to drugs may be a hint of his psychological condition in his old age.

26

The Discovery of the Transference

One of the most significant of Freud's therapeutic discoveries was the transference. Freud recognized in the deeply affective involvement of the patient with the therapist a major vehicle for the cure of the patient.

The phenomenon of the transference had caused Breuer to hesitate. Yet Freud had within his personality the means to cope with and control its consequences. Perhaps it was his apparently excellent marital relationship that made the temptation of sex relations so remote that it was essentially an impersonal event as far as his own libidinous experiences were concerned. Furthermore, his desire to play magician, or healer, or Devil may have made mastery of the transference phenomenon positively rewarding. And he was perhaps more concerned with the fulfillment of the mythico-dramatic role than with the usually associated rewards.

His readiness to permit himself to be involved in the patient's psychosexual life was one of the essential elements of his discovery of the transference. He tells us in "On the History of the Psychoanalytic Movement":

Anyone who reads the history of Breuer's case now in the light of the knowledge gained in the last twenty years will at once perceive the symbolism in it—the snake, the stiffening, the disabling of the arm—and, on taking into account the situation at the bedside of the sick father, will easily guess the real interpretation of her symptom-formation; his opinion of the part played by sexuality in the young woman's mental life will then be very different from that of her physician. In his treatment of her case, Breuer could make use of a very intense suggestible *rapport* on the part of the patient, which may serve us as a prototype of what we call "transference" today. Now I have strong reasons for surmising that after all her symptoms had been relieved Breuer must have discovered from further indications the sexual motivation of this transference, but the universal nature of this unexpected phenomenon escaped him, with the result that, as though confronted by an "untoward event," he broke off all further investigation. . . .[1]

Freud's discovery of the significance of the transference is not a "discovery" in the simple sense of that word. His facility at intellectualization played its part, no doubt, in enabling him to cope with the phenomenon. But his intellectual power is an insufficient explanation.

One day a patient suddenly flung her arms around his neck, an unexpected contretemps fortunately remedied by the entrance of a servant. From then on he understood that the peculiar relationship so effective therapeutically had an erotic basis, whether concealed or overt.[2]

In order to rationalize it as he did, something extremely unusual within himself was required.

In the transference relationship Freud discovered that which he had yearned for in his earlier years, "a master key to open with ease all female hearts," and he no longer stood "helpless at the strange design of the lock," forced to "torment" himself "to discover a suitable key to it." [3]

This does not mean that Freud had ignoble motives in connection with the transference; nor should what we are saying here be interpreted as in any way a criticism of the role of the transference in the therapy relationship. But that it did articulate with some of the deeper aspects of his personality cannot be doubted. The "magic" involved was one of the features of classical magic, the trick or art of making people fall in love. By turning this magic into a therapeutic device Freud made one of the great contributions to modern knowledge. Yet it is important to note that this trick or art is historically associated with the lore of the Devil. As an example, we may cite the affair of Gaufridi, who was burnt at the stake in Aix-en-Provence for having seduced one Magdelaine de la Palud with the supposed aid of the Devil. The Pact that he presumably concluded runs as follows:

> I, Louys Gaufridi, renounce all those benefits, spiritual as much as corporeal, which could in any way be conferred upon me by God and the Virgin Mary and all the saints in Paradise, particularly my patron saint, John Baptist, as also St. Peter, St. Paul, and St. Francis, and I give my body and soul to Lucifer before whom I stand, and all the goods that I shall ever have (save always the benefit of the sacraments touching those who receive them).
>
> And thus do I sign and witness it.
>
> After three days the Devil answered:
>
> By virtue of thy breath, thou wilt inflame with love of thyself all the girls and women whom thou shalt desire to possess, provided that this breath reaches their nostrils.[4]

However, as we will see shortly, when Freud discusses the motives for the Satanic Pact he states specifically that the desire for possession of women is hardly critical. Nonetheless, it cannot be denied that the *ability* to inflame the hearts of women at will is historically associated with Satanic powers.

NOTES TO CHAPTER 26

1. Freud, *Col. Papers,* I, pp. 292-293.
2. Jones, I, p. 242.
3. Cf. p. 197, above.
4. M. Garcon and J. Vinchon, *The Devil: an Historical, Critical, and Medical Study,* trans. S. H. Guest (New York: E. P. Dutton and Co., 1930), pp. 67-68.

27

The "Flectere . . ." of the Interpretation of Dreams

The following is an excerpt from *The Dybbuk*, a dramatic presentation of the Chassidic mood, which is pertinent as indicating the role of Satanic powers in the Jewish mystical atmosphere:

CHENNOCH: When you perform the ablutions, do you also use spells and go through all the ceremonies prescribed by the book of Roziel? [1]

CHANNON: Yes.

CHENNOCH: You aren't afraid to?

CHANNON: No.

CHENNOCH: And you fast from Sabbath to Sabbath—isn't that hard for you?

CHANNON: It's harder for me to eat on the Sabbath than to fast the whole week. [*Pause.*] I've lost all desire to eat.

CHENNOCH: [*Inviting confidence.*] What do you do all this for? What do you expect to gain by it?

CHANNON: [*As if to himself.*] I wish . . . I wish to attain possession of a clear and sparkling diamond, and melt it down in tears and inhale it into my soul. I want to attain to the rays of the third plane of beauty.

I want . . . [*Suddenly in violent perturbation.*]
Yes—there are still two barrels of golden pieces
which I *must* get, for him who can count only
gold pieces.*

CHENNOCH: [*Appalled.*] Channon, be careful! You're on a
slippery road. No holy powers will help you to
achieve these things.

CHANNON: [*Challenging him.*] And if the *holy* powers will
not, then?

CHENNOCH: [*Terrified.*] I'm afraid to talk to you! I'm afraid
to be near you! [*He rushes out. Channon remains
behind, his face full of defiance. . . .*] [2]

In this section we will try to indicate how and in what sense,
Freud's major work, *The Interpretation of Dreams,* was associated with the idea of a Satanic Pact. There is hardly any
question that this work of Freud represents his major breakthrough into the psychoanalytic mode of thought.

On the title page of the book appears the motto: *Flectere si
nequeo superos, Acheronta movebo,* ("if the gods above are no
use to me, then I'll move all hell"). This quotation is from the
Aeneid of Virgil, and the passage from which it is taken is
even more indicative.

Well, if my powers are not great enough, I shall not hesitate—
that's sure—to ask help wherever help may be found. If the
gods above are no use to me, then I'll move all hell.[3]

Freud cites this quotation again in discussing the way in
which the "suppressed material finds methods and means of
forcing its way into consciousness in dreams." [4]

In order to understand how it is possible for the suppressed

---

* For the father of his beloved, so that he might marry her.

material to rise to consciousness, let us consider how this is conceived in the framework of psychoanalytical theory. The reason for the suppression is the action of forces associated with the superego. If God is identified with the superego, then the corresponding antagonistic image is the Devil, who dwells in hell. As we have indicated earlier, in the psychoanalytic relationship the analyst is at one and the same time the representative of the superego as well as a tolerant, understanding father figure. Now what is the Devil, psychologically? The answer is eminently simple, on one level. *The Devil is the suspended superego.* He is the permissive superego. The Devil is that part of the person which permits him to violate the precepts of the superego. Roheim in his discussion of Freud's paper on demoniacal possession says:

> The dream is a refutation or rebuttal of an attack made upon the Ego by the Super-Ego.[5]
> The pact with the Devil is therefore really a pact with the Super-Ego not to help human beings in getting these things but to stop preventing them in doing so.[6]

In dreams then, following Freud, we have the beginning of the rebellion against the superego. However, to strip the dream of its disguise is an even more rebellious act. It is a *conscious* rebellion against the superego, which is perhaps the major reason for *resistance* against interpretation. In becoming conscious, the person risks full punishment by the superego, because the revolt is *avowed*. As Freud recognized in the idea of the Oedipus complex, it is the hostile wish against the parent that is suppressed.

It is the fate of all of us, perhaps, to direct our first sexual impulse towards our mother and our first hatred and our first murderous wish against our father. *Our dreams convince us that this is so* [our italics]. King Oedipus, who slew his father Laius and married his mother Jocasta merely shows us the fulfillment of our childhood wishes. But, more fortunate than he, we have meanwhile succeeded, in so far as we have not become psychoneurotics, in detaching our sexual impulses from our mothers and in forgetting our jealousy of our fathers. Here is one in whom these primaeval wishes of our childhood have been fulfilled, and we shrink back from him with the whole force of the repression by which those wishes have since that time been held down within us.[7]

That Freud was able to cognize this so fully must mean that the forces of repression within him were weakened to such an extent that the full meaning and content of the Oedipus complex could emerge; and some device was necessary whereby the repressive forces could be overcome. In some way the hold of the superego must have been suspended.

Earlier in this essay we discussed the role of Fliess in Freud's psychological development, pointing out that Fliess, as far as general science was concerned, could "play the Devil" for Freud. We have indicated that Fliess had the power to suspend the scientific superego for Freud. Earlier we have also discussed the image of Moses as representing the superego, and we pointed out some of the devices Freud used in order to suspend the threatened punishment inherent in the Moses image. If Moses was the superego, then the Devil was Freud's necessary ally in his fight against him. In our discussion of hypnosis, cocaine, and the transference, indications of suspension of the superego were suggested. Our introduction of the

Devil idea into this discussion rounds out the great drama which was taking place in Freud's mind in his creation of psychoanalysis, a drama which combined the inevitability of the Greek tradition and the moral struggle of the Jewish tradition.

NOTES TO CHAPTER 27

1. There is the possibility that Abulafia's writings make up the part of the *Sefer Razael* from folio 24 onward. Cf. Gershom Scholem, *Cithve Yad Haivrim* Vol. I, *Kabbala* (Jerusalem: Hebrew University Press, 1930), pp. 24-25.
2. *The Dybbuk,* pp. 57-58.
3. Virgil, *The Aeneid,* trans. C. Day Lewis (London: Hogarth Press, 1952), p. 151.
   "... *quod si mea numina non sunt*
   magna satis, dubitem haud equidem implorare quod usquam.
   Electere si nequeo superos, Acheronta movebo."
   —Virgil, THE AENEID ed. J. W. Mackail (Oxford: Clarendon Press), Book VII, lines 310-312.
4. Freud, *The Int. of Dreams,* p. 608.
5. Geza Roheim, *Psychoanalysis and Anthropolgy* (New York: International Universities Press, 1950), p. 469.
6. Roheim, p. 473.
7. Freud, *The Int. of Dreams,* pp. 262-263.

28

Freud's Paper on Demoniacal Possession

Freud begins his paper "A Neurosis of Demoniacal Possession in the Seventeenth Century" [1] by telling us that neuroses which may now appear in a "hypochondriacal guise" would formerly masquerade in "demonological shape." [2] Then he writes, "Despite the somatic ideology of the era of 'exact' science, the demonological theory of these dark ages has in the long run justified itself." [3] The paper is an analysis of a man by the name of Christoph Haitzmann, a painter, who is supposed to have entered into a contract with the Devil. Documents associated with the events surrounding the contract were brought to Freud's attention. The paper attempts to discover the underlying psychological factors involved in such a contract. Early in the paper Freud says:

> What in those days were thought to be evil spirits to us are base and evil wishes, the derivatives of impulses which have been rejected and repressed. In one respect only do we not subscribe to the explanation of these phenomena current in mediaeval times; we have abandoned the projection of them into the outer world, attributing their origin instead to the inner life of the patient in whom they manifest themselves. [4]

With this proviso Freud enters into the spirit of the documents. On the basis of his detailed analysis, he tells us that the essential conditions for making such a contract are (1) *that the man was depressed,* (2) *that the depression resulted from the death of his father,* and (3) *that he was concerned with earning a livelihood.* From the Fliess correspondence we know that these conditions actually coincide exactly with Freud's own state at the time that *The Interpretation of Dreams* was being written.

The question of the *seriousness* of Freud's entry into the Satanic Pact may well be raised. Freud was a modern man who did not believe in supernatural beings. Indeed Freud himself, in this essay on a medieval document, questions the seriousness of the Satanic Pact *even at that time.* He suggests, on the basis of a somewhat tenuous interpretation of the internal features of the document, that some deception may have been involved.

> But then it would all have been a ruse rather than a neurosis, the painter a malingerer and a cheat instead of a man sick of demoniacal possession! But the transition-stages between neurosis and malingering are, as we know, very elastic.[5]

If, in his conception, Christoph Haitzmann may not have been serious about all of this, we can hardly expect Freud to have been fully taken by the metaphor. Yet what Freud is saying is, in effect, that the full acceptance of the supernatural reality of the Devil is not an essential feature of the motivation of the Satanic Pact.

Concerning the motivation of the Satanic Pact, Freud asks, "Why does one sell oneself to the Devil?" He enumerates the possibilities: "Wealth, immunity from dangers, power over mankind and over the forces of Nature, but above all these, pleasure, the enjoyment of beautiful women." [6] Then he says, "Remarkable to relate, it was not for any one of these very natural desires." [7] He cites offers of the Devil to the painter which the painter refuses.

> Now since he refuses magical powers, money and pleasure when the Devil offers them, and still less makes them a condition of the Bond, it becomes really imperative to know what the painter desired of the Devil when he entered into the Pact. Some motive or other he must have had to induce him to have any such dealings at all.
>
> On this point, too, the *Trophaeum* provides us with reliable information. He had become depressed, was unable or unwilling to paint properly and was anxious about his livelihood, that is to say, he suffered from melancholic depression with incapacity for work and (justified) anxiety about his future. [8] [Freud then cites some passages from the documents and freely interprets.] That is to say, his father had died and he had consequently fallen into a state of melancholia, whereupon the Devil had appeared before him, inquired the cause of his dejection and grief, and had promised "to help him in every way and give him aid."
>
> This man sold himself to the Devil, therefore, in order to be freed from a state of depression. Truly an excellent motive, in the judgment of those who can understand the torment of these states and who appreciate, moreover, how little the art of medicine can do to alleviate the malady. [9]

Freud's allusion to the art of medicine is odd. As comment on the art of medicine in the nineteenth or twentieth century, particularly in contrast with psychoanalysis, it might have some meaning. Thus this remark again suggests the contemporaneous reference of this paper for Freud.

He cites some additional supporting material from the document, indicating Haitzmann's sense of himself as a son of the body of the Devil, and specifying the term of the Pact as nine years. Freud says,

> This incomprehensible Pact would then acquire a straightforward meaning which might be expressed thus: The Devil binds himself for a period of nine years to take the place of his lost father to the painter. At the end of this period the latter, as was customary in such dealings, becomes the property of the Devil, body and soul. The train of thought motivating this Pact seems indeed to be as follows: Owing to my father's death I am despondent and can no longer work; if I can but get a father-substitute I shall be able to regain all that I have lost.
>
> A man who has fallen into a melancholia on account of his father's death must have loved that father deeply. The more curious then that he should have come by the idea of taking the Devil as a substitute for the loved parent.[10]

In the preface to the second edition of *The Interpretation of Dreams*, written in the summer of 1908, Freud writes,

> For this book has a further subjective significance for me personally—a significance which I only grasped after I had completed it. It was, I found, a portion of my own self-analysis, my reaction to my father's death—that is to say, to the most important event, the most poignant loss, of a man's life.[11]

It should be noted that *The Interpretation of Dreams* was brought to completion in the summer of 1899, from May to September.[12] Thus this preface, indicating the emotional significance of the death of his father, was written almost exactly *nine* years after the completion of the book! Further, that the number nine is of particular significance to Freud is indicated by his association of nine with *The Interpretation of Dreams* in a paper he published in 1925.

> My *Interpretation of Dreams* [1900] and my "Fragment of an Analysis of a Case of Hysteria" [1905] (the case of Dora) were suppressed by me—if not for the nine years enjoined by Horace—at all events for four or five years before I allowed them to be published.[13]

Having introduced the idea of the Devil "as a substitute for the loved parent," Freud starts a new section which he entitles *The Devil as a Father-Substitute,* and spends over two pages presenting and refuting arguments by imagined "soberminded critics." He argues for his imagined critic,

> Why should we hold aloof from this obvious and natural explanation? The state of affairs would then simply be that someone in a helpless state, tortured with melancholic depression, sells himself to the Devil, in whose healing powers he reposes the greatest confidence. That the depression was caused by the father's demise would then be quite irrelevant: it could conceivably have been due to some other cause. This seems a forceful and reasonable objection. We hear once more the familiar criticism of psycho-analysis that it regards the simplest affairs in an unduly subtle and complicated way, discovers secrets and problems where none exist, and that it achieves this by magnifying the most insignificant trifles to support far-reaching and bizarre conclusions.[14]

Freud goes on to argue, in reply, for the general soundness of the psychoanalytic mode of thought. This protest in the midst of his discussion again suggests his personal involvement in conceiving of the Pact with the Devil as a reaction to the father's death, although we must add that this in no way detracts from the validity of what he says.

Freud goes on to assert:

> ... God is a father-substitute, or, more correctly, an exalted father, or yet again, a reproduction of the father as seen and met with in childhood—as the individual sees him in his own childhood and as mankind saw him in prehistoric times in the father of the primal horde. . . .[15]
>
> It requires no great analytic insight to divine that God and the Devil were originally one and the same, a single figure which was later split into two bearing opposed characteristics. . . .[16]
>
> The father is thus the individual prototype of both God and the Devil. The fact that the figure of the primal father was that of a being with unlimited potentialities of evil, bearing much more resemblance to the Devil than to God, must have left an indelible stamp on all religions.[17]

Perhaps precisely because Freud did not accept the supernatural reality of the Devil, he could permit himself the full exploitation of the metaphor. We may imagine that at times the sense of possession became quite strong; and it is this feeling of possession that Freud is analyzing in his paper.

NOTES TO CHAPTER 28

1. Freud, *Col. Papers,* IV, pp. 436-472.
2. Freud, *Col. Papers,* IV, p. 436.
3. Freud, *Col. Papers,* IV, p. 436.
4. Freud, *Col. Papers,* IV, p. 437.
5. Freud, *Col. Papers,* IV, p. 465.
6. Freud, *Col. Papers,* IV, p. 443.
7. Freud, *Col. Papers,* IV, p. 443.
8. Freud, *Col. Papers,* IV, p. 444.
9. Freud, *Col. Papers,* IV, pp. 444-445.
10. Freud, *Col. Papers,* IV, p. 446.

11. Freud, *The Int. of Dreams*, p. xxvi.
12. Freud, *The Int. of Dreams*, pp. xix-xx.
13. Freud, *Col. Papers*, V, p. 187. This refers to the years before 1899.
14. Freud, *Col. Papers*, IV, pp. 447-448.
15. Freud, *Col. Papers*, IV, p. 449.
16. Freud, *Col. Papers*, IV, p. 450.
17. Freud, *Col. Papers*, IV, p. 451.

29

The Composition of The Interpretation of Dreams

In the next few pages we will present a series of quotations from the *Origins of Psychoanalysis,* Freud's letters to Fliess, which throw some light on Freud's state of mind while he was in the process of working out the material for what is doubtless his greatest work, *The Interpretation of Dreams.* We find confirmation that it was fashioned under conditions specified by Freud as leading to the Satanic Pact: the death of his father, depression and financial pressure. Freud, as we recall, felt that it was his Judaism which supplied him with energy. In our interpretation, it was partly Sabbatian Judaism which helped him overcome his depression, in the metaphor of the Devil.[1] We find that Freud immerses himself in demoniacal literature; and that the desired effects, the liberation from depression and ability to work, are achieved. We find him referring to primitive Semitic sexual cults and one can hypothesize that his Sabbatian tendencies were finding warm echoes as he perused the history of these early Semitic sexual cults. We find him denying the possible effects of his "real father" and asserting the significance of his Catholic nurse; and again we sense in the latter figure an element important for the development of his Sabbatian tendencies, although the available information is insufficient to allow for a detailed analysis of her meaning to him. We have included a quotation showing his reactions after the book is published, in which he relates the dynamics of his own struggles of discovery to the medieval Devil notion, the struggle of Jacob with the angel, as well as a reference to "Lucifer-Amor."

Freud's father died on the night of October 23, 1896. The last sentence of the published version of the letter reporting the death is "It all happened in my critical period, and I am really down over it. . . ." [2]

On December 4, 1896, he tells Fliess, "The first thing I shall disclose to you about my works are the introductory quotations," and cites the "Flectere . . ." Two other quotations which he cites are:

> They are exceeding all bounds, I fear a breakdown; God does not present the reckoning at the end of every week,

and

> Cut it short! On doomsday it won't be worth a . . . ! [3]

On December 6 he tells how "dead tired and mentally fresh" he is "after completing the day's labour and earning the recompense that I need for my well-being (ten hours and 100 florins). . . ." [4]

On January 3, 1897, he writes in a blush of confidence "When I am not afraid I can take on all the devils in hell. . . ." [5] And later in the same letter he says that as a quotation for the section "Sexuality" he will use " 'from heaven through the world to hell'—if that is the correct quotation." [6] On January 17, 1897, he writes,

> By the way, what have you got to say to the suggestion that the whole of my brand-new theory of the primary origins of hysteria is already familiar and has been published a hundred times over, though several centuries ago? Do you remember my always saying that the mediaeval theory of possession, that held by the ecclesiastical courts, was identical with our theory of a foreign body and the splitting of consciousness? But why did the devil who took possession of the poor victims invariably commit misconduct with them, and in such horrible ways? Why were the confessions extracted under torture so very like what my patients tell me under psychological treatment? I must delve into the literature of the subject.[7]

In his next letter of January 24, 1897, exactly three months after his father's death, he discusses the Devil and witchcraft extensively, and refers to a sexual cult in the Semitic East:

> The parallel with witchcraft is taking shape, and I believe it is conclusive. Details have started crowding in, I have found the explanation why witches "fly"; their broomstick is apparently the great Lord Penis. Their secret gatherings, with dances and other entertainment, can be seen any day in the streets where the children play. I read one day that the gold which the devil gave his victims regularly turned into excrement; and next day Herr E., who reports that his nurse had money deliria, suddenly told me (by way of Cagliostro—alchemist—*Dukatenscheisser*) that Louise's money was always excrement. Thus in the witch stories it is only transformed back into the substance of which it originally consisted. If I only knew why the devil's semen in witches' confessions is always described as "cold." I have ordered a *Malleus Maleficarum* [8] and now that

I have put the finishing touches to the children's paralyses I shall study it diligently. Stories about the devil, the vocabulary of popular swear-words, the rhymes and habits of the nursery, are all gaining significance for me. Can you without trouble suggest some good reading from your well-stocked memory? In connection with the dances in witches' confessions you will recall the dancing epidemics of the Middle Ages. . . .*

I am toying with the idea that in the perversions, of which hysteria is the negative, we may have the remnants of a primitive sexual cult, which in the Semitic east may once have been a religion (Moloch, Astarte). . . .†

I am beginning to dream of an extremely primitive devil religion the rites of which continue to be performed secretly, and now I understand the stern therapy of the witches' judges. The links are abundant.

Another tributary into the main stream is suggested by the consideration that to this very day there is a class of persons who tell stories similar to those of witches and my patients; nobody believes them, though that does not shake their belief in them. As you will have guessed, I refer to paranoiacs, whose complaints that excrement is put in their food, that they are abominably maltreated at night, sexually, etc., are pure memory content. . . .*

One more point. In the exacting standards insisted on by hysterics in love, in their humility before the loved one, or in their inability to marry because of unattainable ideals, I recognize the influence of the father-figure. The cause is, of course, the immense elevation from which the father condescends to the child's level. In paranoia compare the combination of megalomania with the creation of myths about the child's true parentage. That is the reverse side of the medal. . . .

I think I have now passed the age boundary; I am in a much more stable state. . . .* [9]

* Our deletions.
† Deletions by the editors of *Origins*.

In a letter on April 28, 1897, Freud speaks of criticizing Fliess "for taking no pleasure in the Middle Ages." [10] On May 31, 1897, he says he has a presentiment that he is "about to discover the source of morality", and tells of a dream which, he says, "of course fulfills my wish to pin down a father as the originator of neurosis and put an end to my persistent doubts." [11]

In his letter of June 12, 1897 he has quite clearly left the biological: "you take the biological, I the psychological." And this is immediately followed with "Let me confess that I have recently made a collection of deeply significant Jewish stories."

He says of himself, "I believe I am in a cocoon, and heaven knows what sort of creature will emerge from it." [12] On October 3, 1897, approaching the anniversary of his father's death he writes,

> I can only say that in my case my father played no active role, though I certainly projected on to him an analogy from myself; that my "primary originator" [of neurosis] was an ugly, elderly, but clever woman who told me a great deal about God and hell, and gave me a high opinion of my own capacities. [13]

On October 15, 1897, he quotes his mother about the old nurse who took care of him when he was very young.

> "Of course," she said, "an elderly woman, very shrewd indeed. She was always taking you to church. When you came home you used to preach, and tell us about how God conducted His affairs." [14]

This Catholic nurse may have had a role to play in the generation of his Sabbatian tendencies. He evidently had an early exposure to Christian religion. The rearousal of these memories, when he was in the wake of the experience of his father's death and as he was growing aware of the significance of the

Oedipus complex and becoming increasingly concerned with the demoniacal, may not be coincidental. The old nurse may have served as some sort of support in rebelling against the superego.

The letter written on October 27, 1897, which relates experiences that Freud had on "Sunday," is of particular interest. October 27, 1897, was actually a Wednesday, and therefore, the Sunday referred to in the letter was October 24, 1897, which was the anniversary of the death of his father. The letter shows the personal importance of Fliess to Freud, the fact of his depression, and his concern over money matters, and refers to the classical story associated with the Satanic Pact, Goethe's *Faust*. He writes,

> I do not seem to be able to "wait" for your answer. The explanation of your silence certainly is not that you have been whirled back by some elemental power to the times when reading and writing were a burden to you, as happened to me on Sunday, when I wanted to write you a letter to mark your not-yet-fortieth birthday; but I hope it was something just as harmless. As for myself, I have nothing to tell you except about my analysis, which I think will be the most interesting thing about me for you too. Business is hopelessly bad, it is so in general, right up to the very top of the tree, so I am living only for "inner" work. It gets hold of me and hauls me through the past in rapid association of ideas; and my mood changes like the landscape seen by a traveller from a train; and, as the great poet, using his privilege to ennoble (sublimate) things, put it:—
>
> *Und manche liebe Schatten steigen auf,*
> *Gleich einer alten, halbverklungnen Sage,*
> *Kommt erste Lieb' und Freundschaft mit herauf—**

* "And the shades of loved ones appear, and with them, like an old, half-forgotten myth, first love and friendship."—From the Dedication of Goethe's *Faust*.

as well as first terror and strife. Some sad secrets of life are being traced back to their first roots, the humble origins of much pride and precedence are being laid bare. I am now experiencing myself all the things that as a third party I have witnessed going on in my patients—days when I slink about depressed because I have understood nothing of the day's dreams, phantasies or mood, and other days when a flash of lightning brings coherence into the picture, and what has gone before is revealed as preparation for the present.[15]

On October 31, 1897, he makes an interesting remark about the state of his sexuality—"Also sexual excitation is of no more use to a person like me"[16]—indicative perhaps of his depressed state, as well as his emotional maturity in the tradition of Kabbala.

In a letter that he wrote on December 5, 1897,* he talks about Rome and Hannibal and cites the quotation from Goethe which we have mentioned. This suggests that Messianic-Kabbalistic[17] feelings are operative, as well the sense of anti-Semitism and a tendency toward obscurantism. The idea of writing the book is first mentioned in May 1897. In the early months of 1898 he completed a first draft of the book, with the exception of the chapter reviewing the literature. The book was actually brought to completion in the period from May to September of 1899. In the year after its completion Freud was evidently depressed by the negligible attention it received. In the six years after its first publication only 351 copies were sold.[18]

On May 7, 1900, the day after his forty-fourth birthday,

---

* The letter is originally dated December 3, 1897, but the December 3rd content is missing in the published version of the letter. The December 5th entry begins "A critical day prevented me from going on."

Freud has a reaction to some of the high spirits he had manifested while writing *The Interpretation of Dreams*. This reaction is describable, to repeat Freud's metaphor, as that which comes upon one when one discovers that "the gold which the Devil gave his victims regularly turned into excrement." [19]

He writes, first about Fliess and then about himself:

> When your book is published none of us will be able to pass the judgment on it which, as in the case of all great new achievements, is reserved for posterity; but the beauty of the conception, the originality of the ideas, the simple coherence of the whole and the conviction with which it is written will create an impression which will provide the just compensation for the arduous wrestling with the demon. With me it is different. No critic . . . can see more clearly than I the disproportion there is between the problems and my answers to them, and it will be a fitting punishment for me that none of the unexplored regions of the mind in which I have been the first mortal to set foot will ever bear my name or submit to my laws. When breath threatened to fail me in the struggle I prayed the angel to desist, and that is what he has done since then. But I did not turn out to be the stronger, though since then I have been noticeably limping.* Well, I really am forty-four now, a

---

* Cf. Goethe's *Faust*, on the limping Devil; and Jacob's limping after wrestling with the angel. It will be recalled that Jacob is to be called Israel, "he who strives with God," because he strove with God and with men and prevailed (Gen. 32:29). The medieval concept of the limping-Jew-Devil has its origin in this verse. Cf. also the limping Dr. M. (Mephistopheles?) in *The Interpretation of Dreams*, pp. 107 ff.

The following Biblical passage may also be of some interest in this connection: "And the sun rose upon him [Jacob] as he passed over Peniel, and he limped upon his thigh. Therefore the children of Israel eat not the sinew of the thigh-vein *(gid ha-nasheh)* which is upon the hollow of the thigh, unto this day; because he [the angel] touched the hollow of Jacob's thigh, even in the sinew of the thigh-vein"— Gen. 32:32-33.

We see here a kind of testimony to the idea of the *eating* of the father and the taboos associated with it as developed by Freud in *Totem and Taboo*. (Note also that Freud's father was Jakob.) This passage in the Bible is an important basis for

rather shabby old Jew [*Israelit* in the German], as you will see for yourself in the summer or autumn.[20]

About two months later, he shows signs of building new defenses. He fantasies a marble tablet on the house where "the Secret of Dreams was revealed to Dr. Sigmund Freud," [21] and says,

> People's opinions on the dream book are beginning to leave me cold, and I am beginning to bewail its fate. The stone is apparently not being worn down by the dripping.[22]

It is then that we have one of the clearest images from Freud of what he is going through. He says,

> It is an intellectual hell, layer upon layer of it, with everything fitfully gleaming and pulsating; and the outline of Lucifer-Amor coming into sight at the darkest centre.[23]

NOTES TO CHAPTER 29

1. Cf. pp. 95 ff., above.
2. Freud, *Origins*, p. 170. It is unfortunate that the published version of the letter does not show what follows after this.
3. Freud, *Origins*, p. 172.
4. Freud, *Origins*, p. 173.
5. Freud, *Origins*, p. 183.
6. Freud, *Origins*, p. 184.
7. Freud, *Origins*, p. 188.

---

the Jewish dietary laws—cf. S. L. Levin and E. A. Boyden, *The Kosher Code,* (Minneapolis: University of Minnesota Press, 1940), p. 184. The word *gid* may mean tendons or blood vessels or nerves. *Gid ha-nasheh* is interpreted to mean the sciatic nerve. It may be completely fortuitous, but "for what it is worth," Freud himself made an investigation of a disturbance of a nerve in the thigh from which he himself suffered. Cf. Jones, I, p. 218, and Freud, "Über die Bernhardtsche Sensibilitätsstörung am Oberschenkel," *Neurolog. Centralblatt* (1895), p. 14, p. 491.

8. Henricus Institorus, *Malleus Maleficarum*, trans. M. Summers (London: Pushkin Press, 1948). This book was the most authoritative work on demonology and the standard handbook for Inquisitors for three centuries after its writing in 1486.

9. Freud, *Origins*, pp. 188-191. Cf. pp. 176 ff., above.

10. Freud, *Origins*, p. 194.

11. Freud, *Origins*, p. 206.

12. Freud, *Origins*, p. 211.

13. Freud, *Origins*, p. 219.

14. Freud, *Origins*, p. 221.

15. Freud, *Origins*, pp. 225-226.

16. Freud, *Origins*, p. 227.

17. Cf. pp. 169 ff., above.

18. Freud, *The Int. of Dreams*, pp. xix-xx.

19. Freud, *Origins*, p. 188.

20. Freud, *Origins*, pp. 318-319.

21. Freud, *Origins*, p. 322. Letter of June 12, 1900.

22. Freud, *Origins*, pp. 323-324.

23. Freud, *Origins*, p. 323.

30

Accretion of Meanings to the Devil Image

The concept of the Devil, because of its ancient history and also because it catches at a significant aspect of human existence, has many accretions. Throughout the Middle Ages the Devil was a star in the great spiritual drama which was then taking place. As Freud had so aptly pointed out, even though the Devil is perhaps no longer a personage in the same sense as in the Middle Ages, the psychological phenomena associated with his image are still current and important. We have already indicated the psychological signicance of the Devil image as an ally against the superego, or better, as its suspension. To further illuminate the role of this image in Freud's thought we turn to a consideration of some other aspects of its meaning.

A. THE PROBLEM OF "DISTANCE"

As we have already indicated we believe that for Freud the idea of the Devil functioned as a metaphor. A metaphor may be more or less "distant" from the person. This phenomenological dimension, although perhaps difficult to specify exactly, is extremely real. The "distance" of which we speak is, on the one hand, at its greatest in scientific literature, if we take the position that scientific constructs are metaphors. In science, presumably, the content of the investigation should be "independent" of the investigator. On the other hand, "distance" is considerably less in works of art, particularly in the Romantic tradition. In certain forms of poetry or music the distance is minimal. We sometimes refer to a work of art as "personal," meaning that the "distance" is small. In our age, the capacity to maintain "distance" is sometimes taken as the measure of intellectual maturity: the greater the "distance" the greater the maturity.

Part of the intellectual genius of Freud was his astounding facility for maximizing "distance" with respect to modes of thought in which minimal "distance" prevailed initially. *The Interpretation of Dreams* is actually a magnificent achievement as a treatment of the problem of "distance"; for it deals with his own life and personality with such "distance" as to create a new methodology.

The image of the Devil is one which is particularly problematical with respect to the matter of "distance." In our discussion of the "Flectere . . ." quotation we saw that Freud took this demonological reference as indicative of the forces within the individual by which the "suppressed material finds methods and means of forcing its way into consciousness." [1] In the religious allegory, God holds the content unconscious, and the Devil is the counterforce which renders the material conscious. The task involved in Freud's self-analysis was that of bringing the unconscious into consciousness. Continuing the allegory, an alliance of the ego with the Devil was necessary to make it possible to achieve the requisite "distance." Thus by permitting successful intervention of the Devil the person wins "distance." Hence, paradoxically, the Devil must cause his own destruction. By bringing the daemonic into the light, the daemonic is stripped of its daemonic character. More prosaically this can be stated as follows: The disease of the neurotic is his guilt. This guilt is, in itself, an evil and its removal is good. However, within the neurosis the guilt is a punishment for evil. Within the neurosis a counterforce to the punishing imago is required. Hence there is an alliance with such a counter-imago as will allow all to become open, accessible to consciousness. If God is the guilt-producing imago, then the Devil is the counterforce. But the Devil's very permissiveness is the cause of his own destruction. Having permitted all to become open, the infantile character of both imagos is revealed and "distance" with respect to each is won.

As Freud said in discussing Anatole France's *Revolt of the Angels,* "War will produce war and victory defeat. God defeated becomes Satan and Satan victorious will become God." [2] It is interesting that in Freud's later writing he separates Eros from the image of the Devil and lets the Devil stand for destructiveness.[3]

B. THE DEVIL AS KNOWER

Classically the Devil is associated with knowing. He is usually depicted as a personage of great knowledge and craft. Man's original sin consisted in eating of the Tree of Knowledge, and therefore God's curse is upon him. When Adam and

Eve ate of the Tree of Knowledge "the eyes of them both were opened." [4] In the Faust legend the contract is made in despair over lack of knowledge. It is interesting that Freud should himself point up the knowing feature of his *The Interpretation of Dreams*. In the preface to the English edition in 1931, he writes,

> It contains, even according to my present-day judgment, the most valuable of all the discoveries it has been my good fortune to make. *Insight such as this falls to one's lot but once in a lifetime* [our italics]. [5]

That our society is saturated with the association of evil with knowing is indicated by our criminal proceedings, in which the critical question is often whether the person "knew" what he was doing. We characteristically identify innocence with ignorance and guilt with knowledge.

When Freud broke the ground in making the most intimate features of man the subject for scientific investigation, it was necessary for him to repeat the very same moral and social struggle which had been engaged in by the early pioneers in the physical and biological sciences. That he was dealing with such intimate matters made the struggle all the more difficult. He could only indirectly avail himself of the "distance" of the other sciences, which, on the surface, are outside the province of the medieval soul. Freud's repeated affirmations that he was a *scientist* may be interpreted, in part, as an effort to draw upon himself some of the fruits of the victories that science had already won.

C. THE CURATIVE POWER INHERENT
IN THE DEVIL

The Devil notion has associated with it a feature which we might call that of aid-in-deep-despair. The Devil is supposed to have great powers and is characteristically called upon *when all else has failed*. He is a terrible cure, but a powerful one nonetheless. Characteristically the Devil is approached, to use the expression Freud used of writing the third part of his *Moses and Monotheism,* "with the audacity of one who has little or nothing to lose." [6]

From a psychological point of view we envisage, on the basis of what Freud has taught us, the individual, in his development, as entering into a kind of social contract, in which the individual agrees to abide by the demands of society in return for certain basic satisfactions and protections. When one's life situation grows too bad, the question arises as to whether the other party is abiding by his part of the contract. If this doubt crosses the line and becomes a conclusion, that the other party has broken the contract, then the individual feels free to do as he pleases.

This is the conflict of Job, and the conflict the Jews have experienced over and over again as they were persecuted. The notion of the Covenant is psychologically the idea of the social contract, that the Jews would accept the yoke of the Law in return for God's favor.

The idea of the contract with the Devil is of course consistent with the contractual feature of both the Covenant and the social contract, but is a new one in its details. The dread of punishment still exists, but it is delayed. The new contract is entered into because, with the loss of hope, the anguish turns into despair; for despair is exactly anguish without hope of relief.

The Devil is then a cure for despair. He is called upon as an assertive act when all hope is gone. And in this sense also, the Devil is always the Tempter. The essential message of the Tempter is that the anticipated rewards associated with resistance to temptation will not be forthcoming, that *faith* is groundless. The Devil presents the new hope, and supports his promise by *immediate* tokens of his favor. But since these tokens themselves bring so much relief, one permits oneself, in his relationship to the Devil, to be thus taken in (by the Devil), since he feels that he has already been taken in (by God).

In more secular terms, Freud suffered from acute depressions. His self-analysis, and his development of psychoanalysis, were the cure for his depression. His practice had already provided him with ample evidence that diseases which other people were suffering from, for which there was no other hope, could be cured by such means. In his despair over making a living, and in his despair over anti-Semitism, he had "little or nothing to lose" by his "audacity." Furthermore, this new set of methods which he was producing held out the promise of bringing patients to him and so solving at least the problem of making a living. That he conceived of psychoanalysis as a means of economic support is indicated by a remark he made in Sachs's presence. Sachs says,

But Freud's expectation did not include any martyrdom: "I would probably succeed in making a living with the help of the therapeutic success of the new technique." [7]

In thus becoming involved in the metaphor of the Devil, Freud certainly risked great sin (or its psychological equivalent, guilt) himself. But in this he had the support of the tradition of the Baale' Shem. These wonder-workers repeatedly risked themselves by invoking God's name in their efforts to cure other people. In order to help people it was necessary for them to thus invoke the Ineffable Name, which was always a possible violation of the third commandment, that "Thou shalt not take the name of the Lord thy God in vain; for the Lord will not hold him guiltless that taketh His name in vain." [8]

NOTES TO CHAPTER 30

1. Freud, *The Int. of Dreams,* p. 608.
2. H. Sachs, "The Man Moses and the Man Freud," *Psychoanal. Rev.,* 1941, 28, 156-162, p. 159.
3. Freud, *Civilization and Its Discontents,* trans. Joan Riviere (London: Hogarth Press, 1955), p. 100.
4. Gen. 3:7.
5. Freud, *The Int. of Dreams,* p. xxxii.
6. Freud, *Moses and Monotheism,* p. 66.
7. Sachs, "The Man Moses . . . ," p. 162.
8. Exodus 20:7.

Part V

Psychoanalysis and Kabbala

31

The Problem of Scholarship

In this section we propose to detail some of the similarities between psychoanalysis as developed by Freud and the Kabbalistic tradition. Up to this point we have emphasized Freud's life and thought as they were an expression of, and a working with, the classical problems associated with Jewish mysticism. We will try to present some features of Kabbala primarily through selected excerpts in order to show at their source the ideas present in the Jewish mystical culture. Despite the similarities of psychoanalysis to Kabbala as a doctrine and method, we are unable to hypothesize that Freud actually read in Kabbalistic literature. The point is actually a minor one. The Kabbalistic spirit pervaded the culture out of which Freud arises. This much is evident: Freud was opened up to Kabbalistic feelings within himself, and this may be a sufficient explanation of the close similarities. In a letter to Fliess, Freud furnishes us with an instance of the ease with which ideas may be transmitted when there is a readiness for them. Freud got the idea of bisexuality, which as we shall see is characteristic of Kabbala, from Fliess. Freud mentioned it to Swoboda, a patient, in the course of treatment. In a letter to Fliess, Freud says Swoboda mentioned the word "bisexuality" to Weininger who "slapped himself on the forehead and ran home to write his book" [1] in which the idea was thoroughly exploited.

Kabbala is extremely old. Through the centuries it has been modified and added to continuously. It has woven itself into the cloth of man's intellectual and spiritual stirrings in complex and strange ways. The attempt to explicate such a doctrine, even to some degree, cannot be undertaken without humility and awe. The hesitation stems perhaps from the essential uncertainty associated with Kabbala, from the taboo on its exposition, and from the sense that its meaning can never be plumbed. The hesitation stems also from the fact that any clear assertion about the nature of its content is somehow denied, as though clarity itself is a denial of what Kabbala affirms. Its allegorical, paradoxical, and obscurant features invite the greatest latitude with respect to interpretation and constrict clear-cut assertions. As it hints of great mysteries and knowledge of precious secrets, so does it warn of inherent risks. We have indicated that the major counterforce to Kabbalistic thought came from the Jewish tradition of disciplined scholarship.[2] Scholarship provides the ballast which Kabbala itself does not have. And the Kabbalistic superego, if we might use such a term, dictates that the flight into Kabbalistic spaces should be held in check by the development of scholarship. The danger of scholarship in this sense, however, is that it may be so heavy that one never gets off the ground.

These difficulties were indeed the very same that Freud faced. He chafed at the problem of scholarship. Sometimes he chose to be wanton with it; sometimes he yielded to it. A few instances of his struggles on the score of scholarship might be cited to make the point:

> The first chapter [of *The Interpretation of Dreams*], dealing with the literature, . . . had always been a bug-bear to Freud.[3]

He wrote it after the other parts of the book, evidently as a kind of appeasement of the scientific superego. He says:

> I shall give by way of preface a review of the work done by earlier writers on the subject as well as of the present position of the problems of dreams in the world of science, since, in the course of my discussion I shall not often have occasion to revert to those topics.[4]

Indeed the editor of the Modern Library edition of Freud's *Basic Writings* simply deletes the bulk of the chapter with a note on its lack of importance.[5] In a postscript to the first chapter added for the 1909 edition, Freud indicates that his failure to extend the account of the literature

> . . . stands in need of justification. It may strike the reader as an unsatisfactory one, but for me it was none the less decisive. The notions which led me to give any account at all of the way in which earlier writers have dealt with dreams were exhausted with the completion of this introductory chapter; to continue the task would have cost me an extraordinary effort—and the result would have been of very little use or instruction.[6]

And although he says in connection with the reading of medieval demonological materials that he "must delve into the literature of the subject," [7] he also writes "what horrifies me more than anything else is all the psychology I shall have to read in the next few years," [8] indicating, perhaps, that he is interested in reading only insofar as it will stimulate the flight. What Freud was, of course, demonstrating with the lengthy scholarly section of *The Interpretation of Dreams* was that he was *capable* of that kind of disciplined scholarship. The fact that *The Interpretation of Dreams* contains only negligible references to the demonological materials, which we know, from his letters to Fliess, he consulted extensively, indicates again his reluctance to discuss live source material.

He says,

> If only one did not have to read! The literature on the subject [of dreams], such as it is, is too much for me already.[9]

His actual writing procedure is the reverse of what the scientific superego would have dictated.

> First I want to get my own ideas into shape, then I shall make a thorough study of the literature on the subject, and finally make such insertions or revisions as my reading will give rise to. So long as I have not finished my own work I cannot read, and it is only in writing that I can fill in all the details.[10]
>
> The literature [on dreams] which I am now reading is reducing me to idiocy. Reading is a terrible infliction imposed upon all who write. In the process everything of one's own drains away. I often cannot manage to remember what I have that is new, and yet it is all new. The reading stretches ahead interminably, so far as I can see at present.[11]

This hostility to pedantic scholarship was characteristic of the Sabbatians in particular, who viewed rabbinic scholarship as something dead and useless. One of the important values the orthodox Jew saw in study was that it kept temptation at a distance. In psychoanalytic terms, study served as a repressive force. The deep immersion in Biblical and Talmudic study was to protect the individual from Satan and "alien thoughts." [12] In the developments that took place within Jewish mysticism, intuitional rather than scholarly ways of appreciating God were emphasized. It was no longer necessary to pore over Talmudic folios in order to attain higher piety.

Generally speaking, there are two principal areas in which Kabbala and psychoanalysis show striking similarity: techniques of interpretation and the importance and meaning attached to sexuality. We will deal with these in order.

NOTES TO CHAPTER 31

1. Richard Pfennig, *Wilhelm Fliess und seine Nachentdecker: O. Weininger und H. Swoboda*. Berlin: E. Goldschmidt, 1906, p. 26.
2. Cf. pp. 90 ff.
3. Freud, *The Int. of Dreams*, pp. xix-xx.
4. Freud, *The Int. of Dreams*, p. 1.
5. Freud, *Basic Writings*, p. 185.
6. Freud, *The Int. of Dreams*, p. 93.
7. Freud, *Origins*, p. 188.
8. Freud, *Origins*, p. 228.
9. Freud, *Origins*, p. 244.
10. Freud, *Origins*, p. 249.
11. Freud, *Origins*, p. 270.
12. Joshua Trachtenberg, *Jewish Magic and Superstition* (New York: Behrman's Jewish Book House, 1939), p. 155.

32

Techniques of Interpretation

A. MAN AS TORAH

The subject matter of classical Kabbalistic interpretation was the Torah. The *Zohar,* for example, is on the face of it a commentary on the Torah, and its order follows the Pentateuch, first citing text and then interpreting it. With the social development of Kabbalistic modes of thought, an extremely interesting transition took place. The idea gradually took hold that the *Messiah was a Torah.* All of the attitudes of reverence towards the Torah transferred themselves to the image of the Messiah. Later the person of the Zaddik, the Holy Man, the center of the Chassidic groups, came to be regarded as a Torah. Every word the Zaddik spoke, every gesture he engaged in, was taken as equal to the Torah in profundity and significance. We may say that Freud carried this transition one step further. *The Kabbalistic forms of interpretation were now to be used in the appreciation of any human being.* This transition on Freud's part may be assigned to the democratic and enlightened trends of modern society. Not only is the Zaddik a Torah, but each person is a Torah!

Actually the *Zohar* itself suggests such an interpretation of man by using man as an analogy for the Torah, and already distinguishes, as Freud does, between what is manifest and latent.

> Thus had the Torah not clothed herself in garments of this world the world could not endure it. The stories of the Torah are thus only her outer garments, and whoever looks upon that garment as being the Torah itself, woe to that man—such a one will have no portion in the next world. David thus said: "Open thou mine eyes, that I may behold wondrous things out of thy law" (Ps. cxix, 18), to wit, the things that are beneath the garment. Observe this. The garments worn by a man are the most visible part of him, and senseless people looking at the man do not seem to see more in him than the garments. But in truth the pride of the garments is the body of the man, and the pride of the body is the soul. Similarly the Torah has a body made up of the precepts of the Torah, called *gufe torah* [bodies, main principles of the Torah], and that body is enveloped in garments made up of worldly narrations. The senseless people only see the garment, the mere narrations; those who are somewhat wiser penetrate as far as the body. But the really wise, the servants of the most high King, those who stood on Mount Sinai,[1] penetrate right through to the soul, the root principle of all, namely, to the real Torah.[2]

If Freud wished to hint, consciously or unconsciously, that the analysis of a person is like the analysis of Torah, it would not have been out of character for him, or inconsistent with psychoanalytical principles, to name a critical case in some revelatory fashion. We are immediately led to the case of Dora,[3] in connection with whom he discovered the transference. "Dora" readily becomes "Torah." The discipline of scholarship should immediately warn us that this may be an instance of *our own* associations, a humorous and inconsequential coincidence, an example of "clang-association" hardly to be admitted as evidence. One is aware that there are innumerable instances of coincidental similarity of words which, because of the limited number of sounds that the human being can make, arise with no other connection between them than their phonic similarity. And thus one would dismiss the similarity between Dora and Torah as "cute" but inconsequential.

But then, it is Freud of whom we are speaking; and it is Freud whose mind inferred profound connections from word similarity. It is quite sober to imagine that if Freud wanted to hint at something without actually saying it, he would have done it in this way.

However, such an argument is still insufficient as a basis for inferring the significance of a Dora-Torah association. We would want something still more specific from Freud on this particular phonic connection, and this he obligingly provides us. The associative links are to be found in his essay on Judaism, *Moses and Monotheism,* where, we would suppose, they belong.

The phonic identification of which we speak is his assertion that the Egyptian Sun God Aton has become the Jewish Adonai. He says,

> There would be a short way of proving that the Mosaic religion is nothing else but that of Aton: namely, by a confession of faith, a proclamation. But I am afraid I should be told that such a road is impracticable. The Jewish creed, as is well known, says: *"Schema Jisroel Adonai Elohenu Adonai Echod."* If the similarity of the name of the Egyptian Aton (or Atum) to the Hebrew word Adonai and the Syrian divine name Adonis

is not a mere accident, but is the result of a primeval unity in language and meaning, then one could translate the Jewish formula: "Hear, O Israel, our God Aton (Adonai) is the only God." I am, alas, entirely unqualified to answer this question and have been able to find very little about it in the literature concerned, but probably we had better not make things so simple.[4]

This identification of Aton with Adonai has been criticized as historically groundless. We are reminded of Leo Strauss's comments to the effect that if a great author commits school-boy errors, that we have reason to search for a deeper meaning behind the apparent blunders.[5] Although Strauss's analysis is restricted to conscious processes, there is no reason to suppose that his considerations cannot be extrapolated to unconscious processes, particularly since the dividing line is often vague. The Aton-Adonai identification may, then, have a deeper significance. It clearly shows that Freud conceived of a ready transition from a *t* to a *d,* consistent with classical linguistics,* a transition which we are hypothesizing in going from Torah to Dora. The Aton-Adonai transition, and, hence, the *t-d* transition, is given to us by Freud in his major essay on Judaism. If Freud, again consciously or unconsciously, wanted to inform us that in psychoanalysis he is analyzing a human being as the Jews have for centuries been analyzing Torah, he could not have chosen a more appropriate place in his writings. That *Moses and Monotheism* constitutes, so to speak, Freud's "dying words" only adds weight to the probability of the hypothesis.

* Actually the *Sefer Yetzirah* already refers to the essential identity or inter-changeability of a *t* with a *d* (Paragraph 17 of *Sefer Yetzirah*). Cf. the Goldschmidt edition, Frankfurt: J. Kauffmann, 1894, p. 54.

We can summarize the presumptive associational links in Freud's thought by a diagram similar to the one Freud uses in his *Psychopathology of Everyday Life:*

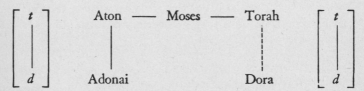

We have direct evidence in Freud's writings for all the associative links (represented by lines) in the diagram with the exception of the broken line. Our point is that this final association of Dora and Torah is strongly suggested by the others.

Furthermore our presumptive identification of Dora and Torah would not be complete without adding that the problem of Dora's name is one with which he was evidently concerned. He discusses the matter in the *Psychopathology of Everyday Life:*

> While preparing the history of one of my patients for publication, I considered what first name I should give her in the article. There seemed to be a wide choice; of course, certain names were at once excluded by me, in the first place the real name, then the names of members of my family to which I would have objected, also some female names having an especially peculiar pronounciation. But, excluding these, there should have been no need to being puzzled about such a name. *It would be thought, and I myself supposed, that a whole multitude of feminine names would be placed at my disposal. Instead of this, only one sprang up, no other besides it, it was the name Dora* [our italics].[6]

Freud then goes on to tell us about a nurse of his sister's children whose real name was Rosa, but who had adopted the name "Dora" in the household because the woman of the house was also Rosa. He says,

> Thus, when I sought a name of a person *who could not retain her own name* [Freud's italics], no other except "Dora" occurred to me.[7]

The Dora-Torah identification makes good sense when we consider the anti-Semitic atmosphere in Vienna in Freud's time.[8] It would have been impossible for Freud to allow that his techniques were associated with interpreting Torah. Indeed, *the Torah could not retain its own name!*

Freud virtually says that he will analyze human productions as though he were analyzing Torah. He writes,

> We have attached no less importance in interpreting dreams to every shade of the form of words in which they were laid before us. And even when it happened that the text of the dream as we had it was meaningless or inadequate—as though the effort to give a correct account of it had been unsuccessful—we have taken this defect into account as well. In short, *we have treated as Holy Writ what previous writers have regarded as an arbitrary improvisation* . . . [our italics].[9]

Elsewhere we find him referring to "the unconscious, the real center of our mental life," in a manner reminiscent of Abulafia, as "the part of us that is so much nearer the divine than our poor consciousness." [10]

This interpretation of man as Holy Scripture was no doubt facilitated by the general attitude of critical scrutiny toward the thought and behavior of oneself and others which prevailed among the Jews for centuries. Its basis is to be found in the fact that for the orthodox Jew every action which he engaged in during the day and night was a satisfaction or a defection with respect to the varieties of commandments and derivations from the commandments. All activities that concerned preparation and eating of food, sexual and social relations, dress, relationship to relatives and strangers, toilet practices, etc. were closely regulated. The way of living like a Jew was prescribed from moment to moment, from sunrise to sunrise, from week to week, from season to season, from birth to death. It was all in fulfillment of the Covenant. Not only did the Jew police himself, but he policed his neighbor also; for if his neighbor defected, God's wrath would fall equally on him and his neighbor. Living was always a full-time religious occupation. We may say that there occurred a ready transfer of this perceptual attitude, the close scrutiny of the human being with inordinate conscientiousness in every detail, from the long Jewish tradition to psychoanalysis.

Even more important, for centuries the Torah had been treated as a document so sacred that every letter, every nuance of style—even the size of the letters in the handwritten scroll—were regarded as having profound hidden meanings, which the mystic and the exegete interpreted in a manner strikingly like that of the psychoanalyst interpreting turns and vagaries of human expression. All that was needed was a transfer of subject matter from the text of the Torah to the "text" of human behavior, a point not even very novel in Jewish tradition.

B. INTERPRETATION EN DETAIL AND EN MASSE

Freud's method of interpreting dreams involves as one of its major technical features an initial breaking up of the dream into parts, and subsequent association to each part separately. He writes:

> Our first step in the employment of this procedure teaches us that what we must take as the object of our attention is not the dream as a whole but the separate portions of its content. If I say to a patient who is still a novice: "What occurs to you in connection with this dream?," as a rule his mental horizon becomes a blank. If, however, I put the dream before him cut up into pieces, he will give me a series of associations to each piece, which might be described as the "background thoughts" of that particular part of the dream. Thus the method of dream interpretation which I practise already differs in this first important respect from the popular, historic and legendary method of interpretation by means of symbolism and approximates to the second or "decoding" method. Like the latter, it employs interpretation *en détail* and not *en masse;* like the latter, it regards dreams from the very first as being of a composite character, as being conglomerates of psychical formations.[11]

This kind of *ad locum* form of interpretation runs through a great deal of the Jewish literature. It is the pattern of the rabbinic literature and the *Zohar,* although the latter may be more freely associative. The way to the hidden or deeper meaning of the Torah is to pluck the passage out of its context, to find, if not the conglomerates of the *psychical* formations, then the conglomerates of the *divine*[12] formations. To show the essential similarity of style, we present a passage written by Freud and a passage from the *Zohar.* It should be apparent, inci-

dentally, that although the associations are "free" in both excerpts, they do not run completely wild.

Presenting his critical dream, the one of Irma's injection,
Freud first relates the whole dream. Then he takes each detail
separately and comments upon it.

The hall—numerous guests, whom we were receiving. We were
spending that summer at Bellevue, a house standing by itself
on one of the hills adjoining the Kahlenberg. The house had
formerly been designed as a place of entertainment and its re-
ception-rooms were in consequence unusually lofty and hall-
like. . . .

*I reproached Irma for not having accepted my solution; I
said: "If you still get pains, it's your own fault."* I might have
said this to her in waking life, and I may actually have done so.
It was my view at the time (though I have since recognized
it as a wrong one) that my task was fulfilled when I had in-
formed a patient of the hidden meaning of his symptoms: I
considered that I was not responsible for whether he accepted
the solution or not—though this was what success depended
on. . . .

*Irma's complaint: pains in her throat and abdomen and stom-
ach: it was choking her.* Pains in the stomach were among my
patient's symptoms but were not very prominent; she com-
plained more of feelings of nausea and disgust. Pains in the
throat and abdomen and constriction of the throat played
scarcely any part in her illness. . . .

She looked pale and puffy. My patient always had a rosy
complexion. I began to suspect that someone else was being
substituted for her.

*I was alarmed at the idea that I had missed an organic ill-
ness.* This, as may well be believed, is a perpetual source of
anxiety to a specialist whose practice is almost limited to neurotic patients and who is in the habit of attributing to hysteria

a great number of symptoms which other physicians treat as organic. . . .

I took her to the window to look down her throat. She showed some recalcitrance, like women with false teeth. I thought to myself that really there was no need for her to do that. I had never had any occasion to examine Irma's oral cavity. What happened in the dream reminded me of an examination I had carried out some time before of a governess: at a first glance she had seemed a picture of youthful beauty, but when it came to opening her mouth she had taken measures to conceal her plates. This led to recollection of other medical examinations and of little secrets revealed in the course of them—to the satisfaction of neither party. . . .[13]

The analysis of the dream continues for several pages in this manner.[14] To indicate its stylistic similarity to the *Zohar,* the latter may be opened virtually at random:

AND JOSEPH WAS BROUGHT DOWN TO EGYPT, AND POTIPHAR BOUGHT HIM, ETC. The expression "was brought down" indicates that God approved of the act, so as to bring to fulfillment the announcement made to Abram between the pieces: "thy seed shall be a stranger," etc. (Gen. xv, 13) AND POTIPHAR BOUGHT HIM, for a sinful purpose. . . .

AND THE LORD WAS WITH JOSEPH, AND HE WAS A PROSPEROUS MAN; AND HE WAS IN THE HOUSE OF HIS MASTER THE EGYPTIAN. R. Jose quoted the verse: "For the Lord loveth justice, and forsaketh not his saints; they are preserved for ever" (Ps. xxxvii, 28). "Observe," he said, "that wherever the righteous walk, God protects them and never abandons them, as David said: 'Yea, though I walk through the valley of the shadow of death, I will fear no evil, for thou art with me, thy rod and staff they comfort me' (Ibid. xxiii, 4); wherever the righteous walk the Shekinah accompanies them and does not abandon them. Joseph walked through the valley of the shadow of death, having been brought down to Egypt, but the Shekinah was with him. . . ."

AND IT CAME TO PASS AFTER THESE THINGS THAT HIS MASTER'S WIFE, ETC. R. Hiya discussed the text: *Bless the Lord, ye angels of his, ye mighty in strength, that fulfil his word, hearkening unto the voice of his word* ([Ps.] ciii, 20). "How greatly," he said, "it behoves a man to guard against sin and pursue the straight path, so that the evil prompter, his daily assailant, should not lead him astray. And since he assails man perpetually, it behoves man to muster all his force against him and to entrench himself in the place of strength; for as the evil prompter is mighty, it behoves man to be mightier still; and those sons of men who do excel him in might are called 'mighty in strength,' dealing with him in his own coin, and they are 'the angels of the Lord' who come from the side of *Geburah* (Might) to deal mightily with him. Such a one was Joseph, who was called 'righteous' and guarded in purity the sign of the holy covenant [the circumcision] which was imprinted upon him." R. Eleazar said: "The word 'after' here alludes to the evil prompter, being the name of a grade as we have laid down. Joseph exposed himself to his accusations because he used to pay great attention to his personal appearance. That gave the evil prompter an opening to say: 'Behold, his father observes mourning for him, and he decks himself out and curls his hair!' Thus the bear was let loose, as it were, and set upon him."

AND IT CAME TO PASS AFTER THESE THINGS. When God surveys the world with intent to judge it, and finds there wicked people, then, in the words of the Scripture, "He shuts up the heaven, so that there shall be no rain, and the ground shall not yield her fruit" (Deut. xi, 17); through the sins of the sons of men heaven and earth are shut up and do not perform their functions. . . .

AND IT CAME TO PASS, AS SHE SPOKE TO JOSEPH DAY BY DAY. R. Eleazar discoursed on the verse: *To keep thee from the evil woman, etc.* (Prov. vi, 24). "Happy," he said, "are the righteous

256

who know the ways of the Almighty and follow them, since they devote themselves to the Torah day and night. . . ." [15]

We note that in addition to the free associations on the Biblical text, the *Zohar* frequently brings in as associative material additional Biblical text. Freud does this too. Thus in his account of the dream of Irma's injection, while "discoursing" on a sentence from the dream, he writes,

> It was as though the replacement of one person by another was to be continued in another sense: This Mathilde for that Mathilde, *an eye for an eye and a tooth for a tooth* [our italics].[16]

We can distinguish among three "grades" of the method of free association as it appears in Jewish tradition. First is the rabbinic literature which has the *ad locum* feature but stays relatively disciplined. Second is the type represented by the *Zohar*. The *Zohar* has its own fundamental idiom, largely sexual-cosmological, whereby its *ad locum* interpretations are less literal and more "free." Third, in Abulafia, whom we have discussed earlier,[17] we have the most unlimited use of the associative methods. Instead of using Biblical text as the starting point for his meditations, he uses his own written productions. Freud, when interpreting dreams, follows the pattern of the *Zohar*. In his general practice of psychoanalysis, however, he is closer to the pattern of Abulafia.

C. DREAM INTERPRETATION IN THE TRACTATE BERAKOTH

Among the various folk-religious practices and beliefs of the Jews, which included the usual repertoire of beliefs in angels and demons and varieties of magical practices, dream interpretation was one of the foremost. Characteristically, the rabbinical attitude was hostile to these activities.

> The rabbis sought to eradicate these practices, or at least to transmute their offensive features. But their efforts met with only indifferent success, and they were often obliged to accord the elements of this folk religion a grudging recognition and acceptance. "Better is it that Israel should sin unwittingly than consciously break the law." [18]

The traveling bookseller was an institution in the Eastern European Jewish community. Among his most popular items were the dream books, which told the meaning of any dream one might have.[19] The dream book of Solomon B. Jacob Almoli, *Pitron Chalomot,* was one of the most sought after. Freud makes a reference to Almoli in a footnote that he added to *The Interpretation of Dreams* in 1914.[20] Almoli's book was first published in 1515 and was republished many times. In 1694 a Yiddish translation appeared which still had a wide circulation in pre-Hitler Europe.

The fundamental principles of dream interpretation used by Freud are already present in the Talmud. We have previously drawn a heavy line of separation between Talmud and Kabbala. This line was primarily drawn socially, and arose particularly in connection with the Sabbatian movement. It did not block diffusion both ways of legalistic and mystical thought; and scholars often concerned themselves with both Kabbala and Talmud.

The tractate *Berakoth,* one of the less legalistic in the Talmud, contains one of the most extensive treatments of dreams and dream interpretation in rabbinic literature. Down through the centuries it served as a basic guide for dream interpretation. The fundamental similarity between its methods and those used by psychoanalysis has already been recognized in the psychoanalytic literature.[21] Although *Berakoth,* in its discussion of dreams, contains many of the primitive notions criticized by Freud in the first chapter of *The Interpretation of Dreams,* we find within it a number of features which are very closely akin to psychoanalytic theory.

Thus we read in *Berakoth:*

> R. Samuel b. Nahmani said in the name of R. Jonathan: A man is shown in a dream only what is suggested by his own thoughts. . . .[22]

On the use of sexual symbolism in the dream we read:

> I saw myself [in a dream] pouring oil on olives. He [the interpreter] replied: [This man] has outraged his mother. . . . He said to him: I dreamt that my eyes were kissing one another. He replied: [This man] has outraged his sister. He said to him: I dreamt that I kissed the moon. He replied: He has outraged the wife of an Israelite. He said to him: I dreamt that I was walking in the shade of a myrtle. He replied: He has outraged a betrothed damsel.* He said to him: I dreamt that there was a shade above me, and yet it was beneath me. He replied: It means unnatural intercourse. . . .[23]

Word play is used, as for example,

> I dreamt that they said to me: You will die in Adar and not see Nisan.† He replied: You will die in all honor [*adrutha*]

---

* The editor's footnote explains "For whom it is usual to make a canopy of myrtle."

† Adar and Nisan are the names of months.

and not be brought into temptation [*nisayon*].[24]

He said to him: I dreamt that people told me: Your father has left you money in Cappadocia. He said to him: Have you money in Cappadocia? No. In that case, he said *kappa* means a beam and *dika* mean ten.‡ Go and examine the beam which is at the head of ten, for it is full of coins.[25]

Although the prophetic feature of dream interpretation is still present, nevertheless intimations of dreams as wish fulfillment, as interpretable by word play, as having sexual significance, as being basically symbolic, as involving a conflict of "good" and "evil" impulses, are clearly present in *Berakoth*. Even the full prophetic nature of the dream is denied: "Neither a good dream nor a bad dream is ever wholly fulfilled";[26] and "While a part of a dream may be fulfilled, the whole of it is never fulfilled."[27]

Of critical importance is the fact that *Berakoth* already uses sexual imagery to symbolize knowing. Thus we read:

> If one dreams that he has intercourse with his mother, he may expect to obtain understanding.* . . . If one dreams he has intercourse with a betrothed maiden, he may expect to obtain knowledge of Torah. . . . If one dreams he has had intercourse with his sister, he may expect to obtain wisdom. . . . If one dreams he has intercourse with a married woman, he can be confident that he is destined for the future world, provided, that is, he does not know her and did not think of her in the evening.[28]

‡ In Aramaic *kappa* and Greek for *dika*.

* This is based on an ambiguity in the text (Proverbs 2:3). The original text does not include pure vowel sounds. Thus the distinction between the word *im*, which means "if," and *aym*, which means "mother," is usually made on the basis of the context. In this instance the context does not help because a sensible sentence is possible both ways. The sentence can mean either "If thou wilt call for understanding [*Binah*]" or "Thou wilt call understanding mother."

Berakoth laid down two fundamental principles of dream interpretation, which became integral to the subsequent tradition. The first is that all dreams have meaning.

A dream which is not interpreted is like a letter which is not read.[29] (This presumably comes from R. Hisda in the third century.) We recall in this connection that Freud calls his book *Die Traumdeutung, The Interpretation of Dreams,* and begins the exposition of his views as follows:

> The title that I have chosen for my work makes plain which of the traditional approaches to the problem of dreams I am inclined to follow. The aim which I have set before myself is to show that dreams are capable of being interpreted. . . . My presumption that dreams can be interpreted at once puts me in opposition to the ruling theory of dreams . . . for "interpreting" a dream implies assigning a "meaning" to it—that is, replacing it by something which fits into the chain of our mental acts as a link having a validity and importance equal to the rest. As we have seen, the scientific theories of dreams leave no room for any problem of interpreting them. . . . Lay opinion has taken a different attitude throughout the ages. . . . Led by some obscure feeling, it seems to assume that, in spite of everything, every dream has a meaning, though a hidden one, that dreams are designed to take the place of some other process of thought, and that we have only to undo the substitution correctly in order to arrive at this hidden meaning.[30]

The second fundamental principle formulated in *Berakoth* was "All dreams follow the mouth" [31] or "All dreams follow their interpretation." This dictum was the basic one in the history of dream interpretation among the Jews for centuries.[32] According to this principle, *the interpretation of the dream had priority over the dream itself,* especially the first interpretation.

Actually this principle is but a carry-over of the traditional view that the interpretation of Torah has priority over the Torah itself with respect to the conduct of the Jews. *The important consequence of this dictum is that it lends tremendous conviction to the interpretation of the dream.* The significance of whatever first comes to the "mouth" is enhanced, thereby encouraging a kind of free association as a technique for ascertaining meaning. On the basis of this second dictum the question of the *validity* of an interpretation, as to whether or not a given interpretation is *really* what the dream means, becomes meaningless.

We see in this feature of the tradition some basis for the sense of conviction Freud showed with respect to his interpretations. Alternative interpretations never disturbed him. In usual scientific thought, one pits one explanation against another in logical counterposition. Freud, however, with his doctrine of overdetermination and overinterpretation of dreams, made such counterposition inappropriate for dream interpretation. In his view, different and contradictory interpretations could be maintained simultaneously, and hence the doctrine that "dreams follow their interpretations" could never be violated. The idea of multiple interpretation is also contained in *Berakoth:*

> There were twenty-four interpreters of dreams in Jerusalem. Once I dreamt a dream and I went round to all of them and they all gave different interpretations, and all were fulfilled, thus confirming that which is said: All dreams follow the mouth.[33]

The doctrine that "dreams follow their interpretations" led historically to certain difficulties. Since any interpretation given was valid, the choice of an interpreter was critical. The authors of *Berakoth* were aware of the dangers inherent in this principle and tell, as a case in point, of an interpreter of dreams: "To one who paid him he used to give a favourable interpretation and to one who did not pay him he gave an unfavourable interpretation." [34]

When Almoli's book came out in the sixteenth century, a radical change was wrought in connection with dream interpretation. Almoli could not accept the view that God's will as expressed in the dream could be so readily determined. Almoli insisted that dream interpretation required intensive training. The dream interpreter must take into account the circumstances and environment of the dreamer. There were, he said, fine shades of meaning in dream symbolism which could be ascertained only by understanding both the principles of dream interpretation and characteristics of the dreamer.[35]

D. WORDPLAY

As we have seen, *Berakoth* uses wordplay to plumb the hidden meaning of dreams. In the mystical tradition wordplay becomes an integral part of the search for the hidden meaning of the Torah. Concerning this hidden meaning, each word is apparently conceived as having its latent content. We read in the *Zohar*:

How assiduously should one ponder on each word of the Torah, for there is not a single word in it which does not contain allusions to the Supernal Holy Name, not a word which does not contain many mysteries, many aspects, many roots, many branches.[36]

On the text,

FEAR AND DREAD FALL UPON THEM. R. Simeon interpreted the word *aymathah* (dread, instead of the usual *aymah*) as *aymath he,* "the fear of *He*" (i.e., the Shekinah), since there is no letter or word in the Torah that does not contain profound allusions.[37]

As another example:

LIGHT, AND THERE WAS LIGHT. These words imply that there had already been light. This word, *awr* (light), contains in itself a hidden significance. The expansive force proceeding from the hidden recesses of the secret supernal ether opened a path and produced from itself a mysterious point (or, rather the *En Sof* [Limitless] clave its own ether and disclosed this point), *Yod.* When this expanded, that which was left of the mysterious AWIR (ether) was found to be AWR (light).*

In addition to simple wordplay, which one finds throughout the *Zohar,* there is also considerable numerological play, based largely on the fact that each Hebrew character has a numerical value. For example,

GET THEE FORTH. R. Simeon said: "What is the reason that the first communion which God held with Abraham commenced with the words 'Get thee forth' *(lech lecha)?* It is that the numerical value of the letters of the words *lech lecha* is a hundred, and hence they contained a hint to him that he would beget a son at the age of a hundred. See now, whatever God does upon the earth has some inner and recondite purpose.[38]

---

* *Zohar,* I, p. 69. The -I- of the transliteration, AWIR, is the *yod.* There is the possibility, as passages such as this suggest, of relations between Kabbala and general science, e.g., the relation of ether and light. But it is beyond the scope of this essay to pursue this.

Freud's use of wordplay as a device for ascertaining unconscious material is well known. In *The Interpretation of Dreams,* for example, he writes:

> A still deeper interpretation led to sexual dream-thoughts, and I recalled the meaning which references to Italy seem to have had in the dreams of a woman patient who had never visited that lovely country: *"gen Italien* [to Italy]"—"Genitalien [genitals]." [39]

As another example—many of these can be cited—he writes:

> One of my women patients told me a short dream which ended in a meaningless verbal compound. She dreamt she was with her husband at a peasant festivity and said: *"This will end in a general 'Maistollmütz'. . . ."* In the dream she had a vague feeling that it was some kind of a pudding made with maize—a sort of polenta. Analysis divided the word into *"Mais"* [maize], *"toll"* [mad], *"mannstoll"* [nymphomaniac—literally, "mad for men"] and *Olmütz* [a town in Moravia]. All these fragments were found to be remnants of a conversation she had had at a table with her relatives. The following words lay behind *"Mais"* (in addition to a reference to the recently opened Jubilee Exhibition): *"Meissen"* (a Meissen [Dresden] porcelain figure representing a bird); *"Miss"* (her relatives' English governess had gone to Olmütz); and *"mies"* (a Jewish slang term, used jokingly to mean "disgusting"). A long chain of thoughts and associations led off from each syllable of this verbal hotch-potch. [40]

As for Freud's use of numerology, the best example is the one which he reported in his *Psychopathology of Everyday Life:*

> In a letter to a friend, I informed him that I had finished reading the proof sheets of *The Interpretation of Dreams,* and that I did not intend to make any further changes in it, "even if it

contained 2,467 mistakes." I immediately attempted to explain to myself the number and added this little analysis as a postscript to the letter. It will be best to quote it now as I wrote it when I caught myself in this transaction:

"I will add hastily another contribution to the *Psychopathology of Everyday Life*. You will find in the letter the number 2,467 as a jocose and arbitrary estimation of the number of errors that may be found in the dream book. I meant to write: no matter how large the number might be, and this one presented itself. But there is nothing arbitrary or undetermined in the psychic life. You will therefore rightly suppose that the unconscious hastened to determine the number which was liberated by consciousness. Just previous to this, I had read in the paper that General E. M. had been retired as Inspector-General of Ordnance. You must know that I am interested in this man. While I was serving as military medical student, he, then a Colonel, once came into the hospital and said to the physician: 'You must make me well in eight days, as I have some work to do for which the Emperor is waiting.'

"At that time, I decided to follow this man's career, and just think, today (1899) he is at the end of it—Inspector-General of Ordnance and already retired. I wished to figure out in what time he had covered this road, and assumed that I had seen him in the hospital in 1882. That would make 17 years. I related this to my wife, and she remarked, 'Then you, too, should be retired.' And I protested, 'The Lord forbid!' After this conversation, I seated myself at the table to write to you. The previous train of thought continued, and for good reason. The figuring was incorrect; I had a definite recollection of the circumstances in my mind. I had celebrated my coming of age, my 24th birthday, in the military prison (for being absent without permission). Therefore, I must have seen him in 1880, which makes it 19 years ago. You then have the number 24 in 2,467! Now take the number that represents my age, 43, and add 24 years to it and you get 67! That is, to the question whether I wished to retire, I had expressed the wish to work

266

24 years more. Obviously, I am annoyed that in the interval during which I followed Colonel M., I have not accomplished much myself, and still there is a sort of triumph in the fact that he is already finished, while I still have all before me. Thus we may justly say that not even the unintentionally thrown-out number 2,467 lacks its determination from the unconscious."

Since this first example of the interpretation of an apparently arbitrary choice of number, I have repeated a similar test with the same result; but most cases are of such an intimate content that they do not lend themselves to report.[41]

Characteristically, letter play—called *zeruf* (combination) in Jewish mysticism—is summarized under three major rubrics, *gematria, notarikon,* and *temurah. Gematria* establishes meaning on the basis of the numerical value of words. *Notarikon* proceeds by making words from the first or last letters of other words. Thus *chen,* which means grace, is the same as the first letters of *chokmah nistarah,* meaning hidden wisdom. *Temurah* changes words by changing the order of their letters. In the *Sefer Yetzirah* we have *oneg,* which means pleasure, and *nega* which means pain, the same letters in different order.[42]

The techniques of *temurah,* in particular, are interesting for their similarity to the word forms Freud discusses in his essay, "The Antithetical Sense of Primal Words." [43] He starts his discussion by indicating that "the word 'No' does not seem to exist for a dream. Dreams show a special tendency to reduce two opposites to a unity or to represent them as one thing." [44] He tells us that the ancient dream interpreters supposed that anything in a dream could mean its opposite. He cites Abel, whose essay on the Egyptian language he is reviewing in the paper, to the effect that the Egyptians had many words which could reverse meaning and sound, and also that the Egyptian language had words of compounded opposites, such as *old-young, farnear, bindloose, outsideinside,* which meant only young, near, bind, and inside, respectively.

Freud's *temuric* penchant is even more aptly shown in the following, which includes a quotation from Abel:

> For comparison with the dream-work there is significance in still another very strange characteristic of the Ancient Egyptian tongue. "In Egyptian, words could—we will at first say, apparently—*reverse their sound as well as their sense.* Let us suppose the word 'good' was Egyptian; then it could mean 'bad' as well as 'good,' and be pronounced *doog* as well as *good.* Of such reversals of sound, which are too numerous to be explained as chance-products, plenty of examples can be produced from the Aryan and Semitic languages. If we confine ourselves at first to Germanic, we find: *Topf* (pot)—pot; boat—tub; wait—*täuwen* (wait); hurry—*Ruhe* (rest); care—reck; *Balken* (club)—*Kloben* (club). If we take into consideration the other Indo-Germanic tongues the number of relevant cases grows accordingly; for example, *capere-packen; ren-Niere* (kidney); leaf—*folium;* dum-a, θυμός—(Sanscrit) mêdh, mûdha, *Mut; rauchen* (to smoke)—(Russian) *Kur-it; kreischen* (to shriek)—shriek; and so on."

The phenomenon of *reversal of sound* Abel tries to explain as a doubling, reduplication, of the root. Here we should find some difficulty in following the philologist. We remember how fond children are of playing at reversing the sounds of words, and how frequently the dream-work makes use for various ends of a reversal of the material to hand for representation. (Here it is no longer letters but visual images of which the order is reversed.) We should therefore rather be inclined to derive the reversal of sound from a factor of deeper origin.[45]

NOTES TO CHAPTER 32

1. Cf. Sachs's image of Freud as standing at Mount Sinai, p. 124, above.
2. *Zohar*, V, p. 211.
3. Freud, *Fragments of an Analysis of a Case of Hysteria,* Standard Edition, VII, pp. 3-122.
4. Freud, *Moses and Monotheism,* pp. 27-28.
5. Cf. p. 142, above.
6. Freud, *Basic Writings,* p. 151.
7. Freud, *Basic Writings,* p. 151.
8. Cf. pp. 25 ff., above.
9. Freud, *The Int. of Dreams,* pp. 513-514. In the German this is ". . . das haben wir behandelt wie einen heiligen Text." Freud, *Gesammelte Werke,* Band II, III (London: Imago Publishing Co., 1948), p. 518.
10. Freud, *Col. Papers,* II, p. 224.
11. Freud, *The Int. of Dreams,* pp. 103-104.
12. Cf. p. 251, above.
13. Freud, *The Int. of Dreams,* pp. 108-109.
14. Freud, *The Int. of Dreams,* to p. 118.
15. *Zohar,* II, pp. 219-223.
16. Freud, *The Int. of Dreams,* p. 112; Exodus 21:24.
17. Cf. pp. 75 ff.
18. Trachtenberg, *Jewish Magic and Superstition,* p. viii.
19. Mark Zborowski and Elizabeth Herzog, *Life Is with People: The Jewish Little-Town of Eastern Europe.* (New York: International Universities Press, 1952), p. 127. (also Schocken Paperback, 1962)
20. Freud, *The Int. of Dreams,* p. 4.
21. I. Velikovsky, "Psychoanalytische Ahnungen in der Traumdeutungskunst der alten Hebräer nach dem Traktat Brachoth," *Die Psychoanalytische Bewegung,* 18, pp. 117-121; B. Cohen, "Über Traumdeutung in der jüdischen Tradition," *Imago* (1932, 1933), 5, 66-69.
22. The Babylonian Talmud, *Seder Zeraim; Berakoth,* trans. M.

Simon, ed. I. Epstein (London: Soncino Press, 1948), pp. 341-342.

23. *Berakoth*, p. 347.
24. *Berakoth*, p. 346.
25. *Berakoth*, p. 347.
26. *Berakoth*, p. 337.
27. *Berakoth*, p. 337.
28. *Berakoth*, p. 351.
29. *Berakoth*, p. 337.
30. Freud, *The Int. of Dreams*, p. 96.
31. *Berakoth*, p. 345.
32. Trachtenberg, *Jewish Magic and Superstition*, pp. 235 ff.
33. *Berakoth*, p. 341.
34. *Berakoth*, p. 342.
35. Trachtenberg, *Jewish Magic and Superstition*, pp. 236-237.
36. *Zohar*, III, p. 172.
37. *Zohar*, III, p. 185.
38. *Zohar*, I, p. 268.
39. Freud, *The Int. of Dreams*, pp. 231-232.
40. Freud, *The Int. of Dreams*, pp. 296-297.
41. Freud, *Basic Writings*, pp. 152-153.
42. Müller, *History of Jewish Mysticism*, pp. 49-50.
43. Freud, *Col. Papers*, IV, pp. 184-191.
44. Freud, *Col. Papers*, IV, p. 184.
45. Freud, *Col. Papers*, IV, p. 190.

33

Sexuality

Against the background of the mores of Western civilization at the turn of the century the Freudian ideas of sexuality and its significance were bold, strange, and unconventional. It is true enough that the old conventionalism with respect to sexuality was breaking. Romanticism had played its part in ennobling sexuality, but it did so through a kind of idealism which can be traced to the Greek tradition. Breaches in conventional attitudes were also being made in connection with the general enfranchisement of women. The steady progress of the enlightenment in the illumination of area after area of human concern had finally reached the problem of human sexuality at the turn of the century. There was a sense in which the world was ready for Freud's ideas. Yet this complex message about sexuality was hardly present in the main stream of Western civilization. We find a conception of sexuality which is startlingly close to Freud's in the Kabbalistic tradition, mixed with many supernatural considerations which tend to turn the modern enlightened mind away from it.

Never in the Jewish tradition was sexual asceticism made a religious value. The commandment to be fruitful and multiply was always taken extremely seriously in both rabbinical and mystical traditions. In contrast with other ascetic forms of mysticism, the Jewish mystics ascribed sexuality to God himself. The Jewish Kabbalist saw in sexual relations between a man and his wife a symbolic fulfillment of the relationship between God and the Shekinah. And drawing from the fact that the Bible uses the same word for both knowledge and sexual relations, knowledge itself is viewed as having a deeply erotic character.[1]

It is to be noted that the ideal form of sexuality is conceived of as heterosexual, and in particular as realized in marriage. Marital sexuality becomes the symbol for creativity. Thus Freud's use of the idiom of sexuality as the basic one for the expression of all the deeper and more profound problems of mankind is entirely in the spirit of Kabbala. Moreover, it should be recalled in this connection that Freud's concept of sexuality is by no means libertine. Freud had as a norm the so-called "genital" form of sexuality, most adequately realized in marriage. The Talmud and the whole orthodox tradition had pressed the marital form of sexuality into a normative position. Kabbala accepted this normative form but turned it into a cosmology and a fundamental idiom.

The soul, according to the *Zohar,* has an unquenchable yearning to be united with its source in God. This union is characteristically discussed in the metaphor of sex. Generally speaking, the union of male and female is taken as the ideal form of existence. Thus human sexual relations become symbolic vehicles of Divine acts; and the Divine creativity is understood as of a deeply erotic character itself.

One of the theological ideas in Judaism is the Shekinah, God's Divine Presence. In Kabbala this becomes highly feminized, the female counterpart of God, and part of God himself. It is perhaps about this idea that the whole mystery of the Kabbala revolves. The notion of the Shekinah is really a complex of many meanings. But somehow the sexual runs through all of the meanings associated with this maternal figure. In the complexity of meaning associated with the Shekinah we have much the pattern for the appreciation of the nature of sexuality as understood by Freud. For in Freud, sexuality is not the simple physical act of copulation, but is rather a complex metaphor in which all human meanings are somehow involved.

The Shekinah is also identified as the Community of Israel,[2] with God as her spouse.

> In the Book of Rab Hamnuna the Elder it is written that so long as the Community of Israel is in the Holy One, blessed be He, the latter, so to speak, is complete and pleased with himself from sucking the milk of the supernal Mother, and from that draught He waters all the others and gives them suck. We have learnt also that R. Simeon said that as long as the Community of Israel is in the Holy One, blessed be He, the latter is complete and joyful, and blessings abide in Him and issue from Him to all the others, but when the Community of Israel is not in the Holy One, blessed be He, then, as it were, blessings are withheld from Him and from all the others. The secret of the matter is that wherever male and female are not found together, blessings do not rest. Hence the Holy One, blessed be He, laments and weeps. . . . And when the Community of Israel

273

went into exile, she said to Him, "Tell me, O thou whom my soul loveth, how shalt thou feed thyself from the deep river that ever flows, how shalt thou feed thyself from the light of the supernal Eden, how shalt thou feed all the others that depend on thee, just as I too was fed from thee every day and watered all those below, and Israel too were fed by me? And now how shall I be as one that is veiled, as one that fainteth without blessings for lack of the blessings that I require and have not? How shall I be able to lead without feeding the flocks of thy companions, to wit, Israel, the children of the patriarchs, who are a holy chariot above?" [3]

Man is created at the instigation of the Shekinah. She it is who takes the burden of the sin of man.

She replied, "Since his guilt is referred to the mother and not the father, I desire to create him in my likeness." [4]

On account of the darkness, which was destined to sin against the light, the Father was not willing to share in man's creation, and therefore the Mother said: "Let us make man in our image after our likeness." [5]

A distinct sense of the fundamentality of the Oedipus complex emerges in the following passage:

. . . the created Torah is a vestment to the Shekinah, and if man had not been created, the Shekinah would have been without a vestment like a beggar. Hence when a man sins it is as though he strips the Shekhinah of her vestments, and that is why he is punished; and when he carries out the precepts of the Law, it is as though he clothes the Shekinah in her vestments. [6]

According to the *Zohar,*

Moses cohabited with the Shekinah, who is symbolized by the man, even while the spirit dwelt in his body, and he subjected her to his desires. [7]

274

We are reminded here of Freud's reference to Oedipus as "that mythical lawbreaker."

We are aware of the criticism leveled against Freud for his assertion of the *universality* of the Oedipus complex; and that Freud continued to maintain his assertion in spite of this criticism. With the Kabbalistic tradition opened to us as a background, we believe that we can better appreciate this element in Freud's thought. The basic criticism against the doctrine of the Oedipus complex is that it is modeled along the lines of the particular type of family constellation to be found in Freud's immediate culture. It is claimed that Freud committed the fallacy of ethnocentrism, that he overgeneralized on the basis of a particular culture.

We recall in this connection the significance that Freud attached to the actual witnessing of the "primal scene." We believe that the essential truth in Freud's doctrine lies in the fundamental curiosity displayed by children concerning the nature of their own being. As the child's self-consciousness develops, as he begins to wonder and seek answers to questions concerning the origin of things, he asks also about his own origins. This question is perhaps more universal among children than the Oedipus complex in the particulars as sometimes outlined by Freud. But with the metaphor of the Oedipus complex, Freud was able to seize upon the much more critical question that is in the life history of each person, the question "Where did I come from?" If the Oedipus complex does not exist cross-culturally in its limited form, it exists cross-culturally in the more general form of the sense of wonder at one's own being. The Oedipus complex is a profound metaphor which catches at the deep mystery of human existence. *That this sense of mystery should be referred to the sexual is one of the great insights Freud provided. But this insight, that being has its origins in the sexual, that the sexual is thus one with the metaphysical and the theological, is central to Kabbala.*

The mystery of the Oedipus complex is the mystery of the story of genesis, creation. As Freud says in discussing the development of sexual consciousness,

> Corresponding with the history of this awakening, the first problem with which he [the child] occupies himself is not the question as to the difference between the sexes, but the riddle: Where do children come from? In a distorted form which can be easily unraveled, this is the same riddle which was proposed by the Theban Sphinx.[8]

In Freud's use of the story, the secret of the origin of things is the secret of the creation of the individual. What the child wants to know is how he was created; and the secret which he discovers is that the moment of his creation was the moment in which his father and mother were having sexual intercourse. There is thus a sense in which the essential feature of the Oedipal wish is the wish to have been present to witness the act of one's own creation. This wish is transformed into the fantasy of the primal scene, and the urge to replace the father in the act of creation.

As Jones and others have pointed out, the Oedipus complex was one of Freud's most important contributions. According to Kabbala it is as the father is beheld that great knowledge is received. (Kabbala means "received.") We recall in this connection that Freud wrote of his *The Interpretation of Dreams* that it was a reaction to his father's death,[9] and that "Insight such as this falls to one's lot but once in a lifetime." [10] The *Zohar,* in speaking of Joseph, with whom Freud avowedly identified himself, says,

> So Joseph, in whatever he was about to do, used to contemplate in the spirit of wisdom the image of his father,* and so he prospered and an augmentation of spirit came upon him with a higher illumination. When that sinner said to him: "Behold, a vine was before me," Joseph was alarmed, not knowing what import it might have; but when he continued, "and in the vine were three branches," straightway Joseph's spirit was astir and received an influx of energy and illumination, because, at the same time he gazed at the image of his father, and knew the meaning of the words he heard.[11]

Kabbalistic profundity with respect to sexuality is evident also in the idea of the *ninth Sephira.* According to the tradition there are ten *Sephiroth,* which are the mystical emanations and dominions of God. Each of the *Sephiroth* is associated with a part of God. The ninth Sephira is called *Y'sod,* which means foundation, and the *Y'sod* is located at God's genitalia. The word *Y'sod* means not only foundation, but contains within it also the word *sod* meaning secret. The sexual is the secret foundation of all things. The *Malkuth,* the Kingdom, issues from the *Y'sod;* and all of the higher *Sephiroth* of God flow into it. Thus the *Y'sod* is the locus and fountain of all life and vitality, and from it the world is nurtured.

The *Zohar* refers repeatedly to the union of God with His Shekinah, the "celestial mother." Out of the *Y'sod* the major

* Whose name was Jacob like that of Freud's father.

life forces flow into the Shekinah. Scholem says that the *Y'sod* fascinated the author of the *Zohar,* and the phallic symbolism used in connection with the discussions of the *Y'sod* is, suggestive of a psychological problem in the author, if one takes into account the piety which is manifest in the *Zohar*.[12]

A parallel to the Freudian doctrine of libido, the conception of sexuality as the source of all energy pervades the *Zohar*. Moreover even what may be regarded as a "peculiarity" of Freud's doctrine of the libido is to be found in Kabbala. The peculiarity of which we speak is Freud's conception of the libido as *masculine*. Thus in Freud's discussion of libido, we find in spaced type * in editions prior to 1924 of the *Three Essays on Sexuality,*

> . . . libido is invariably and necessarily of a masculine nature whether it occurs in men or in women and irrespectively of whether its object is a man or a woman.[13]

An example of the *Zohar*'s conception of male sexuality follows.

> Now, when a female becomes pregnant from a male, it is mostly the result of an equal and reciprocal desire, or less often of the predominating desire of the female. But when the desire of the male predominates then the soul of the child that is born has unusual vitality, inasmuch as the whole of its being is the result of the desire and yearning for the tree of life.[14]

Thus vitality is traced to the male component.

Of particular interest is the Kabbalistic conception of *Daath* or knowledge. In Kabbala *Daath* is a semi-*Sephira* which re-

---

* Spaced type is sometimes used in German publications for greater emphasis and corresponds to italics.

sults from the union of the two *Sephiroth, Chokmah,* or wisdom, and *Binah,* or understanding. *Chokmah* is a male principle and *Binah* a female principle. *Daath* is the divine offspring of their mystical union.

The word *Daath* is also used for sexual intercourse. The Torah characteristically uses this word to mean copulation, as, for example, "And the man knew Eve his wife, and she conceived. . . ."[15] Thus knowledge and sexuality are identified in a syncretism through which they merge and are one and the same thing.

The basic paradigm of knowledge is union or penetration. Sexual union in the *Zohar* is spoken of as "uncovering of nakedness." *Binah* is understanding and *Binah* is Mother. Thus when a man sins sexually he "uncovers the nakedness of the Mother (*Binah*)."[16] Kabbalistically speaking, Freud came to *Binah* in his discovery of the unconscious forces in man. He had, in the idea of the Oedipus complex, an image of the "mother lying in her nakedness." We actually find this association in a paper of his called "A Religious Experience."[17] This paper is based on a letter from an American physician who reported a religious experience when he saw the body of an old woman being carried to a dissecting table. Freud says of this experience,

> We may suppose, therefore, that this was the way in which things happened. The sight of a woman's dead body, naked or on the point of being stripped, reminded the young man of his mother. It roused in him a longing for his mother which sprang from his Oedipus complex, and this was immediately completed by a feeling of indignation against his father. His ideas of "father" and "God" had not yet become widely sepa-

rated, so that his desire to destroy his father could become conscious as doubt in the existence of God and could seek to justify itself in the eyes of reason as indignation about the ill-treatment of a mother-object. It is of course typical for a child to regard what his father does to his mother in sexual intercourse as ill-treatment. The new impulse, which was displaced into the sphere of religion, was only a repetition of the Oedipus situation and consequently soon met with a similar fate. It succumbed to a powerful opposing current.[18]

Here, perhaps, is some clue to the significance of *The Interpretation of Dreams,* being, as Freud said, a reaction to his father's death. The Kabbalistic conception of knowledge brings knowing to an Oedipal-type violation. With the death of his father, he was able to marshal his forces to "uncover the nakedness" of the mother, which, in the Kabbalistic spirit, is the winning of understanding. He could penetrate the unconscious, uncover the nakedness of the mind, win its understanding, with the "audacity"—to use his word—involved in beholding *Binah* in her nakedness.

Freud was well aware of the relationship between knowledge and sexuality, pointing out that

At about the same time as the sexual life of children reaches its first peak, between the ages of three and five, they also begin to show signs of the activity which may be ascribed to the instinct for knowledge or research. This instinct cannot be counted among the elementary instinctual components, nor can it be classed as exclusively belonging to sexuality. Its activity corresponds on the one hand to a sublimated manner of obtaining mastery, while on the other hand it makes use of the energy of scopophilia. Its relations to sexual life, however, are of particular importance, since we have learnt from psycho-analysis that the instinct for knowledge in children is attracted unexpectedly early and intensively to sexual problems and is in fact possibly first aroused by them.[19]

Somewhat later in the same essay, he writes,

Finally, it is an unmistakable fact that concentration of the attention upon an intellectual task and intellectual strain in general produce a concomitant sexual excitation in many young people as well as adults. This is no doubt the only justifiable basis for what is in other respects the questionable practice of ascribing nervous disorders to intellectual "overwork." [20]

A further implication of the doctrine of *Daath* has to do with the nature of psychoanalytic therapy. In Freud's psychoanalytic theory the diagnosis of the problem is sexual, but simple sexuality is not rendered as the solution to the problem. If Freud were really following in the footsteps of Chrobak, who, Freud said, had suggested the prescription "a normal penis in repeated doses," [21] he would have regarded the solution to the problems of neurosis as just sexual in nature. Instead, Freud's "prescription" was insight. Kabbala provides us with a resolution of this difficulty. Insight is *Daath*, knowledge that comes from union—in this instance of conscious and unconscious; and *this kind of knowledge is a deeply erotic experience*. The most profound insight experience is, of course, the discovery within one's self of the Oedipus complex, which brings into the open not only the unconscious in its more general sense, but the image of the father and mother having sexual intercourse, and the substitution of oneself, in fantasy, in the act.

It is relevant to note that the fall of man as developed in the *Zohar* emphasizes the role of knowledge in sin. The passage

281

containing the idea of Moses cohabiting with the Shekinah [22] appears almost immediately before "And God said, Let us make a man." The *Zohar* interprets the Tree of *Daath*, the Tree of Knowledge, as the key to creation. R. Jose interprets the speech of the serpent to Eve,

> With this tree God created the world; eat therefore of it, and ye shall be like God, knowing good and evil, for through this knowledge he is called God.[23]

R. Judah says that the serpent said,

> Therefore, eat of it and you shall create worlds. It is because God knows this that He has commanded you not to eat of it, for every artisan hates his fellow of the same craft.[24]

And R. Jose points out that this sin was symbolic of all sin, idolatry, murder, and adultery.

> Hence all the prohibitions had reference to this tree, and when he ate of it he transgressed them all.[25]

Another pervasive feature of the *Zohar* is its view of the bisexual character of man. We have already seen a female as part of the Deity in the doctrine of the Shekinah and that Adam was supposed to have been created in the image of God and Shekinah, or God as containing the Shekinah within Him. So Adam, out of whose rib Eve was made, contains both male and female within him.

> Adam was created as a double personality (male and female), as previously explained. "And he took one of his ribs. . . ." (Gen. II, 21).[26]
>
> The first man consisted of male and female, for it says: "Let us make man in our image after our likeness" (Gen. I:26), which indicates that male and female were originally created as one and separated afterwards.[27]

282

Thus the doctrine of bisexuality, which Fliess took pains to assert as original with him, and of which Freud writes to him, "I seized eagerly on your notion of bisexuality," [28] contains its harbinger in the Kabbalistic tradition.

In Kabbala, male and female are simply two poles of an essential unity, although a disturbance of the balance of the male and the female elements leads to sin and defection.

> Observe that all spirits are compounded of male and female, and when they go forth into the world they go forth as both male and female, and afterwards the two elements are separated. If a man is worthy they are afterwards united, and it is then that he truly meets his mate and there is a perfect union both in spirit and flesh.[29]

In the *Zohar* we also read,

> "Male and female he created them." From this we learn that every figure which does not comprise male and female elements is not a true and proper figure. . . . Observe this, God does not place His abode in any place where male and female are not found together, nor are blessings found save in such a place, as it is written, AND HE BLESSED THEM AND CALLED THEIR NAME MAN ON THE DAY THAT THEY WERE CREATED: note that it says *them* and *their* name, and not *him* and *his* name. The male is not even called man till he is united with the female.[30]
>
> . . . a man who is not married is defective, and the holiness of the King flees from him.[31]

Modern thought as contrasted with Kabbala draws a sharp distinction between male and female. This difference between Kabbala and modern thought illuminates another "peculiarity" of Freudian theory. As we know, Freud made the Oedipus complex of the male in Western civilization the central feature of his *whole* theory. The fact that the Oedipal paradigm was of the male child never seemed to disturb him. He talked of it as characterizing *man* in general, not so much, we believe, as though he were ignoring women, but rather, like Kabbala, as a denial of essential distinction between the sexes. We recall in this connection Freud's concept of libido, whether in the male or female, as masculine in nature.

In sexual relations the individual loses his "alienation" in the fullest sense of the word. Generally speaking, the whole set of doctrines associated with Freud's psychoanalytic theory is opposed to this alienation, and it is perhaps, in part, as a reaction to our own contemporary alienation that Freud's ideas have won the acceptance they have. In Freud's view, the individual is a part of the larger society in an integral way. He made the relationship of the patient to the therapist one of profound intimacy. He pointed out that the transference phenomenon was a love relationship; and, in connection with love, Freud wrote:

> Normally there is nothing we are more certain of than the feeling of our self, our own ego. It seems to us an independent unitary thing, sharply outlined against everything else. That this is a deceptive appearance, and that on the contrary the ego extends inwards, without any sharp delimitation, into an unconscious mental entity which we call the id and to which it forms a façade, was first discovered by psycho-analytic research, and the latter still has much to tell us about the relations of the ego and the id. But towards the outer world at any rate the ego seems to keep itself clearly and sharply outlined and delimited. There is only one state of mind in which it fails to do this—an unusual state, it is true, but not one that can be judged as pathological. At its height the state of being in love threatens to obliterate the boundaries between ego and object. Against

all the evidence of his senses the man in love declares that he and his beloved are one, and is prepared to behave as if it were a fact.[32]

He then goes on to sketch the developmental pattern of the ego.

Originally the ego includes everything, later it detaches from itself the external world.[33]

The concept of development formulated by Freud holds that the individual is born with a bisexual constitution, that this separates later and that the person fulfills himself in heterosexuality, as is suggested by the Kabbalistic doctrine.

Freud regarded all other forms of sexual expression as in some way indicative of unhealthy psychological functioning. The following quotations show some of his views. He defined perversions as

. . . sexual activities which either (a) extend, in an anatomical sense, beyond the regions of the body that are designed for sexual union, or (b) linger over the immediate relations to the sexual object which should normally be traversed rapidly on the path towards the final sexual aim.[34]

With the arrival of puberty, changes set in which are destined to give infantile sexual life its final normal shape. The sexual instinct has hitherto been predominantly auto-erotic; it now finds a sexual object. . . . Now, however, a new sexual aim appears, and all the component instincts combine to attain it, while the erotogenic zones become subordinated to the primacy of the genital zone. Since the new sexual aim assigns very different functions to the two sexes, their sexual development now diverges greatly. . . .

The new sexual aim in men consists in the discharge of the sexual products. The earlier one, the attainment of pleasure, is by no means alien to it; on the contrary, the highest degree of pleasure is attached to this final act of the sexual process. The sexual instinct is now subordinated to the reproductive function; it becomes, so to say, altruistic. If this transformation is to succeed, the original dispositions and all the other characteristics of the instincts must be taken into account in the process. Just as on any other occasion on which the organism should by rights make new combinations and adjustments leading to complicated mechanisms, here too there are possibilities of pathological disorders if these new arrangements are not carried out. Every pathological disorder of sexual life is rightly to be regarded as an inhibition in development.[35]

We also find in Jewish tradition an adumbration of Freud's ideas on social development. Characteristic of Jewish tradition is the idea that the prepubertal stages are dominated by evil impulses. In the *Zohar* it is expressed as follows:

... the moment a child is born into the world, the evil prompter straightway attaches himself to him. ... But the good prompter first comes to man only ... when he reaches the age of thirteen years. From that time the youth finds himself attended by two companions, one on his right and the other on his left, the former being the good prompter, the latter the evil prompter.[36]

Freud regarded all that we ordinarily conceive to be unhealthy and immoral in man as lodged in the pregenital stages and, in adults, as due to a regression to these pregenital stages. Thus, for example, he writes:

The cruel component of the sexual instinct develops in childhood even more independently of the sexual activities that are attached to erotogenic zones. Cruelty in general comes easily to the childish nature, since the obstacle that brings the instinct for mastery to a halt at another person's pain—namely a capacity for pity—is developed relatively late. ... *It may be assumed that the impulse of cruelty arises from the instinct for mastery*

286

and appears at a period of sexual life at which the genitals have not yet taken over their later role [our italics]. It then dominates a phase of sexual life which we shall later describe as a pregenital organization.[37]

The *Zohar* contains advice on the proper tenderness in the conduct of sexual relations.

We make a similar reflection on the verse, "And he prayed in the place and tarried there" (Gen. xxviii, II), viz. that Jacob sought permission first. From this we learn that a man who desires his wife's society must first entreat and coax her; and if he cannot persuade her, he must not stay with her, for their companionship must be loving and unconstrained. It says further of Jacob that "he tarried there because the sun had set," which shows that sexual intercourse is forbidden during the day. Further it says that "he took of the stones of the place and put it under his head." From this we learn that even a king who has a bed of gold and precious coverings, if his wife prepares for him a bed of stones, must leave his own bed and sleep on the one which she prepares, as it is written, "and he lay down in that place." Observe that it says here AND THE MAN SAID, THIS TIME, ETC., to show that he spoke to her lovingly so as to draw her to him and win her affections. See how tender and coaxing is his language—"bone of my bone and flesh of my flesh"—to prove to her that they were one and inseparable. Then he began to sing her praises: THIS SHALL BE CALLED WOMAN, this is the peerless and incomparable one; this is the pride of the house, who surpasses all other women as a human being surpasses an ape. This one is perfect in all points, and alone merits the title of woman. Every word is inspired by love, like the verse "Many daughters have done valiantly, but thou excellest them all" (Prov. xxxi, 29). THEREFORE A MAN SHALL LEAVE HIS FATHER AND HIS MOTHER AND CLEAVE TO HIS WIFE, AND THEY SHALL BE ONE FLESH: all this, too, was to win her affection and to draw her closer.[38]

The following passage from Freud shows how close he is to the tradition, even to the point of quoting the same Biblical verse!

> These fixations of the child's feeling of affection are maintained through childhood, continually absorbing erotic elements, which are thus deflected from their sexual aims. Then, when the age of puberty is reached, there supervenes upon this state of things a powerful current of "sensual" feeling the aims of which can no longer be disguised. It never fails, apparently, to pursue the earlier paths and to invest the objects of the primary infantile choice with currents of libido that are now far stronger. But in relation to these objects it is confronted by the obstacle of the incest-barrier that has in the meanwhile been erected; consequently it seeks as soon as possible to pass on from these objects unsuited for real satisfaction to others in the world outside, with whom a real sexual life may be carried on. These new objects are still chosen after the pattern (imago) of the infantile ones; in time, however, they attract to themselves the tender feeling that had been anchored to those others. *A man shall leave father and mother—according to the Biblical precept—and cleave to his wife* [our italics]; then are tenderness and sensuality united. The greatest intensity of sensual passion will bring with it the highest mental estimation of the object (the normal over-estimation of the sexual object characteristic of men).[39]

The *Zohar* hints, at least symbolically, at the psychoanalytic notion that the depths of sexual satisfaction are in having intercourse with the Mother. The sex act in the *Zohar* is symbolic of the relationship to the supernal Mother. If a man goes on a journey,

> When he does reach home again, it is his duty to give his wife some pleasure, because it is she who procured for him this heavenly partner [the Shekinah]. It is his duty to do this for

two reasons. One is that the pleasure is a religious pleasure, and one which gives joy to the Shekinah also, and what is more, by its means he spreads peace in the world, as it is written, "thou shalt know that thy tent is in peace, and thou shalt visit thy fold and not sin" (Job. v, 24). (Is it a sin, it may be asked, if he does not visit his wife? The answer is that it is so because he thereby derogates from the honour of the celestial partner who was joined him on account of his wife.) [40]

The identification of peace with Eros, which is Freud's point in his conception of Eros as opposed to the death instinct, as he expressed it in *Civilization and Its Discontents,* is suggested by the above quotation. In addition, the following passage from the *Zohar* also suggests that the pleasure of sexual relations has an Oedipal basis and is a force for peace.

Hence "thou shalt know that thy tent is in peace," since the Shekinah comes with thee and abides in thy house, and therefore "thou shalt visit thy house and not sin," by performing with gladness the religious duty of conjugal intercourse in the presence of the Shekinah. In this way the students of the Torah who separate themselves from their wives during the six days of the week in order to devote themselves to study are accompanied by a heavenly partner in order that they may continue to be "male and female." When Sabbath comes, it is incumbent on them to gladden their wives for the sake of the honour of the heavenly partner, and to seek to perform the will of their Master, as has been said. . . . When his wife is purified [after menstruation], it is his duty to gladden her through the glad performance of a religious precept. . . . The esoteric doctrine is that men of true faith should concentrate their whole thought and purpose on this one (the Shekinah). You may object that, according to what has been said, a man enjoys greater dignity when he is on a journey than when he is at home, on account of the heavenly partner who is then associated with him. This is not so. For when a man is at home, the foundation of his house is the wife, for it is on account of her that the Shekinah departs not from the house. So our teachers have understood the verse, "and he brought her to the tent of his mother Sarah" (Gen. xxiv, 67), to indicate that with Rebecca the Shekinah came to Isaac's house. Esoterically speaking, the supernal Mother is found in company with the male only at the time when the house is prepared, and the male and female are joined. Then the supernal Mother pours forth blessings for them. Similarly the lower Mother is not found in company with the male save when the house is prepared and the male visits the female and they join together; then the lower Mother pours forth blessings for them. Hence the man in his house is to be encompassed by two females, like the male above.[41]

The sixth day is the most appropriate one for sexual intercourse. We quote the following passage to show that "genitalization" is regarded as a great blessing.

> The sixth day has more blessings than the rest, for on this day, as R. Eleazar has said, the Shekinah prepares the table for the King. Hence the sixth day has two portions, one for itself and one in preparation for the joy of the union of the King with the Shekinah, which takes place on Sabbath night, and from which all the six days of the week derive their blessing. . . . Those who are aware of this mystery of the union of the Holy One with the Shekinah on Sabbath might consider, therefore, this time the most appropriate one for their own marital union.[42]

The sexual act draws its religious significance as a symbol of the termination of the Exile. The Shekinah, who is identified with the Community of Israel, has been cast aside by her King.

> Imagine a king who was wroth with his queen and banished her from his palace for a certain time. When that time arrived

she at once returned to the king. So it happened several times. Finally, however, she was banished from the king's palace for a very long time. Said the king: "This time is not like the other times when she came back to me. This time I shall go with all my followers to find her." When he came to her he found her in the dust. Seeing her thus humiliated and yearning once more for her, the king took her by the hand, raised her up, and brought her to his palace, and swore to her that he would never part from her again. So the Community of Israel, on all previous occasions in which she was in exile, when the appointed time came, used to return of herself to the King; but in this exile the Holy One, blessed be He, will himself take her by the hand and raise her and comfort her and restore her to his palace.[43]

Concerning the man "who is improperly alone, without a wife," the *Zohar* says

... "and he hath not a second," no one to uphold him, no son to establish his name in Israel, or to bring him his due meed; "yet there is no end of all his labour," as he is always labouring, day and night; "neither is his eye satisfied with riches" [Eccl. IV, 8] and he has not the sense to reflect: "for whom, then, do I labour and bereave my soul of pleasure?" [Eccl. IV, 8]. You may say that he has pleasure in that he eats and drinks and feasts every day; but it is not so, inasmuch as his soul (*nefesh*) does not share in his pleasure, so that assuredly he bereaves his soul of pleasure, of the blissful illumination of the world to come; for it is left stunted without attaining its full and proper growth.[44]

Freud's writing is, of course, replete with similar ideas. For example,

A certain degree of direct sexual satisfaction appears to be absolutely necessary for by far the greater number of natures, and

frustration of this variable individual need is avenged by manifestations which, on account of their injurious effect on func-
tional activity and of their subjectively painful character, we
must regard as illness.[45]

We may also observe in the above quoted Zoharic passage
the notion of sublimation and substitute gratification, and its
inadequacy as a complete solution to the problem of sexual
frustration.

We turn now to the role of the incest theme in the history
of the Jews, for whatever light it may shed on Freud's repeated reference to it. The Jews, because of their endogamy,
characteristically had an incest *problem,* and part of the role
of Jewish mysticism was to provide devices for coping with the
intense feelings of guilt associated with incest wishes.

When we say that the Jews had an incest problem, what we
mean is that the incestual temptations, which are perhaps, as
Freud indicated, quite universal, were particularly exaggerated
among the Jews, causing the development of intense counterforces and consequently an exaggerated sense of guilt. The
reason for the intense incestual temptation may be traced to
two characteristics of the Jewish people. On the one hand, the
taboo against intermarriage with Gentiles was one of the se-
verest. To this day, if a member of an orthodox family marries a Gentile, the family may engage in the ritual of sitting
shib'ah, which is ordinarily performed when a person dies.
The act of sitting *shib'ah* is a declaration that he is, to all in-
tents and purposes, considered dead. On the other hand, the
Jews, particularly in eastern Europe, usually lived in small

communities so that the number of persons available for marriage was extremely limited. With the field of legitimate sex objects so highly circumscribed, existing incestual feelings could not be easily redirected, and hence called for a redoubled effort at repression. Landes and Zborowski, in their anthropological study of the eastern European Jew, tell, for example, of the extensive avoidance pattern between brother and sister, and that, for example, the parents often acted as intermediaries in cross-sex sibling relationships.[46]

To appreciate this state of affairs it might be instructive to contrast it with the romantic ideology of the free selection of mates. This ideology could take hold in a very large community, bolstered, of course, by a democratic ethic, encouraging marriages among different classes, etc. The romantic idea of free sexual selection is made possible by the low probability that the selected partner would involve one in an incestuous relationship. In the classical Oedipus story, it will be recalled, incest takes place as a result of a freak event which separated the partners so that they did not recognize each other as adults. The major reason for the customary *arrangement* of marriages by the elders of the Jewish community may very well be that the elders were the bearers of the essential information concerning consanguinity. Similarly, the tendency toward early marriage may have found its justification not only in the general realism concerning sexual impulses which existed in Jewish culture at large, but also as a device to cope with incestuous tendencies.

The *Zohar*'s comment on sibling incest is ambivalent.

For so we have affirmed in the secret doctrine of the Mishnah, that "If a man taketh his sister, his father's daughter or his mother's daughter, it is *hesed* (lit. lovingkindness); * truly so, and after *hesed* had appeared, roots and stocks came forth from beneath the highest, and branches spread and that which was near receded afar. This was at the beginning, in the hidden development of the world, but subsequently human beings who behave so 'shall be cut off before the eyes of the children of their people.' " [47]

In Freud, who conceived of Eros as lodged in incestual feelings and as the major force for love among mankind, we find exactly this relationship between incest and *hesed*.

The *Zohar* tells the following tale concerning sibling incest and relief from its associated guilt.

THE NAKEDNESS OF THY SISTER . . . THOU SHALT NOT UNCOVER. R. Abba was once going from Cappadocia to Lydda in company with R. Jose. As they were going they saw a man approaching with a mark on his face. Said R. Abba: "Let us leave this road, because that man's face testifies that he has transgressed one of the precepts of the Law against illicit intercourse." Said R. Jose: "Suppose this mark was on him from his boyhood; how can it show he has transgressed by illicit intercourse?" R. Abba replied: "I can see that he has by his face." R. Abba then called him and said: "Tell me, what is that mark on your face?" He replied: "I beg of you, do not punish me further, because my sins have caused this." "How is that?" said R. Abba. He replied: "I was once travelling with my sister, and we turned in to an inn, where I drank much wine. All that night I was in company with my sister. When I got up in the morning I found the host quarreling with another man. I interposed be-

---

* Leviticus 20:17. The appearance of the word *hesed* in this connection has been problematical, and is usually rendered as meaning that it is a *shameful* thing. The reference is also interpreted as the early necessity for such incest in the children of Adam.

tween them and received blows from both, one on one side and one on the other, and was severely wounded, but was saved by a doctor who was living among us." R. Abba asked who the doctor was, and he replied: "It was R. Simlai." "What medicine did he give you?" asked R. Abba. He replied: "Spiritual healing. From that day I repented, and every day I looked at myself in a mirror and wept before the Almighty for my sin, and from those tears my face was healed." Said R. Abba: "Were it not that you might cease repenting, I would cause that scar to be removed from your face. However, I will say over you the verse, 'And thine iniquity is taken away and thy sin purged' (Isa. vi, 7). Repeat that three times." He repeated it three times and the mark vanished; whereupon R. Abba said: "In sooth, your Master was fain to remove it from you, which shows that you have truly repented." He said: "I vow from this day to study the Torah day and night." R. Abba asked him what his name was, and he said "Eleazar." Said R. Abba: "Eleazar, God is thy help; as thy name is so art thou." He then sent him away with a blessing.[48]

The theme of the incest problem in the history of the Jews, and the special role of the mystical tradition in relieving guilt associated with incestual wishes, bring us to a consideration of *Totem and Taboo*,[49] Freud's major essay on the incest theme. We believe this essay should be grouped with Freud's *Moses and Monotheism* and his *The Moses of Michelangelo*.[50] He was evidently working on both the *Totem and Taboo* and *The Moses of Michelangelo* at the same time, the latter having been published just after the former.[51] As in the case of his Moses writings, Freud hesitated about publication, even though he regarded it as his best written work.[52] *Moses and Monotheism* is a continuation of *Totem and Taboo* according to Freud's own statement, and represents a fulfillment of what was already contained there.[53] In a very real sense *Totem and Taboo* and *Moses and Monotheism* are parts of the same essay, even though their publication is separated by about twenty-five years.

Totem and Taboo was translated into English, Hungarian, Spanish, Portuguese, French, Japanese, and Hebrew. To the Hebrew edition only did Freud feel impelled to add a new preface, in which he reaffirms his Jewish identity. In this preface Freud indicated that he had become "estranged" from the Jewish religion, but that he had not repudiated the Jewish people. He further indicated that although he did not accept the Jewish religion he was still Jewish in "essence"; and although he did not know exactly what that "essence" was, he hoped that it would become scientifically apprehensible some day.[54]

Discussing how the *Totem and Taboo* might be accepted, he once said to Abraham that it "would serve to make a sharp division between us and all Aryan religiosity. For that will be the result of it.[55]

As is well known, the book was poorly received by anthropologists, who in general felt that its assertions were not borne out by extant anthropological materials. It is not in order here to enter into a detailed consideration of the criticisms. We believe, however, that this much can be said in favor of the book: although it may fail with respect to other cultures, it deals with Jewish culture in a very profound way. It is, in effect, a treatment of two major features of Jewish culture, the problems of incest and taboo. In this essay Freud interweaves these problems, deriving taboos from incestual wishes. The taboos of which Freud speaks are readily interpreted in terms of the various taboos of Jewish orthodoxy. In Freud's essay the most important nonsexual taboos are associated with food, strongly suggestive of the food taboos, the laws of *Kashruth*, of Jewish orthodoxy. If the food taboos, for example, are interpreted as the laws of *Kashruth*, then what Freud is doing is to trace the food taboos of the Jews to incestual feelings and their associated guilt on the basis of the psychology of the Jews as he knew it. So, in *Moses and Monotheism* he used the psychology of the Jew to infer an ancient Oedipal violation. The historical allusions serve as a way of analyzing the psychology of the contemporary Jew. The fact that Freud drew so heavily from, and found essential confirmation in, Robertson Smith's *Religion of the Semites* cannot be considered fortuitous. For we believe that the essential reference points of *Totem and Taboo* are the ancient Semitic religions, as Freud understood them to have been carried on in Jewish life through the centuries. The question of the validity of Freud's analysis of religion, even with respect to Jewish religion and culture, is outside the scope of this essay. It cannot be doubted, however, that the work is directed to the acute problems faced by the Jew as he comes into the mainstreams of Western civilization, bearing the residue of the most severe sexual and dietary taboos.

To understand this work of Freud, we must again refer to the Sabbatian tendencies within Judaism. As we have pointed out, Sabbatianism provided the window—made the breaches in the old culture—through which the Jews could participate in the modern world. In complicated ways the tradition of mysticism was placed in the service of this movement. Freud may be regarded as continuing this process. In his *Totem and Ta-*

boo he uses the methods which arose in connection with individual analysis to show that the severe restrictions of spirit and action are based on archaic problems, historically inherited. In a profound sense, these restrictions are no longer appropriate to the world of the "redemption," the world of democracy, the world of enlightenment, the world of growing enfranchisement for all discriminated-against groups. The Jews might be freed from their taboos and relieved of their guilt by an understanding of the historical origins of these taboos, just as the individual may be freed from his inhibitions and guilt by an understanding of their infantile origins in psychoanalysis.

We have attempted to show in this section, partially through excerpts from written Kabbala, how close Freud's views run to the spirit of Jewish mysticism. As we have already indicated, the question of whether Freud had actually read such works as the *Zohar* is not of primary importance. What we wish to demonstrate is that somehow Freud had rewon and spoke from the vantage point of Kabbala and Jewish mysticism generally. We have shown that he had social access to this complex tradition through his family, and the Jewish milieu in Vienna, possibly through his friend Fliess, and possibly in more direct ways; and that if he were conscious of the role of this tradition in his thought it would have been well for him to conceal such a fact in view of the intense anti-Semitism that surrounded him.

It is essential to note, however, that Kabbala is only one ingredient in Freudian theory. Another element is the attitude of scientific analysis. Thus we may say of Freud that he subjected Kabbala to fine analysis. The yield may be conceived of as the integration of science and Kabbala, or the secularization and systematization of the intimate psychological features of Kabbala. From the point of view of Jewish culture this secularization is anti-Mosaic. Mysticism, being closer to rationalism, is inherently antiauthoritarian. Freud carried this antiauthoritarianism to some of its consequences.

Thereby, under the ruse of "playing the Devil" he served Sabbatian interests. He narrowed the gap between Jewish culture and Western enlightenment. In this respect, however, just as Freud may be regarded as having infused Kabbala into science, so may he be regarded as having incorporated science into Kabbala. Sabbatian-wise, by closing the gap between Jewish culture and Western enlightenment he acts as the Messiah not only for Jewish culture but for the Western culture as well.

NOTES TO CHAPTER 33

1. Scholem, p. 235.
2. Cf. pp. 278 ff., below.
3. *Zohar,* IV, pp. 354-355.
4. *Zohar,* I, p. 91.
5. *Zohar,* I, p. 92.
6. *Zohar,* I, p. 95.
7. *Zohar,* Folio I: 22a. This is not included in the Soncino English translation. The translation here is from Waite.
8. Freud, *Basic Writings,* p. 595.
9. Freud, *The Int. of Dreams,* p. xxvi.
10. Freud, *The Int. of Dreams,* p. xxxii.
11. *Zohar,* II, p. 230.
12. Scholem, pp. 227-228.
13. Freud, *Three Essays on Sexuality,* in The Standard Edition of the *Complete Psychological Works of Sigmund Freud,* trans.

and ed. James Strachey (London: Hogarth Press, 1953), VII, p. 219.

14. *Zohar,* II, p. 291.
15. Genesis 4:1.
16. *Zohar,* IV, p. 355. On *Binah* as mother, cf. footnote, p. 260, above.
17. Freud, *Col. Papers,* V, pp. 243-246.
18. Freud, *Col. Papers,* V, pp. 245-246.
19. Freud, Standard Edition, VII, p. 194.
20. Freud, Standard Edition, VII, p. 204.
21. Freud, *Col. Papers,* I, p. 296. Cf. p. 14, above.
22. Cf. p. 274, above.
23. *Zohar,* I, p. 134.
24. *Zohar,* I, p. 134.
25. *Zohar,* I, p. 135.
26. *Zohar,* III, p. 169.
27. *Zohar,* III, p. 170.
28. Freud, *Origins,* p. 242.
29. *Zohar,* V, pp. 5-6.
30. *Zohar,* I, p. 177.
31. *Zohar,* IV, p. 333.
32. Freud, *Civilization and Its Discontents,* trans. Joan Riviere (London: Hogarth Press, 1955), pp. 10-11.
33. Freud, *Civil. and Its Dis.,* p. 13.
34. Freud, Standard Edition, VII, p. 150.
35. Freud, Standard Edition, VII, pp. 207-208.
36. *Zohar,* II, p. 134.
37. Freud, Standard Edition, VII, pp. 192-193.
38. *Zohar,* I, pp. 156-157.
39. Freud, *Col. Papers,* IV, pp. 205-206.
40. *Zohar,* I, pp. 158-159.
41. *Zohar,* I, pp. 159-160.
42. *Zohar,* III, p. 198.
43. *Zohar,* IV, p. 337.
44. *Zohar,* II, pp. 214-215.
45. Freud, *Col. Papers,* II, p. 83.

46. R. Landes and M. Zborowski, "Hypotheses concerning the Eastern European Jewish Family," *Psychiatry* (1950), 13, 447-464, p. 451.
47. *Zohar,* V, p. 83.
48. *Zohar,* V, pp. 78-79.
49. Freud, Standard Edition, XIII, pp. 1-161.
50. Cf. pp. 121 ff., above.
51. Cf. Jones, II, pp. 350-367.
52. Freud, Standard Edition, XIII, p. xi.
53. Freud, *Moses and Monotheism,* p. 65.
54. Freud, Standard Edition, XIII, p. xv.
55. Jones, II, p. 350.

Epilogue

Heimlichkeit

In the speech that Freud prepared for delivery at the B'nai B'rith Lodge in Vienna on the occasion of his seventieth birthday, he sought to give some explanation for his early joining of that group. Among other reasons he said,

> But there remained enough other things to make the attraction of Judaism and Jews irresistible—many dark emotional forces, all the more potent for being so hard to group in words, as well as the clear consciousness of our inner identity, the intimacy that comes from the same psychic structure *(die Heimlichkeit der gleichen seelischen Konstruktion)*.[1]

The word *Heimlichkeit* is a difficult one to translate. It is, as a matter of fact, the subject of a detailed analysis by Freud in an essay the title of which has been translated as "The Uncanny."[2] The fact that this word is used by Freud to characterize his Jewish feeling, and that it is at the same time the subject of one of the most thorough and exhaustive treatments of a single word he ever made, places us in an unusual position for ascertaining some of the significance of Freud's Jewish feeling. Spanning Freud's expressed thoughts over a seven-year period—the essay "The Uncanny" was published in 1919, and the B'nai B'rith speech was written in 1926—we might gain some insight into the nature of Freud's Jewish identity.

A manifest difficulty immediately arises which vanishes once we have read Freud's essay. The essay is, as far as its title is concerned, about the *Unheimlich,* and his comment on his Judaism is about the *Heimlich.* This difficulty vanishes, however, because Freud says,

> Thus *heimlich* is a word the meaning of which develops towards an ambivalence, until it finally coincides with its opposite, *unheimlich. Unheimlich* is in some way or other a sub-species of *heimlich.*[3]

The essay is an attempt to plumb the nature of the experience of the uncanny. Freud gives a number of examples of uncanny experiences and what produces them and asserts that the uncanny results from something being both familiar and unfamiliar:

> . . . the "uncanny" is that class of the terrifying which leads back to something long known to us, once very familiar.[4]

It is essentially due to the rearousal of

> . . . a hidden, familiar thing that has undergone repression and then emerged from it. . . .[5]

Among the considerations in the paper, we find a detailed and scholarly etymological analysis of the word itself,[6] a discussion of death, and an assertion about psychoanalysis itself as being uncanny. He writes,

> Indeed I should not be surprised to hear that psycho-analysis, which is concerned with laying bare these hidden forces, has itself become uncanny to many people. . . .[7]

The essay "The Uncanny" is extremely rich. Many ideas are contained within it, some of which are very suggestive of the kinds of things we have been talking about throughout this essay. We will try to separate out some of the lines in the web of Freud's essay with the object of clarifying the nature of his Jewish feeling.

1. We consider first the fact that Freud regards psychoanalysis as generative of the experience of uncanniness. We recall in this connection that Freud says in *Moses and Monotheism* that

> . . . among the customs through which the Jews marked off their aloof position, that of circumcision made a disagreeable, uncanny impression on others.[8]

As we have noted earlier, Freud felt that one of the factors associated with resistance to psychoanalysis was the fact that he was a Jew. In "On the History of the Psychoanalytic Movement" he says that Janet's charge of psychoanalysis as being a peculiar product of Vienna makes him

> . . . inclined to suppose that the reproach of being a citizen of Vienna is only a euphemistic substitute for another reproach which no one would care to put forward openly.[9]

Thus we have in Freud's thought a complex which can be expressed as psychoanalysis-Jews-circumcision-uncanniness-rejection.

2. We note that this essay deals with death. In this connection we encounter a "peculiarity" which strongly suggests its autobiographical character—that somehow it relates to Freud's own sense of oncoming death. In citing examples of the uncanny, he writes:

> . . . For instance, we of course attach no importance to the event when we give up a coat and get a cloakroom ticket with the

number, say, 62; or when we find that our cabin on board ship is numbered 62. But the impression is altered if two such events, each in itself different, happen close together, if we come across the number 62 several times in a single day, or if we begin to notice that everything which has a number—addresses, hotel-rooms, compartments in railway trains—always has the same one, or one which at least contains the same figures. We do feel this to be "uncanny," and unless a man is utterly hardened and proof against the lure of superstition *he will be tempted to ascribe a secret meaning to this obstinate recurrence of a number, taking it, perhaps, as an indication of the span of life allotted to him* [our italics].[10]

We may recall in this connection Freud's demonstration that the citation of a specific number is never whimsical; and that in his analysis of such an instance the numerological significance is in terms of his age.[11] We also know that

Throughout his life Freud was much preoccupied with thoughts about death. There were reflections on its significance, fears of it and later on the wish for it. He often spoke and wrote about it to us, the burden of his remarks always being that he was growing old and had not long to live. Fliess's "periodic" calculations had given Freud fifty-one years to live. As soon as this time had passed uneventfully, Freud adopted another superstitious belief, which he told Ferenczi in 1910 he had held "for a long time": *that was that he had to die in February 1918* [our italics]. He kept looking forward to that date, usually with resignation and occasionally, in the dark days of 1917, with a sense of welcome. When that date in its turn passed quietly he made the characteristically dry comment: "That shows how little trust one can place in the supernatural." [12]

Finally we point out that the date of the publication of "The Uncanny" is 1919, which means that it was written at some time close to Freud's sixty-second birthday![13] Thus the occurrence of the number 62 in this essay points to its autobiographical character—in particular, Freud's preoccupation with his own death.

3. Freud in this essay makes inconsistent remarks about his own experience of the uncanny. At the beginning of the essay he writes:

> Jentsch quite rightly lays stress on the obstacle presented by the fact that people vary so greatly in their sensitivity to this quality of feeling. *The writer of the present contribution, indeed, must himself plead guilty to a special obtuseness in the matter, where extreme delicacy of perception would be more in place. It is long since he has experienced or heard of anything which has given him an uncanny impression,* and he will be obliged to translate himself into that state of feeling, and to awaken in himself the possibility of it before he begins [our italics].[14]

Yet he reports such experiences in himself and in connection with one of these experiences provides information which clearly dates the experience as recent and not "long since," as he avows in the above quotation. In the part of the essay which just precedes the discussion of 62, quoted above, he relates an experience of his own in Italy in which he kept trying to walk away from and kept returning against his will to the quarter where the prostitutes were located. On his third arrival, he writes, "a feeling overcame me which I can only describe as uncanny."[15]

The story of his experience in Italy is not dated for us in any way. But in relating another story he makes it very clear that the experience of the uncanny is quite recent with him at the time of the writing of the essay.

In the midst of the isolation of war-time [our italics] a number
of the English *Strand Magazine* fell into my hands. [He tells
of a story he read in the magazine and concludes:] It was a
thoroughly silly story, but the uncanny feeling it produced was
quite remarkable.[16]

On the basis of these facts it is evident that he is quite ambivalent about wanting to confess his sense of *Unheimlichkeit;*
and since he tells us that *Unheimlichkeit* and *Heimlichkeit* are
essentially the same, and characterizes his Jewish feeling as
Heimlichkeit, we are perhaps not taxing the logic of associations too much to infer an ambivalence about informing the
world about the nature of his Jewish identification.

4. In the course of this essay, we have attempted in various
ways to show the possibility of an essentially unrevealed and
perhaps unconscious Jewish base to the developments in
Freud's thought. We have also pointed out that secrecy, for
various reasons, is historically characteristic of the Kabbalistic
tradition itself, although violations of the taboo on its revelation have occurred since Maimonides. It should be noted that
Freud cites with evident favor Schelling's idea of the uncanny:

> ... we notice that Schelling says something which throws quite
> a new light on the concept of the "uncanny," one which we
> had certainly not awaited. According to him *everything is un-*
> *canny that ought to have remained hidden and secret, and yet*
> *comes to light* [our italics].[17]

Freud's paper gives us an extended quotation from Sander's
German dictionary on the definitions of the word *heimlich.*
He italicizes portions of the passages from it for stress. Among
these is the comparison of *heimlich* with *geheim* [secret] and

Heimlichkeit with *Geheimnis* [secret].[18] Among Freud's summary statements he says of the word *heimlich*

> "on the one hand, it means that which is familiar and congenial, and on the other, that which is concealed and kept out of sight."[19]

This would suggest, among other things, that if being Jewish is something *heimlich* it is both congenial and secret. We are reminded of Freud's comment on Eliot's *Daniel Deronda* to the effect that things Jewish are things that "we speak of only among ourselves."[20]

We are also reminded that one of the major characterizing features of psychoanalysis is that it attempts to divine the nature of secret things. In his "Psycho-analysis and the Ascertaining of Truth in Courts of Law,"[21] Freud indicates that

> In both [psychoanalysis and law] we are concerned with a secret, with something hidden. . . . In the case of the criminal it is a secret which he knows and hides from you, but in the case of the hysteric it is a secret hidden from him, a secret he himself does not know. . . .
>
> The task of the therapeutist is, however, the same as the task of the judge; he must discover the hidden psychic material. To do this we have invented various methods of detection, some of which lawyers are now going to imitate.[22]

It would not be unfair to characterize the whole of psychoanalysis, then, as the study of *Heimlichkeit:* that which is familiar and hidden.

5. Freud associates the uncanny with the female, with the female genitals, and with home.

. . . I will relate an instance taken from psycho-analytical experience; if it does not rest upon mere coincidence, it furnishes a beautiful confirmation of our theory of the uncanny. It often happens that male patients declare that they feel there is something uncanny about the female genital organs. This *unheimlich* place, however, is the entrance to the former *heim* [home] of all human beings, to the place where everyone dwelt once upon a time and in the beginning. There is a humorous saying: "Love is home-sickness"; and whenever a man dreams of a place or a country and says to himself, still in the dream, "this place is familiar to me, I have been there before," we may interpret the place as being his mother's genitals or her body. In this case, too, the *unheimlich* is what was once *heimisch,* home-like, familiar; the prefix "un" is the token of repression.[23]

We have already become acquainted with the Kabbalistic doctrine of the Shekinah.[24]

6. Freud retells in great detail the story of *The Sandman* by Hoffmann as an example of the uncanny. In Freud's analysis of the story he points out that the Sandman is to be understood as "the dreaded father at whose hands castration is awaited"; pointing out that the Sandman appears three times to interfere with the hero's union with the object of his love.

Let us attempt to draw these strands together. We note, to begin with, that if Judaism is *heimlich,* then it has undergone repression. On the basis of our general knowledge concerning Jewish families who are moving into Western civilization, it is probable that Freud had a number of characteristically Jewish experiences, or experiences he probably felt to be associated with Jewishness, as a child. Later, with the entry into the secular world, this material is repressed because of its incompatibility with the new ideas, concepts, and emotions which are generated by the larger culture.*

That the word *heimlich* in its meaning of "home" should thus apply is completely understandable, for the old culture is the culture of the "home." That also there should be a threatening aspect associated with the reminder of the old and the familiar is also completely understandable in less than psychoanalytic terms. For the old culture is not, at least not obviously, well suited for the new adjustments which have to be made. The threat of the old culture is the threat to the various hard-won adjustments to the new mode of life, which are tenuous enough—for they are superimposed upon a set of childhood experiences which are quite different.

The concern with impending death, which evidently absorbed Freud periodically, may also be understood in terms such as these. As Freud tells us in "The Uncanny," there are phenomena which the modern mind is not too well equipped to handle. He indicates that when such events take place (e.g., the repeated appearance of a number) which are not readily explicable by modern conceptions, there is a tendency to regress to older forms of thought, the varieties of superstitions, etc., which are characteristic in primitive culture. On the subject of death he writes,

> There is scarcely any other matter, however, upon which our thoughts and feelings have changed so little since the very earliest times, and in which discarded forms have been so com-

* Nor is the phenomenon which we are here discussing uniquely associated with being Jewish. It is characteristic, for example, of the children of many immigrant groups in America, in which the parents come from a foreign culture, as well as rural people moving into urban settings.

pletely preserved under a thin disguise, as that of our relation to death. Two things account for our conservatism: the strength of our original emotional reaction to it, and the insufficiency of our scientific knowledge about it. Biology has not been able to decide whether death is the inevitable fate of every living being or whether it is only a regular but yet perhaps avoidable event in life. It is true that the proposition "All men are mortal" is paraded in text-books of logic as an example of a generalization, but no human being really grasps it, and our unconscious has as little use now as ever for the idea of its own mortality. Religions continue to dispute the undeniable fact of the death of each one of us and to postulate a life after death; civil governments still believe that they cannot maintain moral order among the living if they do not uphold this prospect of a better life after death as a recompense for earthly existence. In our great cities, placards announce lectures which will tell us how to get in touch with the souls of the departed; and it cannot be denied that many of the most able and penetrating minds among our scientific men have come to the conclusion, especially towards the close of their lives, that a contact of this kind is not utterly impossible. Since practically all of us still think as savages do on this topic, it is no matter of surprise that the primitive fear of the dead is still so strong within us and always ready to come to the surface at any opportunity.[25]

On the strength of these remarks about the association of death with primitive emotions and on the basis of Freud's reliance on such examples as the significance of the number 62, representing his own age at the time of writing, and his absorption with the Sandman story, it may not be too far-fetched to say the following: *Unheimlichkeit* was associated with his sense of impending death. But if *Heimlichkeit* is associated with being Jewish, and *Unheimlichkeit* with death, and these two are, as Freud tells us, to be identified, then Freud's Jewish feeling is related to his sense of impending death.

We turn now to a speculative explication of what this relationship might mean. Syncretizing, we may say that Freud's sense of *Heimlichkeit* is a return to the classical legends of a life after death, which, in Judaism, is associated with the mystical cultural atmosphere. This is not to say that he accepts them rationally. The evidence is quite clear that he does not. Rather, it is an emotional return in the sense which he indicates in the above-quoted passage, a reversion to his own primitive hidden modes of thought.

To say that Freud returns to Jewish mysticism with his sense of approaching death in any simple sense is a violation of the complexity and integrity that we know were characteristic of him. We must take very seriously the distinction which Freud made over and over again, the distinction between being a Jew, and the acceptance of doctrine. His identification was rather with Jews as people and as a continuous historical line.

As we have seen, the Jewish mystics, in the course of the development of a complex system of thought to extract the deeper, hidden, and truer meaning of God's word, developed a "secret" tradition which included the notion of a female counterpart of God, the Shekinah, who accompanied the Jews in their exile. We have pointed out that the Shekinah is identified with the whole body of Israel—in a sense, the Jewish people themselves. The Shekinah is the wife of God who has been cast aside by her Lord, and the time will soon come when He will again look with favor upon her.[26]

From a cultural point of view, especially in view of the fact

315

that this kind of mystical thinking had become an integral part of the common thought of the Jews by the seventeenth century, the actual body of Jewry—more specially the actual community, the actual family, and most specially the actual mother—becomes the *home*. Friday night, the eve of the Sabbath, is in the culture the time at which the mother becomes the queen. The traveler hastens his steps on Friday afternoon to be home by sundown, the time when the Jewish mother lights the candles, and after which he will partake of the food that the woman of the house has prepared. Friday night is so blessed it is regarded as the most appropriate time for realizing marital union.

In the light of this tradition, that Freud should refer to the female genitals as *home* is not at all strange. For the Jews, who in the diaspora had no land, who always had a sense of temporariness in connection with their dwelling places, the mother, the wife, is the home. With his sense of impending death Freud is then *returning home*. As is suggested by his speech to the B'nai B'rith, he is returning to membership in the body of Israel. And his remarks concerning the female genitalia as home can be understood in terms of the Kabbalistic tradition.

The persecution of the Jews not only produced, as reaction, affirmation of Judaism in one form or another, but also the opposite, what the Devil sought to produce in Job, the denunciation of a God who so mistreated his chosen one. In the modern world even some of the most orthodox Jews, witnessing the massacre of the 6,000,000 Jews in Europe, began to wonder whether the Jews have not been the buffoons of the history of

316

civilization, whether the Covenant to which they clung for thousands of years, and whose letter and spirit they attempted to follow with inordinate conscientiousness, was but a mockery. The most important sin which Freud committed was the breach of the first commandment,* which he achieved by its translation into the fifth commandment,† and his nullification of the latter by an appeal to "natural law." The Oedipal violation, understood as a religio-cultural element in the history of the Jews, as a fundamental violation of the Mosaic-Rabbinic tradition of the Jews, as we have seen in our discussion of the theme of Moses in Freud's thought, is, in actuality, a violation of the first commandment, a denunciation by a Jew of his God.

The sense of sin in connection with the violation of the Mosaic father-God of the rabbinic tradition is evidently quite strong in Freud. In the essay "The Uncanny" he refers to Oedipus as "that mythical law-breaker." [27] That he should so characterize Oedipus indicates, as we have seen, that he understands the Oedipal violation as a violation of the major feature of the Mosaic tradition, the Law.

In the fulfillment of the Oedipal metaphor, Freud is then returning to the Mother who will provide him with forgiveness or acceptance in spite of the "audacity" of his rebellion against the father-image. The sense of his oncoming death is the sense of punishment for his violation, and he permits himself, however so slightly, to accept the Mother's forgiveness in the form of immortality. As he suggests, he is approaching "the dreaded father at whose hands castration is awaited," and

* "I am the Lord thy God, who brought thee out of the land of Egypt, out of the house of bondage."
† "Honour thy father and thy mother . . ."

he seeks comfort and safety in the Mother, the Holy Shekinah, the Community of Israel. That he, as Messiah, fought against the Father for the Mother's sake, makes him feel all the more that She will save him. And it is largely in this that the significance of *Heimlichkeit* lies.

NOTES TO THE EPILOGUE

1. Freud, "On being of the B'nai B'rith," *Commentary* (March, 1946), pp. 23-24, p. 23. This is translated perhaps more effectively by Reik as "the secret of the same inner construction."— T. Reik, "Freud and Jewish Wit," *Psychoanalysis* (1952), 2, (No. 3), 12-20, p. 12.
2. Freud, *Col. Papers,* IV, pp. 368-407.
3. Freud, *Col. Papers,* IV, p. 377.
4. Freud, *Col. Papers,* IV, pp. 369-370.
5. Freud, *Col. Papers,* IV, p. 399.
6. Done with the assistance of Theodor Reik.
7. Freud, *Col. Papers,* IV, p. 397.
8. Freud, *Moses and Monotheism,* p. 116.
9. Freud, *Col. Papers,* I, p. 325.
10. Freud, *Col. Papers,* IV, pp. 390-391.
11. Cf. pp. 265 ff., above.
12. Jones, II, p. 392.
13. Freud was born May 6, 1856.
14. Freud, *Col. Papers,* IV, p. 369.
15. Freud, *Col. Papers,* IV, p. 390.
16. Freud, *Col. Papers,* IV, p. 398.
17. Freud, *Col. Papers,* IV, pp. 375-376.
18. Freud, *Col. Papers,* IV, pp. 373-374.
19. Freud, *Col. Papers,* IV, p. 375.
20. Jones, I, p. 174.
21. Freud, *Col. Papers,* II, pp. 13-24.
22. Freud, *Col. Papers,* II, p. 18.

23. Freud, *Col. Papers,* IV, pp. 398-399. Cf. footnote, p. 165.
24. Cf. pp. 273 ff., above.
25. Freud, *Col. Papers,* IV, pp. 395-396.
26. Cf. pp. 290-291, above.
27. Freud, *Col. Papers,* IV, p. 383.

Index